# Innovation in Music II

*Edited by*

R.Hepworth-Sawyer, J.Hodgson, J.L.Paterson and R.Toulson

Future Technology Press, UK

Innovation in Music II

*Editors*

R. Hepworth-Sawyer
York St John University, UK

J. Hodgson
University of Western Ontario, Canada

J. L. Paterson
London College of Music, University of West London, UK

R. Toulson
University of Westminster, UK

Copyright © 2016 Future Technology Press and the authors of contributed articles,
Virtual Knowledge Solutions Ltd,
PO Box 2115, Shoreham-by-sea,
BN43 9AF, United Kingdom

Print Version
ISBN 978-1-911108-04-7

This work is subject to copyright. All rights are reserved by the publisher and the authors. No part of this work may be reproduced, stored in a retrieval system, or transmitted, in any form or by any means, electronic, mechanical, photocopying, recording or otherwise, without prior written permission from the publisher.

# Preface

Innovation in Music II (InMusic'15) was an international conference organised by KES International and a multi-disciplinary International Programme Committee. Hosted by Conference Chair Dr Rob Toulson, the conference took place over the 7th to 9th June 2015 at Anglia Ruskin University, Cambridge, UK.

Innovation in Music broadly represents all aspects of innovation in the field of music, particularly encompassing music performance, audio technology, music production and the commercial music industries. The conference acted as a forum for industry experts and professionals to mix with researchers and academics to report on the latest advances and exchange ideas.

Award-winning industry experts including David Wrench, Tim Exile, Peter Jenner, Mandy Parnell, Gary Bromham, Bryan Martin and Simon Gogerly contributed to the conference keynote presentations. This book includes articles developed from presentations delivered at the conference and subsequently invited for peer-reviewed inclusion as chapters in this text. It also contains the transcript of the music production keynote interview with mix-engineer David Wrench, who was recently award the UK Music Producers' Guild award for 'Mix Engineer of the Year'. This book therefore gives a broad and detailed overview of modern and cross-disciplinary innovations in the world of music.

We thank all speakers and delegates to the conference for their support, and intend that the articles published will be a lasting record of the event and a resource of research information for the future.


R.Hepworth-Sawyer, J.Hodgson, J.L.Paterson and R.Toulson (Eds)

# Contents

| | |
|---|---|
| Interview with Mix Engineer David Wrench<br>*Rob Toulson* | 1 |
| Mixing Popular Music in Three Dimensions: Expansion of the Kick Drum Source Image<br>*Bryan Martin, King Richard* | 14 |
| A System of Reactive Backing for Live Popular Music<br>*Tim Canfer* | 26 |
| Exploring the sound quality dimensions of hyper-compression<br>*Malachy Ronan, Ward Nicholas, Sazdov Robert* | 36 |
| Paradigms of Music Software Interface Design and Musical Creativity<br>*Mark Marrington* | 52 |
| Loompianola: A Contemporary Hybrid Instrument<br>*Esthir Leml, McRae Colin, Esslinger Reed* | 64 |
| Gestalt Theory and Mixing Audio<br>*Matthew Shelvock* | 75 |
| Formless Form as Forma Efformans<br>*Chang Seok Choi* | 88 |
| New Acoustic Technology for Indoor Live Music Events<br>*Niels Adelman-Larsen* | 103 |
| Interactive Algorithmic Composition<br>*Edward Averell, Knox Don* | 116 |
| Triple Helix Partnerships for the Music Sector: Music Industry, Academia and the Public<br>*Carola Boehm* | 128 |
| Crowd-Sourced Learning of Music Production Practices Through Large-Scale Perceptual Evaluation of Mixes<br>*Brecht De Man, Reiss Joshua* | 144 |
| You Need Me Man, I Don't Need You: Exploring the Debates Surrounding the Economic Viability of On-Demand Music Streaming<br>*Mathew Flynn* | 157 |

Contents

Real-time long-distance music collaboration using the Internet   174
*Paul Ferguson*

Integrating the Spatiality of Live Performers within the Imaginary Spatial   179
Image of a Pre-Recorded Electroacoustic Part as a Compositional Premise
*Timothy Cooper*

Interactive Digital Music: Enhancing Listener Engagement with Commercial   193
Music
*Justin Paterson, Toulson Rob, Lexer Sebastian, Webster Tim, Massey Steve, Ritter Jonas*

# Interview with Mix Engineer David Wrench

Rob Toulson

CoDE Research Institute, Anglia Ruskin University, Cambridge, UK.
rob.toulson@anglia.ac.uk

## Abstract

*David Wrench has become one of the most celebrated and sought-after mix engineers, not least because two of his 2014 projects were nominated for the Mercury Music Prize; those being two of the most contemporary albums of the year - FKA Twigs' LP1 and Jungle's self-titled debut. He has since been awarded the Music Producers Guild's Mix Engineer of the Year award in 2016. David is a multi-talented Producer, Recording Engineer and Mix Engineer and an exceptionally well regarded musician and multi-instrumentalist. His credits for mixing and engineering include Bat For Lashes, Everything Everything, Caribou, Guillemots, Philip Selway and Glass Animals. During the keynote interview at Innovation In Music 2015, David Wrench gave an overview of his pathway into music production, his approach to innovative projects and an insight into some of the varied projects he has worked on. This article is a transcript of the David Wrench's interview with Conference Chair, Dr Rob Toulson.*

## 1. Pathways into music production

**RT: What were your first steps towards being a musician and working in the studio environment?**

DW: I was a musician and I played piano when I was young. I had a couple of experiences in studios when I was in school, for which I was very lucky. In two of the schools that I went to, there were teachers who had recording studios and one was a producer called Gorwel Owen who had a little label. He ended up producing a lot of albums for the Super Furry Animals in the 90s. He was my physics teacher. He'd let me come into the studio with him, and he also put out the 12-inch of my own music while I was still in school, so that was the beginning. Then I got an Atari ST with one megabyte in it, Cubase, a soundcard and a little 4-track. I made a lot of music on that setup.

**RT: So you were already working on a hybrid analogue/digital system from the start?**

DW: Yeah that seemed like the only sensible way to do it, because the computer wouldn't run enough on its own. It was just a little MIDI sequencer, but I wanted to throw some stuff on it, so the 4-track made sense. There was a little thing that you could attach to the side of the computer that would allow one of the tracks to be the time code, and you could lock it together, so it was definitely the beginning of people being able to do stuff at home and with the home recording setup.

**RT: And what happened when you finished at school?**
DW: I sort of went to University at that point, but it went a bit wrong because I got kicked out! So I just listened to lots of records for a few years and didn't really know what I was going to do with myself. I made a record on a Welsh label, and that was in this studio called Bryn Derwen, which was at the time a really tiny place, but in this big beautiful country house. I loved it there, and the person who ran it was a guy called Lori Gane. We just sort of got on, and I pestered him to let me come there and engineer. I told him I knew what I was doing but I had never worked a desk before. Eventually he just said, "yeah come in", and I spent a week there just looking at the desk manual, and was thrown into my first session. It was a heavy metal band and I knew very little about heavy metal music, and the biggest drum kit that I've seen to date. I was just thrown in and had to work it out for myself.

**RT: And then, did that studio bring in bigger and more recognized clients?**
DW: Yeah, we sort of grooved together really. Lori kept building new rooms and it turned into a really brilliant studio. I started a really long relationship with this guy called Jackie Leven, and we did 14 albums together over the years. He was an amazing musician, one the most incredible singers and guitarists I've ever worked with. Most of the time you start recording with local bands, maybe not very good musicians, but I think that teaches you how to mic things up properly, because you've got to get it right, otherwise it just sounds terrible. Then suddenly, when you get to work with a brilliant musician, it sounds amazing, and you can sort of put a mic anywhere on a brilliant musician, it will sound good, because most of your job is done for you. If someone has really tuned a drum kit well, and plays it well, you hardly have to do anything, but it's sort of all that previous hard work that translates when you work with someone who really plays well, and so it turns out to be amazing.

**RT: You've released your own records and you're a multi-instrumentalist, what are your own creative works like?**
DW: It's all sorts of things really. When I was in school I got really excited about the Acid House music that was coming out, and I made Welsh Acid House records, which was a fairly niche market. Then later on I made an album that was very doomy, long songs. I also made an Electro-Pop album in the mid-2000s. I worked on and off with this amazing artist called Julian Cope over the years, and sometimes played mellotron in his band, but he sort of got me to do a record without me knowing. He sorted out the time for me to do another record and I was procrastinating, so he got me to come down and have some jams, and on the second day, he's like, "so this album of yours is going quite well".

**RT: How did you then evolve from being an artist, producer, engineer, to nowadays where in the commercial world, you're known as a specialist mix engineer?**
DW: Partly by accident, and partly through circumstance. A few years ago, I started working with an artist called Caribou. The second album I worked on with him,

'Swim', I did the mix on that, and that really took off. People were really commenting on the mix for that record, especially the track 'Odessa', which became a club hit. So I started getting asked to do a lot of mixing work just on the back of that one song. I realized that can happen; just one song can really change the trajectory of where you're going. But also I've had a child a couple of years ago, and I decided I wanted to try focusing on mixing for a year so I could be home a lot more. I have my own set-up at home and do the bulk of my work there, whereas going off on production jobs could take you out for months, and long days, but I just wanted to be around the baby, and it happened that those two things coincided. I still take on production jobs and I've got a couple going, but I've decided on about one or two a year. I still find that emotionally it's hard to take on more than one production project at a time. I can dip in and out of mix projects, and have multiple mix jobs at once and that's okay, in fact that's actually quite useful, refreshing my ears over time. However, with production, I've got to get really into it and I feel like it's got to take you over a bit, and when I had overlapping production jobs I found that quite confusing for me. Some people are okay with that, but I found it just worked better for me when I had one thing at a time to produce.

## 2. Approaches to mixing and production

**RT: Often mixers don't meet the artists they work with but it seems like you really get to know your artist and get to work with them, as opposed to pushing your own stamp of anything in particular over them. Is that correct?**
DW: I wouldn't feel comfortable taking a project and saying, "well look, this is what I do, and this is what your record is going to sound like" - that's not for me. I'd get bored doing that. I like to find a different method of working for each artist, that works for them and that makes a new record. I'm best when I feel slightly uncomfortable with it. By that I mean not with the person but that I'm doing something I feel I haven't quite done before, or that's not sounding quite like another record. I think, the way I often work these days is to prepare the tracks up to a certain extent and then maybe mail them back a couple of times, but then get into the studio with the artist and spend some time trying stuff out. I find that you can get away with doing more radical things like that. I think if you send someone an email and it's got a really crazy level, they're just like, "why have you done that?" - but if you're in the studio and you try it out together, it's less confrontational in regards to trying new things. It's more collaborative, and you can have mixes that are a bit more exciting that way.

**RT: I'm really interested in the workflow, because everyone works differently. When a project kicks off, what's the first thing that happens?**
DW: Well, I won't agree to anything until I've heard the demos, because I've got to like it. Even if an artist is big, it's important to do that because if I'm not feeling it, there's no point in doing i, and sometimes I have to say, I'm not the right person for this. So that's the first stage, listening to it and making sure I like it, or that there's something exciting me. Then, when it's got the go-ahead, I'll talk to whoever is in

charge of the files, whether it's the producer or the artist themselves. I seem to work with a lot of self-producing artists, which is quite a thing nowadays, especially within the electronic world, but maybe the expertise isn't there for mixing or finally putting it together. Then I'll discuss how they recorded the files, because stems can be quite complicated, especially with a lot of dance music. People use side-chaining on the master busses and major effects of the song, and then it gets quite complicated getting good stems off people because you're losing something that is intrinsic to the song. So unless they've done it in Pro Tools, which is the only thing I work in, we've got to find a way of getting that out. It's usually by me replicating those effects on my own master bus.

**RT: So they'll give you really dry stuff, well ideally anyway, unless they've got a full Pro Tools session in which case you'll happily take that and clean it up?**
DW: Yeah, and sometimes we're talking even before they've got in to record the stuff, if it's really planned in advance. That's quite useful because I can talk then about formats. I'm a massive convert to 96k sessions, I think they sound fantastic. The first album I did like that was the Glass Animals album and I was able to get this extra space out of the mix. It was recorded at 96 kHz all the way through and I had to buy a new computer just to open up the session They were huge sessions, and a lot of plugins, so yeah I was really converted to it - I just think it sounds brilliant. I think reverb sounds good at 96 kHz, and there was a space and depth that I just couldn't get before.

**RT: So it's about getting the right source recordings at the end of the day still?**
DW: So if I'm in conversation before the recording takes places then I'll suggest that 96 kHz is the way to go, but then it's a matter of taking delivery of the stems, and looking through them. Stems arrive in all sorts of states, from brilliant and you just put them in, like Caribou, or Jamie XX, the stems are always in great shape, it sounds good from the start. However, some other stuff comes in and you're just thinking, "what is this?" There's reverbs rendered onto vocals, with clicks on them, and all sorts of stuff, and sometimes you make the call and they say, "no we really don't have it any other way, you're going to have to work with this". Other times I'm saying, you're going to have to re-record this because I can't work with this. So you've got that process to start with, just looking at what's there, what state it's in, sometimes trying to decipher, especially if people have not come through either a studio way of learning or university way of learning, they've just taught themselves. They might have some quite eccentric ways of recording, which might sound good, but quite hard to get your head around as a mixer to start with, and then maybe their ways of explaining it are quite complicated too.

**RT: So understanding the recording process really helps your early decision making in the mix?**
DW: It informs how to set up the mix and what they're hearing in the tracking mixes; I'll always get a rough mix out of them. I've got a PreSonus Central Station

switching unit, so I can have my mix on 1 and 2, and I just flip to their mix on 3 and 4. I'm always going back and forth between those, right through the mixing process, just to see if I'm making it worse, or losing something that's not technically correct in their mix, but is part of the atmosphere of it. It's really easy to polish it up too much or to take the life out of it. There's often good things in their demo music, that's not what you would instinctively do as a mixer, but you have to listen out for those things.

**RT: When you take a single song, do you kind of listen to it and think about how that song evolves - what its life span is from start to finish?**
DW: Sort of. I'll listen to it a few times. When it comes to the actual mix, I work quite quickly and quite instinctively for certain sections of it, but I will listen to it a couple of times and just get an overall feel for where the peaks and troughs are, what I like about the demo, what I don't like about it. Then I'll just do a very quick balance, which is just drums, bass, keyboards, guitars, atmospherics, vocals, backing vocals, but I'll just go through them, soloing them. So unless there's something really horrendous that needs sorting with EQ, I'll just try and get a balance that works well so it feels good just from volume. I think volume is the main thing about mixing. I mean often you can sort stuff just by changing the level, so I'll just do basic volume and panning and then I'll do a second pass where I start EQ-ing. Then it's just EQ-ing, bits of compression, and starting to add basic reverb onto stuff, so trying to create a bit of a 3D image. Then it's into the boring bit of cleaning it all up, going through the vocals, getting rid of any clicks, any sort of unwanted noise, dodgy edits and things; that's the sort of time-consuming boring bits. Then I'll go through and I'll really start doing the intricate little rides on stuff. I'll pretty much ride every word of a main vocal, and it'll be really sculpted so that it keeps its presence in the song, even though I'll have compression on it and possibly multiband compression on it, I'll also ride it so it feels natural, and sits there. It's about trying to get the vocal to be really clear, but to sit in the track and not be in front of it, because once you've really compressed the vocal, it can often just sound like it's plonked on top of a track, and it's separate to it. Just trying to get it to be in the track, but also every detail to be clear in it. If you do the rides manually, you can get that, and then sort out backing vocals, and the detailing, and just keep listening, keep listening, and just tiny little rides on things. I like movement and I'll try and find some things so they sound wrong. I think mixes where everything's really nice and nicely placed becomes a little boring to listen to. I like to have somethings that are slightly out of place, for example, if a solo comes in and it's 2 or 3 dB louder than you think it should be, that's probably about right, or if you're going to have reverb on something then make it a little bigger than you would naturally want it to be. I think it's about creating elements of excitement, and finding points in the mix that are key transitional points and making features of them. Although, with all of this, it's about listening to the lyrics as well and working out what's been said, because if what you're doing with the other mix things is taking away from the narrative of the song, then it's not helping at all. You've always got to ask, is this helping what this person is saying at this point?

**RT: Susan Rogers used to be Prince's in-house engineer, and now she's a Behavioral Psychologist. She lectures on the psychology of music production and I remember she used the phrase "violating people's expectations". It sounds like you try to bring a bit of that into your mixing?**
DW: Yeah, definitely. You either create an expectation, and then you give something slightly different, or you delay the giving of the expectation, which works as well.

**RT: Do you find some imagery in the lyrics or the story that you can then tell maybe a little bit through the structure of the mix?**
DW: Yeah definitely, especially with someone like Twigs. It's definitely the music supporting the story that she's telling and creating, because she's singing about images, and you can really strengthen what emotion is being felt at that time, if it's unrest, or tension, or if it's calm - you can definitely do that with the mix and how it's unfolding at that point.

3. **Mix tools and technical considerations**

**RT: You do a lot of your mixing 'in the box'. So was the FKA Twigs album mixed that way?**
DW: It was all in the box. We cross-referenced with an analogue console, and chose to mix completely in the box.

**RT: Do you think that if you've got the ears and the skills it doesn't matter how you work, you can make it sound good regardless?**
DW: Yeah, though I thought there was a change in Pro Tools 10, I don't know if anything really changed, but to me it suddenly sounded better. Mixes I had done in the box with Pro Tools 9, there was sort of something not quite right about them. I don't know if I got better or if the technology changed in version 10, but it suddenly sounded pretty good to me, and it's a matter of practicality most of the time. Especially working remotely from artists a lot, and there's so many recalls these days, so much stemming that needs to be done, and how quick they want the turnaround to be, as well as how quick they need extra stuff, and how many versions you need, there's various radio mixes required for example.

**RT: What sort of alterations do you make for the radio?**
DW: For FKA Twigs, one radio asked us to take the word 'thighs' out because it was too strong, and obviously 'motherfucker' had to come out as well, but you can't have any trace of the word in it, you can't even have 'mother-blank', it has to be totally got rid of, they're really strict.

**RT: I'm interested in some of your go-to tools and techniques that have helped you out on a number of occasions. I think you mentioned multiband compression in the mix, which is almost always left for the mastering engineers to play with, so how do you use that?**

DW: I'm a big fan of multi-band compression. I think it's a really useful tool. I use it on bass instruments because often when you're compressing, what you want to actually be controlling are certain frequencies, and so just setting it up to a certain band, let the top end of the bass come through as it wishes, but hold the low-mids, and then maybe hold the low-end even more. Vocals, sometimes you think you can be compressing, but all you want to be doing is controlling the harshness that comes through on certain loud sections, so it makes sense to be using the multi-band compression at the top end, maybe around sort of high-mids, just to control it when it gets peaky. If you just hear something that's peeking out, instead of EQ-ing that out for the whole track, just control it when it gets too much. Yeah, I nearly always use multi-band across the mix too. In fact something I often do across the mix is I'll have an EQ, and a compressor, then a multi-band, and actually that's how it goes for listening purposes, with a limiter as well.

**RT: So you do give listening copies that have been pushed up a bit in loudness?**
DW: You have to, otherwise people just complain that it's too quiet, but I'll often be riding the level of one compressor into another, on the master mix. So I'll automate compression settings for different parts of the song, so that maybe. I mean, when I used to mix at the desk I'd often be riding the master fader throughout the mix to sort of lift it up a bit for the chorus, but I tend to ride the output of just an SSL type compressor into a multiband compressor.

**RT: Would you push that through the song and then at various points bring it back?**
DW: Yeah, at various points I'll bring it back and forth, just so it feels more intense at certain points.

**RT: What kind of modulation effects do you go to regularly?**
DW: The Waves MondoMod, I use that a lot. So I'll mix a tiny bit of that on synths to sort of create a bit of stereo movement.

**RT: What kind of effects do you use on the reverb channel or the delays?**
DW: There's the new Soundtoys MicroShift, that's really good, I've used it a lot on backing vocals. It's gives the tiny little pitch shifting delay effect that you used to be able to do with the Eventide H3000 or the AMS. It gives it this stereo width, by changing the phase a bit on the left or right, but I just mix a bit of that in and it can help. It has a slight chorusing effect as well. Delays I use quite a lot, often really quietly and buried in the mix, especially on the vocal, almost imperceptible, but it helps the vocal settle in. I'm also a big fan of a company called Valhalla DSP and it's just one guy. He makes some amazing reverbs, especially the VintageVerb, I think it's brilliant, and it's $50, I use that a lot. Actually that's the main reverb on all of the records we've talked about. It's just a really good sounding reverb, and he's really approachable, a very helpful person, and just keen to make something that people will use.

**RT: You mentioned mastering, how do you communicate with the mastering engineer?**
DW: Usually mastering engineers would want to communicate with whoever's mixed the record. [Mastering Engineer] Mandy Parnell is brilliant, she's great at making records that have a real depth and space, and bringing that out in them, and being true to what I've handed her. The Philip Selway album was quite complicated because I had done a rough master just for him to listen to and he had fallen in love with it, so then it was quite difficult for Mandy because he kept referring back to this even though what she was doing was technically way better than what I had thrown together. But he had sort of gotten used to that and she was great working through that challenge. The Glass Animals album - she really got that to sit together, which was quite of an in-depth record, it had a lot of detail on it, which had previously gotten lost.

**RT: I suppose a big part of the mix is knowing what a mix sounds like versus what a master sounds like, which is sometimes kind of hard for the artist to understand. Do you find that at all?**
DW: I think it should go to mastering sounding pretty good. If someone is not happy with how it's sounding, I continue to work on it, not depending on that it's going to sound better in the mastering. I think it should go to mastering just needing some technical tweaks, that it shouldn't be a creative process at that point. I'd rather continue working on it as a mix, because you have much more control.

**RT: That means taking a lot more responsibility on dynamics and things like that?**
DW: Yeah, I think that's alright, I think that's part of the job.

**RT: I agree, I've heard lots of mix engineers, maybe in academia, leaving dynamics purely for the mastering engineer to resolve.**
DW: I think if you're starting off and you're really uncomfortable about it, some mastering engineers would probably be fine with you taking a portable mix setup and having to mix there so they could make tiny tweaks to it if needed. I personally always fight against it if a mastering engineer asks for stems, I say no, especially as I do a lot of mix-bus alteration. It's like that's taking it out of its creative thing; I'd rather they just say what's wrong with it.

**RT: You mentioned that you're working on surround sound projects at the moment, could you talk about that?**
DW: Yeah, it's Jamie XX, he's done music for a ballet that's going to be in the Manchester Arts Festival coming up in July [2015] and that's going to be in surround in the theatre. So it's 6.1, which is 3 stereo pairs and a low-frequency channel, but yeah the music's beautiful.

**RT: Do you feel like there's more surround sound projects coming around these days or is that still kind of a niche thing?**

DW: For me it's niche, the focus of most records is stereo, especially now because of headphones, and budgets being so small, I can't see it particularly expanding to surround.

## 4. Working with FKA Twigs, Philip Selway and Jungle

**RT: Let's talk about FKA Twigs' *LP1* record. I noticed it's built around percussion and even the harmony, the bass and the keys are all very percussive. It struck me that it must have been difficult to make it work in the mix without just a load of things happening all at the same time. How did you approach that?**
DW: It was a really difficult record to mix, especially because the big challenge with it was that Twigs had worked with a number of different producers, and she's a producer herself - a really good producer. She does all the drum programming on a Dave Smith Tempest [analogue drum machine], so nearly all of the drums, most of the bass, and a lot of the synths are just the Tempest on that record. Then there's other real instruments, and synths as well, but it arrived in all sorts of formats, from 44 kHz / 16-bit files, to 96 kHz / 24-bit files, Pro Tools sessions, to stems with reverb ending on, it had just been through so many people, different engineers, and different producers. Twigs works very quickly, so none of it was particularly cleaned up, and it all sounded quite different. When I first met Twigs, she said, "I really just want someone to bring this all together into something cohesive, and it needs to sound like an album, not a collection of different songs". So that was the key, to find something that enlightened the record, and it was there, because it has her vocals. I could see that it was possible and, as soon as I heard the demos, I realised I'd never heard music like that - it was amazing. Then once I got into it, I realized how tricky it was. We tried different things, although her main instruction was to make it to sound more hip-hop than soul, and she wanted to have hard-hitting bass drums. She likes it when the percussion comes in; she wants it to somewhat painful and aggressive. The whole thing was to make a record that wasn't at all tame or soft, that it was going to be quite of an intense record. Bits of it were like Music Concrète, bits of it were like Scott Walker, in that there are moments of just noise, there are moments where it's all about movement of these complicated rhythms, while it's got something beautiful going on underneath, but it hinges on these beats in there, and the melodies too. I'm a massive fan of Captain Beefheart, and I could see bits of that in it, in that you'd have these melodies like he used to, it would start on one instrument and end on another while passing through percussion, and they would sort of intertwine, but it wouldn't be necessarily obvious to start with. Twigs is very creative in the mix process and really involved. She'd know every tiny little detail, and there might be hundreds of tracks of material. For example she'd know there's a little thing that's meant to go "ff-ff-ff", she searches through everything and finds it, and it perhaps doesn't even register, and she says, "that's got to be loud and panned to the left because I make a movement at that point with my hand". So she thinks about it all as movement as well - she's a dancer, and she has everything planned out, so it makes even more

sense when you see her dancing to it. It's very much a complete vision that she's got.

**RT: I was really pleased that you said that this was an album and not a collection of songs, and again the albums of yours that I own, I've bought all of them on vinyl because they felt like pieces of art that actually deserved to be listened to as an album. Do you find that with the artist's you work with, they hold the album as quite a strong concept?**
DW: Yeah, and I do as well. I like listening to albums, I find it disconcerting when an album sounds just like disparate songs, and that can happen a lot with pop music, especially once you start working with different producers and albums that are mixed by different people. I find it hard to connect with those at times. I might not even know when I put it on but there's something about it, so I'll look at the notes and think oh that's probably why.

**RT: What were the real challenges and interesting points mixing the song *Two Weeks* by FKA Twigs?**
DW: The vocals were challenging on that. It doesn't sound it, but there were a lot of tracks of vocals, like 30-40 tracks of vocals, but a lot of them are doing the same thing. The key to it was tightening everything up, just create that one thick sound, because it was sounding quite messy, even though they were really well tightened up, there were a lot of breaths.

**RT: There are clearly vocal phrases that layer over other phrases.**
DW: Yeah, getting everything to be clear so that you could tap into it if you wanted to, so a lot of that has to do with an intricate stereo placement.

**RT: And percussion, there's a lot of sub in there, because it goes quite low.**
DW: It's that kick when it goes into the chorus.

**RT: There is a real kind of euphoric lift when the chorus kind of drops in.**
DW: That would also be a master fader push as well, just a slight change in compression settings when the chorus comes in. The vocals were the thing on that, and later on in the song it gets even more complicated - there were a lot of intertwining vocals, and all of the little percussive elements. There was a lot of detailing on the song, but there was also this aspect of how to get it on radio.

**RT: So there were a few kind of rules that you had to follow?**
DW: Yeah it had to be about loud vocal - that's Twigs, right? She wanted it loud, she likes a lot of 3k in the mix, probably a lot more than I put into the mix, but she likes it sort of cutting, and quite sparkly. Then that low end and it is quite tricky because there isn't a lot of harmonic content in the music, there are bits that come in and it's a bit of relief when they do come in, it's a moment, because she's created so much tension before that.

**RT: Maybe there's something in that approach - you take away and then you get more when you give it back?**
DW: Yeah, but there is a lot of percussion and bass and vocal, there's only moments in the album when you get harmony.

**RT: How did you approach the mix of [Radiohead drummer] Philip Selway's solo *Weatherhouse* album.**
DW: That was a slightly different way of working to normal, in that the tracks were about 80% complete when I started mixing them. Radiohead had their own private studio in the middle of nowhere, and we went in there, and there were a couple of rooms. So I'd be mixing in there and Philip would still be doing vocals and other bits in the other room, but I'd be sending mixes through so he could sing to something that was a bit more complete and immediately hear how it was all sounding. So it was quite a nice process of finishing it off. Everyone who was there, Ardem Ilhan, who was producing, and Quinta [musician Katherine Mann] - they were also there finishing the stuff in one room, while I was mixing in the other - it was just going back and forth.

**RT: The drums sounds really beautiful on the album, particularly the opening track *Coming up for Air*.**
DW: Well, Philip's an amazing drummer, I mean a really amazing drummer. I think that track went through quite a few mixes of trying different ways of making it sound good and I think eventually the thing that worked on it was getting the sidestick through a space echo that was lying around; it just opened it up. I'm a massive fan of reggae records and the sounds of them. I listen to a lot of 70s reggae records, Lee Perry mixes, and I think that just sort of worked on that.

**RT: What's great about working in the box is that you can try stuff and throw it away if you don't like it. You said that you did quite a lot of mixes. Is that because sometimes you don't really know what you're looking for, but if you look for long enough you'll find it?**
DW: Yeah, just keep trying stuff out until it feels right. There were various sorts of iterations of that song, it just didn't sound right. I think we had it a bit dry and distorted at one point and it just didn't feel right against the vocal, but then you sort of eventually find something that feels right.

**RT: Vocals are interesting as well aren't they, very layered. Is there quite a lot going on there?**
DW: That's actually one vocal but it's got quite a bit of processing on it; there's some distortions on it and then quite a thick delay on it. I think because it had some really nice delay units, I had to do some passes where I was playing with the reverb as it was going down, but it recorded in and then have it sort of coming in and out of places.

**RT: What was the approach to mixing Jungle's [self titled] debut album?**

DW: That's quite a strange record - the whole album. Every single vocal on that album is run through a Leslie speaker simulator in Logic. There's not a single vocal on the record that hasn't been run through that, and that's just their sound. I asked to hear it without it and it didn't sound like them. My initial mix of that was probably a bit more normal-sounding and they thought it sounded a bit too clean. It came with the Leslie effect on it, and without it, and actually the final sound is a mixture of both, I used the clean vocals to just put a tiny bit more clarity, because what they initially had was just a bit muddy. However, their instruction was to try and make the mix sound like someone had thrown a blanket over the speakers. They wanted it to sound muddy, but in a clear way. They worked in a room with these Barefoot monitors - a small room, and it was so bass heavy in there. I went and had a listen in the room they were working in and I couldn't tell what it was going to be like. There were all sorts of muddy low-end frequencies that needed to stay to some extent, because it was their sound, but it also needed to be tamed. Also in the studio they listen to the mix incredibly loud on headphones, but then eventually I had to explain that they needed to listen to it quietly, because they kept wanting the vocal down, and it was just getting lost. So I suggested we put it through the speakers really quietly, like it is on the radio - we want this record in the charts, and they were like, "oh yeah, it's disappeared", so we got it eventually to a point where everyone was happy that it was characterful enough, but still clear enough to get on the radio.

## 5. Monitoring at home, in clubs and at Strongroom Studios

**RT: What's your preferred approach in regards to monitoring?**
DW: I have a few monitors that I know well, that I'm happy with wherever I go. So some Neumann KH310s - those are my main monitors at home. Also Adam A7Xs, because I've had them for a while and I'll always mix with the sub unless it's with the Neumanns in a small room, in which case you don't always need it, but in big studios I always get a sub in. If I have to use monitors I'm not used to I just have to listen to a load of stuff first; I have to spend a couple of hours listening to records.

**RT: That's why you often mix at Strongroom Studios, purely for sound?**
DW: I know it sounds good in there. I mean, lots of studios sound good, it's just what you know. Although some studios have lumpiness in the low-end and with the sort of music I'm working with, often dance music, it often has quite heavy low-end. There's a lot more low-end in records than there used to be, and I love bass. I'll really try to push it as much as I can, without it sounding messy. I think you can get away with a lot of bass if you haven't got clashes and you've got defined frequencies, like the kick is in one frequency and the bass is in another. If it's all mushed together into similar frequencies, you get a kind of phasing and peaks and troughs, and it starts to sound a bit messy, but you can get away with a lot of bass if you take control of it. You've got to know what's there in your mixing room, and I think a lot of places have set up for mixing guitar music and there's not that level or that depth of bass, and so the monitoring isn't set up for that.

**RT: You also mentioned that there were some records you take into the club and have a final listen too?**
DW: Yeah with the Caribou record we took it into The Plastic People nightclub. They had a great sound system, it's gone now - it's a real shame. It was a good fun nightclub and listening to it at that volume, you could feel the bass like you could in the club. We definitely tweaked the mix to make it sound good in the club.

**RT: So are you using Strongroom pretty much as just a playback room?**
DW: We do creative things in there too. With the Hot Chip mixes we ended up using the AMS, delays, and stuff like that. Yeah, I mean the equipment is there if you want to do it, but sometimes things will get recorded in the mix as well because you realise it's missing something. However, I go there predominantly because it's somewhere I can go in London where I know it sounds good. I also like the feeling in there, they're really nice people there.

## 6. Acknowledgements

Thank you to Jay Hodgson and Amaal Bhaloo for arranging and conducting the transcription of the interview audio recordings.

# Mixing Popular Music in Three Dimensions: Expansion of the Kick Drum Source Image

Bryan Martin[1], Richard King[2]

[1]Enhanced Reality Audio Group (ERA), McGill University, Montreal, Canada
bryan.martin@mcgill.ca

[2]Centre for Interdisciplinary Research in Music Media and Technology (CIRMMT), Montreal, Canada

## Abstract

*Three dimensional sound is being implemented in cinema, automobiles, codecs, and in new domestic listening specifications, but there is little investigation into the tools and methods needed to create music mixes in multiple dimensions. Commercial releases of popular music beyond stereo have been limited to 5.1 and 7.1 formats with no height channels present. The sound-stage architecture varies widely in these offerings, and the small number of releases has constrained the dialog for the artistic evolution of the sound-field presentation. This paper discusses evolving 3D mix architectures being developed for 22.2 multi-channel surround sound systems by McGill University's Sound Recording Program. The major topic discussed is the expansion of the size of sonic objects in two- and three-dimensional planes.*

## 1. Introduction

The presentation of audio in three-dimensions is the next horizon in professional audio. It is being examined for delivery in cinema [6, 18], home [5], automobiles [2, 3, 9], headphones [1, 4], via codecs [12, 13] and upmixing [11, 15, 19]. The bulk of the investigations in actual recording have largely been focused in classical music recording [8, 17, 23], broadcast [10, 16, 18] and live event capture [21, 22], with little or no address of conventionally recorded popular music.

Multi-channel commercial releases of popular music have been limited to 5.1 and 7.1 formats [14] with no height channels present. The sound-stage architecture varies widely in these offerings and the small number of releases has constrained the dialog for the artistic evolution of the sound-field presentation.

The introduction of multi-channel audio (beyond stereo and excluding quadraphonic) largely began when Dolby Labs created the 5.1 array as a format for cinema sound delivery in 1976 [20]. The industry has lately experienced the expansion of immersive formats that include height channels. Some of the most notable formats are Dolby Atmos for cinema sound, with a home theatre specification of 7.1 channels [5, 6], Auro 3D specifying 13.1 channels [19] and the 22.2 multi-channel sound system developed by the Japanese broadcaster NHK [7]. It should be noted that the above formats are for sound with picture, and were not developed for the exclusive delivery of musical content.

## 2. Goal of Three-Dimensional Mix Investigation

The goal of the discussed mix investigation was to discover and develop effective mixing techniques for the presentation of popular music reproduced in a playback array that included height channels. The aims were to develop methods for expanding the size of sonic objects into two- and three-dimensional planes; methods and strategies for the design and implementation of early and late reflections in a three-dimensional sound field; strategies and architectures for the design of three-dimensional reverberant fields; and best practices for the distribution of the audio spectrum in hemispherical multi-dimensional playback systems.

## 3. Test Environment

This research was conducted at McGill University Schulich School of Music's Studio 22 (Figure 1). Studio 22 is a music mixing control room with an RT60 of 200 milliseconds ±50 ms at all frequency bands (Figure 2). This is coupled with a full-range playback system comprised of two-way loudspeakers. The room/reproduction system displays a flat response, with a level deviation of ±3dB between 20 Hz and 18kHz. This studio is optimized for multichannel recording and playback, with up to 30 discrete channels and loudspeakers available in the control room.

The NHK 22.2 multi-channel sound system (Figure 3) consists of a ten-loudspeaker surround middle layer, an eight-loudspeaker surround upper layer, an overhead VOG (Voice Of God) loudspeaker, a front LCR (Left, Center, Right) lower layer and two subwoofers.

Figure 1. McGill University Studio 22.

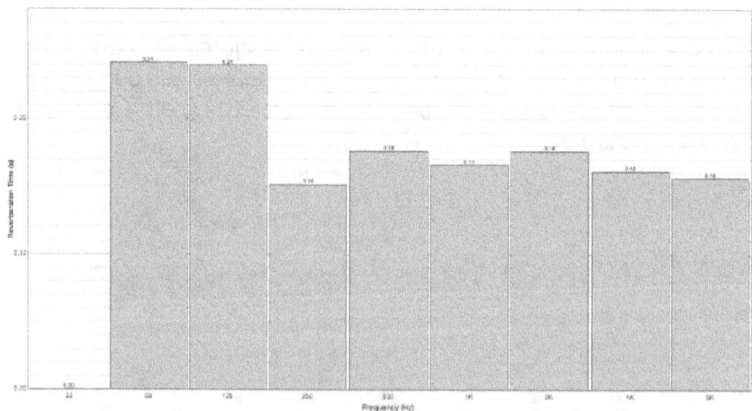

Figure 2. Studio 22 reverberation time (T30). The lowest octave band is excluded due to noise introduced by the measurement computer

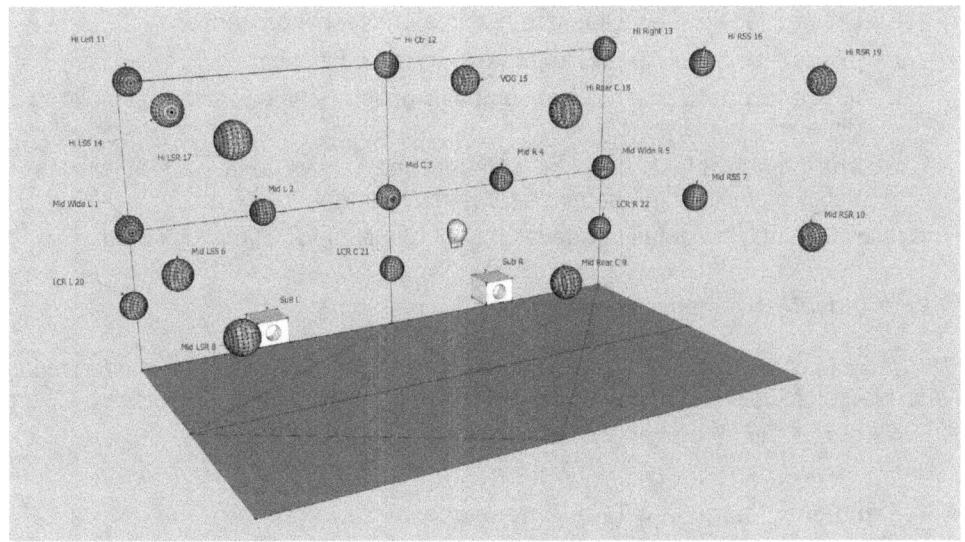

Figure 3: 22.2 multi-channel sound system loudspeaker configuration.

## 4. Experimental Design

The source material used for this investigation was a commercially released track recorded in the early 1980s. The sources were largely recorded via direct injection (DI) and those recorded with microphones contained little or no natural ambience.

The processing and plugins used in this mix study were conventional tools developed for monophonic and stereo use. Commercially available reverberation, delay and processing plug-ins were used in the design of the three-dimensional spatial architecture. Multi-channel reverberation from McGill University's Virtual Acoustics Technology Laboratory (Space Builder) was the only dedicated multi-channel tool employed. It was used in the design of the hemispherical spatial architecture.

The approach taken for this investigation was to create a believable three-dimensional presentation of the source material within the 22.2 array, and afterwards examine the strategies and techniques that proved effective. Critical listening assessment was done by faculty and graduate students of the McGill Sound Recording department. The mix platform was Protools 10, and all processes (excluding Space Builder) were performed within the DAW.

The requirements set out for the creation of an effective 3D sonic image from a monophonic source as perceived from the mix position were:

1. Defined localization within the hemispherical environment.
2. Image size should be appropriate to musical function.
3. Image expansion should encompass optimally three, and minimally two-dimensional planes.
4. The image must have a coherent immersive aspect that places it believably within the hemispherical environment.

The following sections detail the development of the image of the kick drum:

## 4.1. Original Monophonic Source Track

The monophonic source image of the kick drum was located in the middle center loudspeaker of the 22.2 array. Conventional equalization and compression were employed as in standard mix practice (Figure 4).

## 4.2. Expanding Image into Two Dimensions

The original source track was bussed to a separate channel strip within Protools and assigned to the center loudspeaker in the lower LCR (Figure 5). This increased the perceived size of the image and expanded it into two dimensions. Separate equalization and compression was used on this track.

## 4.3. Increasing Immersive Content

The original source track was bussed to a third channel strip within Protools, and sent to the center rear loudspeaker of the middle ring (Figure 6). Discrete compression and equalization were again used on this channel. The purpose of this technique was to add an immersive aspect to the kick drum. No listeners reported localization of the kick drum image from the rear. This technique expanded the image of the kick drum into three dimensions, and also served to distribute low frequency energy to multiple loudspeakers throughout the array. Localization of the image to the front center was maintained, image size was increased to three dimensions, but the result was judged to lack both the desired immersion and power appropriate for believability.

## 4.4. Expanding Perceived Size and Power

Figure 7 illustrates the addition of the left and right subwoofers to the kick drum image. The monophonic source track arrived there via a stereo send, and was panned center. This localized the image downward, and added extended low frequency response within the sound field.

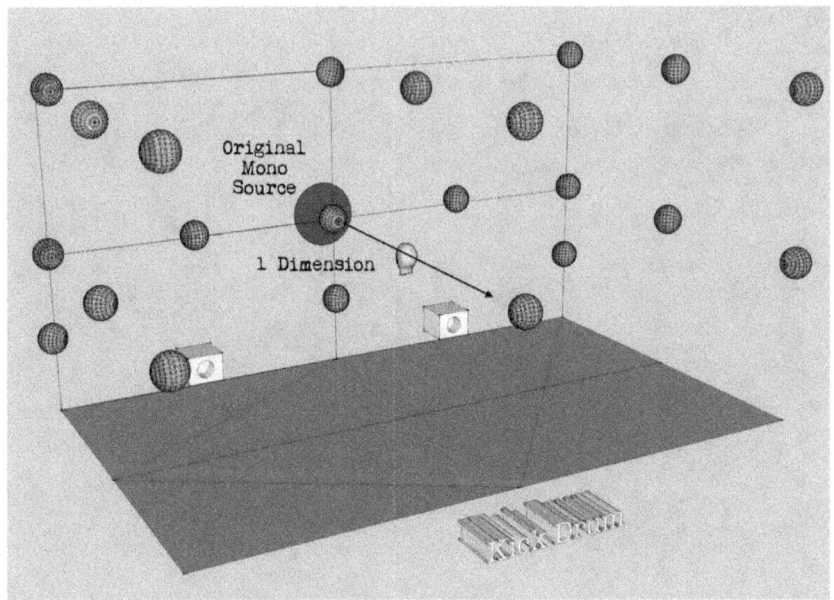

Figure 4: Original monophonic source image.

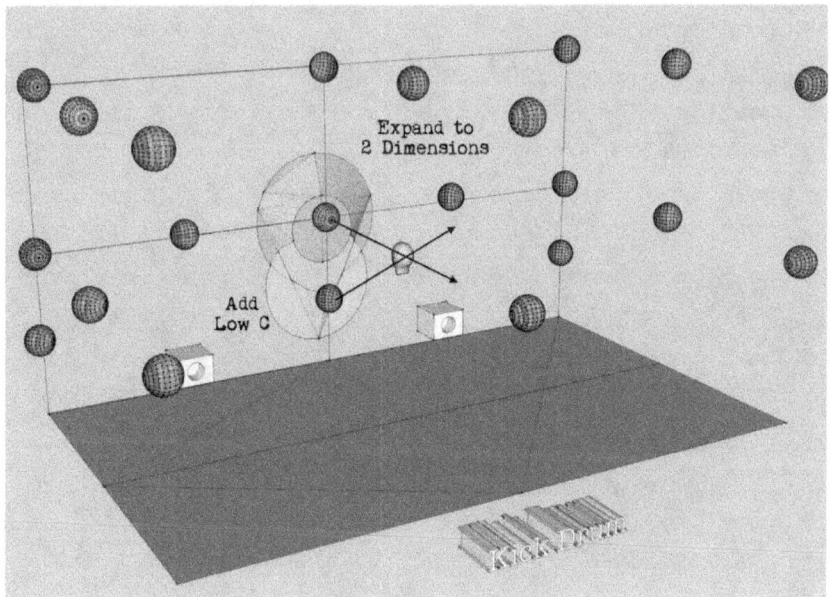

Figure 5: Low center loudspeaker added to image.

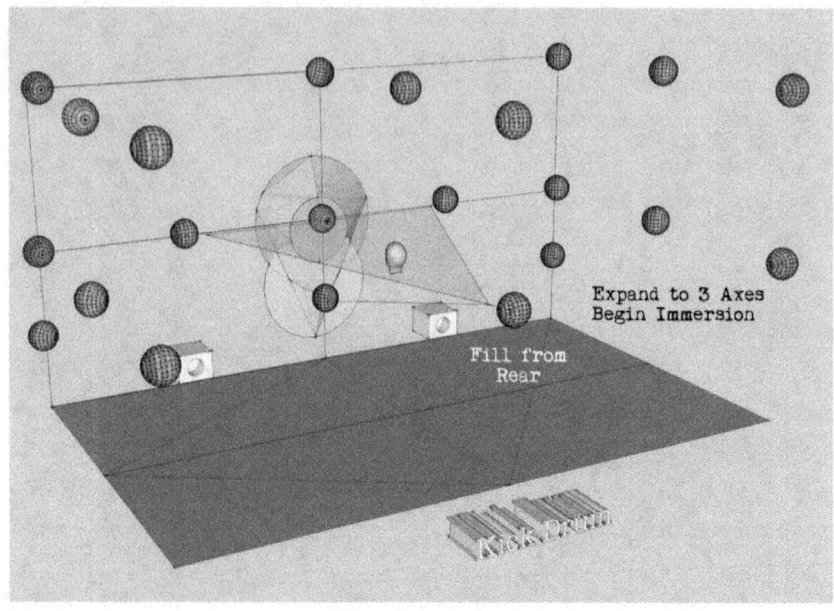

Figure 6: Rear middle center loudspeaker added to image.

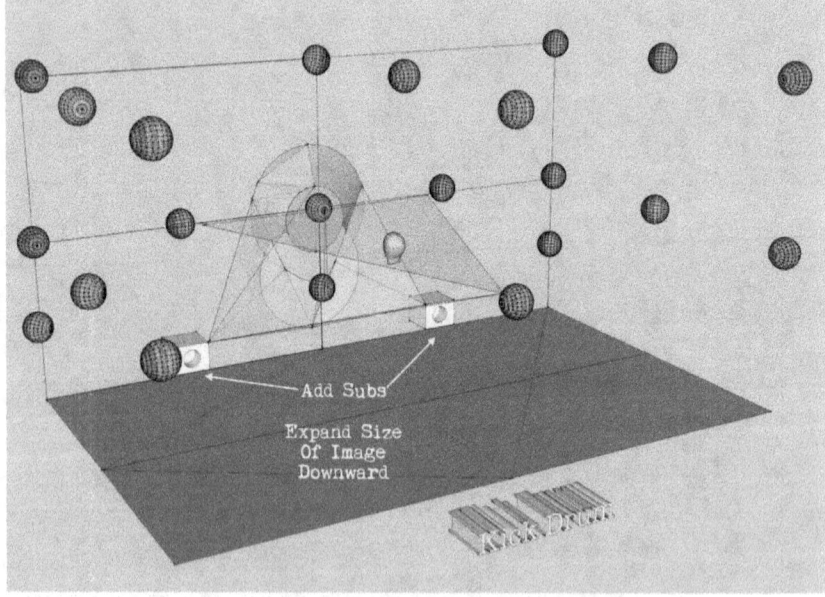

Figure 7: Subwoofer loudspeakers expand image.

## 4.5. Focusing Impact of Image

At this stage in the development of the 3D image, the kick drum was judged to have acceptable size, but lacked detail. The solution was to buss the original source track to a fourth channel strip and add a high degree of compression. This track was panned center in the narrow left and right loudspeakers of the middle ring and blended with the expanded 3D image, (Figure 8).

## 4.6. Surround Image Expansion

The final step was to expand the immersive aspect of three dimensional image of the kick drum. The original monophonic source track was bussed to the middle rear left and right surrounds, (Figure 9). The final addition improved immersive perception, distributed additional low frequency energy, and added weight to the image without detracting from the frontal localization.

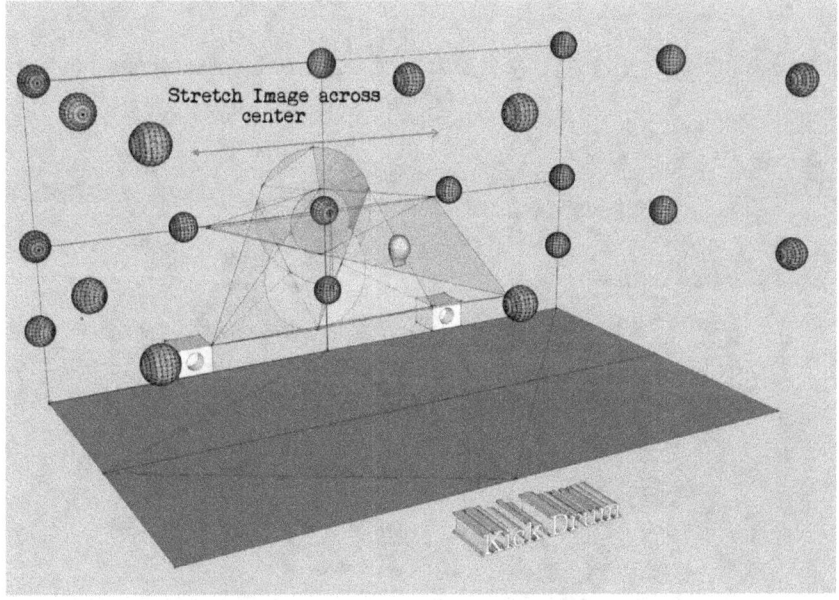

Figure 8: Narrow left and right middle loudspeakers adds focus to image.

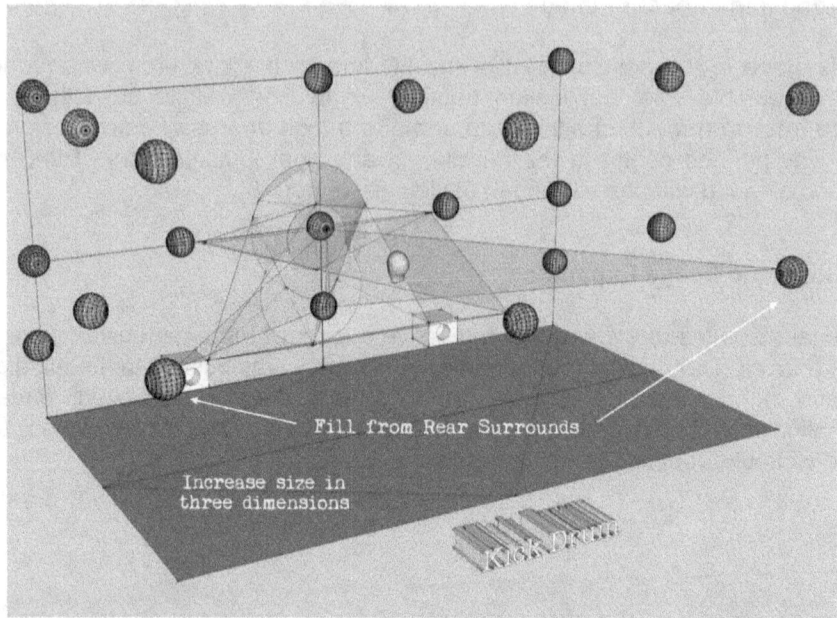

Figure 9: Middle left and right rear surround speaker increase immersive content of image.

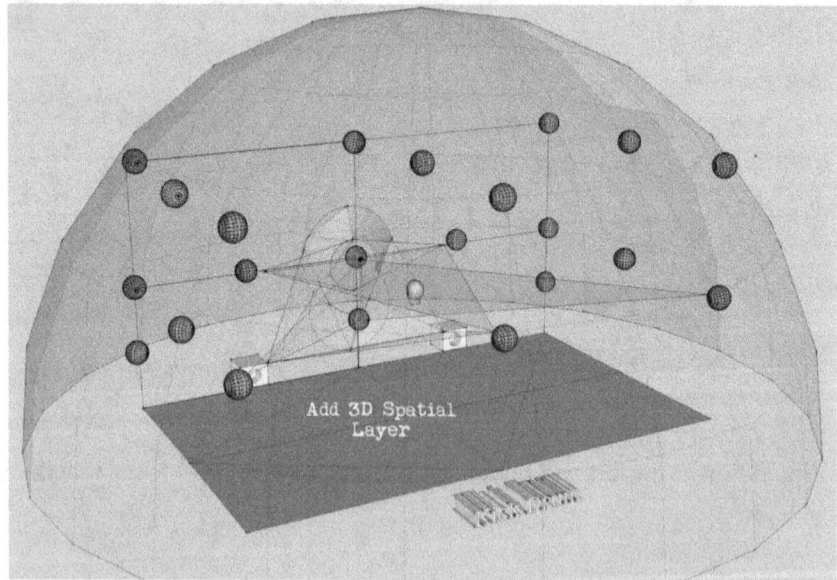

Figure 10: Expanded image is placed in hemispherical acoustic.

## 4.7. Hemispherical Integration

The last step in the creation of the kick drum image was to integrate it into the global spatial architecture. This was achieved by the addition of the Space Builder multi-channel reverberation, (Figure 10).

The final immersive, three-dimensional image of the kick drum within the 22.2 sound field contained information from nine discrete loudspeakers: (1) middle center, (2) LCR center, (5, 6) stereo subwoofers, (7) rear center, (8, 9) rear left and right surround. Separate processing (equalization and compression) was used on the track information routed to loudspeakers 1-6.

## 5. Conclusions

The level of image development required to achieve three-dimensional believability and immersion is far greater than that required for conventional stereo presentation. It was found that believability was achieved when the source image was spread into three distinct planes during playback, essentially sound radiation in the $X$, $Y$ and $Z$ axes. It was also the observation of the author that low frequency power and immersion increased when spread between multiple loudspeakers that did not necessarily create the source localization.

The lack of multi-dimensional tools in the discussed mix investigation, and the subsequent use of conventional monophonic and stereo tools, necessitates a large time investment and tedious workflow that must be performed on each and every musical element of the mix. This workflow is not commercially viable, and would be improved with a simple, non-rendering 3D panning tool, and multi-channel (4-8), non-rendering equalization and compression processors.

## 6. Future Work

The mixing and recording of popular music for three-dimensional presentation is in its infancy. Every aspect of this type of capture and presentation will require much work to be understood and mastered.

Future work to propel this area forward will include the development of studio recording techniques and practices, the continued development and improvement of multi-channel mixing tools for the manipulation of the source tracks and the development of spatial processing handling early and late reflections, reverberation and other effects processes.

In the current climate, much effort for 3D sound creation is being focused on post-processes to generate the immersive experience. It is the opinion of the author that a fundamental understanding of the basic principles derived from the practice of both mixing and recording in loudspeaker arrays with height channels will aid, enhance, and help define the development and architecture of future 3D tools.

## 7. References

[1] Auro 3D Beautifyer, http://www.auro-3d.com/consumer/experience/, (2015).
[2] Auro Technologies, http://www.auro-3d.com/consumer/technology/ (2015).
[3] Bang & Olufsen Car Audio, http://www.bang-olufsen.com/en/car-audio, (2015).
[4] DTS Headphone X, http://listen.dts.com/pages/headphone-x, (2015).
[5] Dolby Laboratories, Inc. "Dolby Atmos Home Theater Installation Guidelines." In, (2014).
[6] ———. "Dolby® Atmostm Next-Generation Audio for Cinema." Dolby Laboratories, Inc., 2013.
[7] Hamasaki, Kimio; Hiyama, Koichiro; Okumura, Reiko. "The 22.2 Multichannel Sound System and Its Application." In *AES Convention:118*. Barcelona, Spain: Audio Engineering Society, 2005.
[8] Hamasaki, Kimio; Shinmura, Toru; Akita, Shoji; Hiyama, Koichiro. "Multichannel Recording Techniques for Reproducing Adequate Spatial Impression." In *AES Conference:24th International Conference: Multichannel Audio, The New Reality*. Banff, Alberta, Canada: Audio Engineering Society, 2003.
[9] Harman Automotive, http://www.harman.com/EN-US/Solutions/Home/Pages/AutomotiveBrandedAudio.aspx, (2015).
[10] Hinata, Tsuyoshi; Ootakeyama, Yuichi; Sueishi, Hiromi. "Live Production of 22.2 Multichannel Sound for Sports Programs." In *AES 40th International Conference: Spatial Audio: Sense the Sound of Space*. Tokyo, Japan: Audio Engineering Society, 2010.
[11] Jot, Jean-Marc. "Two-Channel Matrix Surround Encoding for Flexible Interactive 3-D Audio Reproduction." In *Audio Engineering Society 125th Convention*. San Francisco, CA, USA: Audio Engineering Society, 2008.
[12] Jot, Jean-Marc; Fejzo, Zoran. "Beyond Surround Sound – Creation, Coding and Reproduction of 3-D Audio Soundtracks." In *Audio Engineering Society 131st Convention*. New York, NY, USA: Audio Engineering Society, 2011.
[13] Nuntius. "Multimedia - Streaming Audio Codecs." In, *Nuntius.com* (2015).
[14] Rumsey, Francis; McCormick, Tim. "Sound Recording Applications the Theory." Chap. Chapter 17: Surround Sound. Oxon, UK: Focal Press, 2014.
[15] Staff, AES. "Automotive Audio Quality." *J. Audio Eng. Soc* 53, no. 6 (June 2005 2005): 542-48.
[16] Stenzel, Hanne; Scuda, Ulli. "Producing Interactive Immersive Sound for Mpeg-H: A Field Test for Sports Broadcasting." In *137 AES Conference*. Berlin, Germany: Audio Engineering Society, 2014.
[17] Theile, Günther; Wittek, Helmut. "Principles in Surround Recordings with Height." In *130 AES Convention*. London, UK: Audio Engineering Society, 2011.

[18] Union, International Telecommunications. "Itu-R Bs.2159-4 Multichannel Sound Technology in Home and Broadcasting Applications." Geneva, Switzerland, 2012.
[19] Van Baelen, Wilfried; Bert, Tom; Claypool, Brian; Sinnaeve, Tim. "Auro-3d a New Dimension in Cinema Sound." Auro Technologies NV, 2013.
[20] Wikipedia. "5.1 Surround Sound." In, (2015).
[21] Williams, Michael. "The Psychoacoustic Testing of the 3d Multiformat Microphone Array Design, and the Basic Isosceles Triangle Structure of the Array and the Loudspeaker Reproduction Configuration." In *Audio Engineering Society 134th Convention*. Rome, Italy: Audio Engineering Society, 2013.
[22] "Microphone Array Design for Localisation with Elevation Cues." In *Audio Engineering Society 132nd Convention*. Budapest, Hungary: Audio Engineering Society, 2012.
[23] Woszczyk, Wieslaw; Beghin, Tom; de Francisco, Martha; Ko, Doyuen. "Recording Multichannel Sound within Virtual Acoustics." In *AES Convention:127*. New York, NY: Audio Engineering Society, 2009.

# A System of Reactive Backing for Live Popular Music

Tim Canfer

University Campus Barnsley, Church Street, Barnsley, UK
timcanfer@gmail.com

## Abstract

*This paper presents a new type of system of Reactive Backing for live Popular Music, specifically for a Singer/Songwriter. A plugin device is presented, which adjusts the tempo of a sequencer (Ableton Live) using foot tapping, so that syncing to a click track is unnecessary. Other secondary devices are also presented to adjust the dynamics and transport of the sequencer so that the separate instruments of the backing track react in real time in the manner of live musicians. The context of this work is also discussed, drawing upon the relevant work in the area.*

## 1. Introduction

Current trends for the use of technology as accompaniment in Popular Music are still very much stuck in the pre-recorded backing track tape technology of the 1960s and 1970s, requiring the musician(s) to slavishly follow the click track to stay in sync. Playing at the same tempo with the same music for every performance takes much of the life out of it and is a restriction that has not been widely addressed in the field of Music Technology. In Art Music there are many technological systems for augmenting accompaniment, but these are generally systems of Score Following, which are inherently unsuitable for the more flexible requirements of Popular Music.

The terms Art Music and Popular Music, used within this article, are broadly based on the distinctions offered by Tagg [1]. That is, Popular Music, including such genres as Rock and Pop, is music generally created for mass production, explicitly as a commodity. Popular Music is generally not stored or distributed in written form and does not have a history of theoretical and aesthetic analysis. This is in contrast to Art Music, including Classical Music and Electroacoustic Music, which is music that generally *does* have a history of theoretical and aesthetic analysis, *is* commonly stored or distributed in written form, but is *not* created explicitly for mass production as a commodity.

This work presents a novel solution to restrictive backing tracks. It aims to demonstrate new ways in which a laptop computer can provide a system of flexible and effective Reactive Backing to enhance performance and to explore the feasibility of using live foot tapping data in contrast to live audio to drive a tempo control device.

## 2. Background and Related Work

There is a wide range of automatic accompaniment solutions available for Art Music. These mainly employ the technique of Score Following, that is, anticipating known musical events and following them using a variety of note detection methods. Current commercial Score Following programmes include: Tonara, SampleSumo, and Cadenza. Current academic systems include IRCAM's Antescofo [2] and the IMuSE [3] system.

In Popular Music however, a score is not generally used. A musician playing Popular Music will usually be expected to play from memory and by ear and have a far greater degree of flexibility than a musician playing Classical Music. Because of this, a system of Reactive Backing for Popular Music must try to track the beat of the music without the reference of a score. This is done using the technique of Beat Tracking. It is because there is no knowledge of when the notes occur that this is inherently a far more difficult technique with which to drive a reliable system of Reactive Backing.

There has only been one notable commercial attempt to employ Beat Tracking, which was Circular Logic's InTime. InTime was released in 2005, has not been commercially successful enough to be updated since then and is no longer supported. The only significant mention of the software is a review in the music technology magazine Sound on Sound in 2005 [4]. The method that InTime used was to run as a MIDI sync master, calculating the tempo from MIDI information such as piano keyboard or electronic drums. The Sound on Sound review reported that the system is: 'perfectly capable and in fact very clever at tracking tempo changes.' This is, however, with significant restrictions: 'it takes some practice to get the hang of it, and in the beginning you are likely to experience runaway situations when it just seems to go faster all the time.' (p. 1)

There have been several Max MSP patches that use a variety of Beat Tracking methods to calculate the tempo from incoming live audio. However, the only current and notable system is B-Keeper, created by Andrew Robertson at Queen Mary University [5]. B-Keeper is specifically designed for a rock band set-up, taking the microphone input from the Kick and Snare drum and calculating the tempo for Ableton Live.

Another particularly notable system is the 2014 Human Computer Music Performance (HCMP) system by Dannenberg et al [6]. The Dannenberg system uses foot tapping on a custom-built pedal to control the tempo playback of an audio file. The taps are acquired at half time (every other beat) and the tempo is calculated from linear regression of the last six taps. This system is reported to have worked well in performance and demonstrates the potential effectiveness of foot tapping as a driving function.

Additionally, it is worth noting that there is also the very widely implemented and simple process of Tap Tempo, which calculates the tempo based on the time between successive taps. Tap Tempo is included as a part of live Popular Music applications such as Ableton Live and Mainstage and is able to control the tempo of these applications in real time. Tap Tempo's main use is as a rough tempo identification tool. As a live tempo varying tool, it suffers from several significant drawbacks:

1. The tempo initially changes in large instantaneous jumps.
2. Every beat must be tapped for it to work.
3. The tempo generally gets progressively averaged, making the system less and less responsive as you continue to use it.

## 3. Discussion of Foot Tapping Data

The main focus of this work is to examine the feasibility of foot tapping data (instead of analysed audio), to drive a device that varies the tempo of a backing track in real time. The three main reasons for using foot tapping are discussed below:

1. The tactus (or beat) of music is defined concisely by Davies and Plumbley as 'the rate at which humans are most likely to tap' (p. 1010) [7]. The idea of using foot tapping information is to cut out the audio analysis and go straight to the musician's own physical interpretation of the beat.
2. Foot tapping to music is widely encouraged in Popular Music teaching to ensure a more consistent performance. (In comparison, foot tapping is widely discouraged in Classical Music. While this contrast is interesting, its discussion is outside the scope of this work.)
3. There is an inherent difficulty in achieving a Beat Tracker reliable enough for a live system of accompaniment (especially compared with Score Following). This is compounded when considering the audio signal of a guitar and vocal, which is particularly rhythmically ambiguous in comparison with a drum kit.

The process of tapping your feet along with music is a typical example of what is known in Psychonomics as Sensorimotor Synchronisation (SMS), defined by Repp [8] as 'the rhythmic coordination of perception and action.' (p. 969) There are many studies of SMS and they give an idea of how useful or reliable foot tapping may be as a means to drive a system of Reactive Backing.

One of the oldest and most consistently backed-up findings in SMS research is the anticipation tendency, or the mean negative asynchrony (MNA). As Repp points out, this is the evidence that in tapping in time with an auditory metronome the taps tend to precede the tones by a few tens of milliseconds [9].

In an early experiment published initially in 1971, Fraisse and Voillaume demonstrated that if the metronome sound is switched mid-experiment to be generated by the tapping itself by an unsuspecting listener, the tempo steadily accelerates. In their conclusion, regarding the subjects of the experiment who were unaware of the change in tap generation, they found that the subjects didn't like to tap with the beat, they preferred to tap ahead of the beat [10].

With regard to the synchronisation to music by musicians there are two relevant studies. Firstly, Aschersleben's evidence that the MNA of the trained musicians she tested was 14ms compared with 40 to 50ms for non-musicians [11]. Secondly, and most importantly, the work of Wohlschläger and Koch which showed that the MNA tends to disappear when additional tones or movements are inserted in between metronome tones or the taps. They go on to suggest that the MNA might only occur under artificial laboratory conditions [12].

Clearly there is a wealth of tones and movements in between the beats when playing music live. These experiments and summaries strongly support foot tapping as a method of driving a system of tempo control, particularly with trained musicians. It is also noted that an offset function to allow for consistent asynchrony would be desirable for this system.

## 4. Devices

### 4.1 Relative Tap Tempo

The tempo control element of this system of Reactive Backing is called Relative Tap Tempo. This is similar to Tap Tempo however, Relative Tap Tempo works by comparing the position of a foot tap to the existing beat of the backing track while it plays, rather than simply counting the time in between taps.

This is shown graphically below in Figure 1. The foot taps are represented as diamond shapes on a timeline of one bar of music split into four beats. A new tempo is calculated for each foot tap within the deviation window range (set by the Dev % control), using the time interval from the last beat that is more than half a beat away from the foot tap. If the foot tap occurs before the beat (foot tap a), the new beat interval is used to generate a faster tempo. If the foot tap occurs after the beat (foot tap b), the new beat interval is used to generate a slower tempo. The new tempo is updated immediately and the amount of change can be scaled down by the sensitivity setting (set by the Sens control) and smoothed by the moving average setting (set by the Ave control), see controls below Figure 3. Any foot tap outside the deviation window range is ignored (foot tap c).

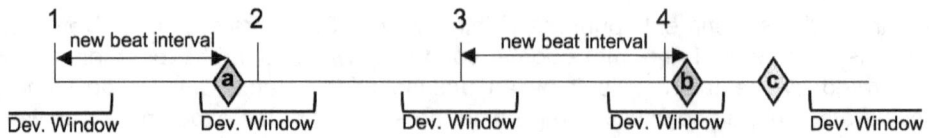

Figure 1: Graphical representation of foot tap timing in relation to beats in a bar.

This design works towards the ideal of the computer acting as another musician to be interacted with.

In the initial stages of development, a footswitch was used to register the foot taps. However, it became clear that this interface was a significant restriction to performance, so a tapping sensor using an accelerometer from a Wii remote nunchuk gaming controller strapped to the musician's shoe was developed (see Figure 2).

Figure 2. Photograph of the accelerometer strapped onto a shoe.

The data from the Wii remote nunchuk is captured using a third-party program called OSCulator and a new part of the device was created to interpret the movement and extract foot taps. The accelerometer, rather than a foot switch, allows for much more freedom of movement and the tapping is far more natural.

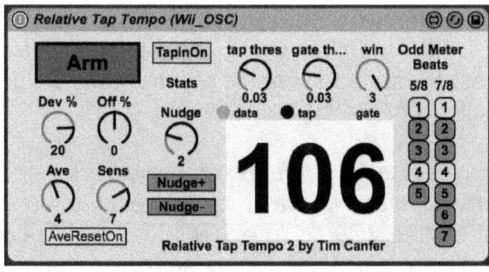

Figure 3. User Interface of the Relative Tap Tempo (Wii_OSC) device.

The controls for this device are as follows:

**Arm**: This button readies the device. If transport is stopped it will use the first four taps as a count in (as tap tempo, but only if the Tapin button is on), then it will play. If transport is running it will operate as normal.

**Dev %**: The maximum percentage deviation window range of tempo per foot tap.

**Off %**: The offset as a percentage of ticks relative to 100 BPM to allow for consistent asynchrony.

**Ave**: The number of moving average per beat to allow basic smoothing of changes.

**AveReset**: When on this resets the averaging after a bar of no tapping.

**Sens**: Allows reduction of sensitivity of the tempo change in tens of per cent.

**Nudge +** and **-**: Switches to increase or decrease tempo by the number of BPM set on the **Nudge** control above.

**Stats**: This button will open a text window showing a table containing the following information per tap so far 'index' 'ms' 'bar' 'beat' 'ticks' 'Offset' 'BPM' 'newBPM'.

**tap thresh**: The threshold at which accelerometer registers a foot tap.

**gate th…**: The threshold for the gate to reject any data from the accelerometer if it senses movement other than tapping (e.g. walking).

**win**: The size of time window away from the beat that the threshold will be operating. (The circle to the left of the thresh control will light red when gate is closed.)

### 4.2 Dynamic Control

As well as changing the tempo of the backing track as real musicians do, it is also clear that real musicians will vary their dynamics as they play, in response to the other musicians.

The dynamic control element of this system of Reactive Backing is achieved by using three devices linked together using the Ableton Live Application Program Interface. The devices are called Dymanic Control and Gain Drive (developed by the author) and Velocity (an Ableton Live device).

The Dynamic Control device is a master control device that is placed into the controlling track's effect insert where it measures the volume of the incoming audio. It then compares this volume to either a constant value, or a programmed set of values depending on position, then adjusts either the velocity (for MIDI tracks) or volume (for Audio tracks) of up to five different tracks.

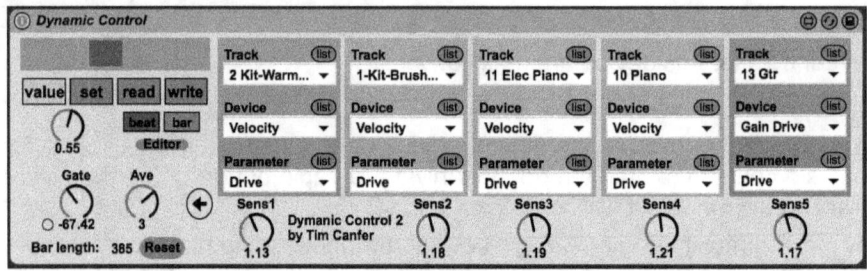

Figure 4. User interface of the Dynamic Control device.

MIDI track velocity is controlled using the Ableton Live device Velocity, which adjusts the velocity of the MIDI parts, much like a compressor and expander. Audio track volume is controlled by the purpose made Gain Drive device, which as the name suggests adjusts the gain of the track. As can be seen below, the main control for both of these devices is the Drive control, which is slaved to the Dynamic Control device.

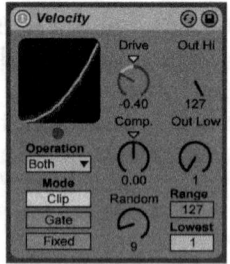 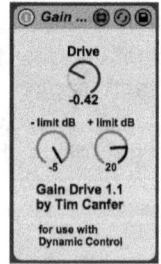

Figure 5. User interfaces of the Velocity and Gain Drive devices.

## 4.3 Arrangement Control

As well as musicians having the ability to manipulate both tempo and dynamics, there is also the more limited possibility of varying the arrangement of the music, generally by using prearranged signals such as watching the band leader for a pointed nod to progress to the next section.

The arrangement control element of this system of Reactive Backing is a device called Four Loops. Most sequencers allow a single loop function; however, multiple loops are useful to select areas that musicians may want to repeat playing, for example the later phrases of a Verse, Chorus or Bridge. Cue points (generally referred to as Markers in other Sequencers), are set for the start of four available loops and the bar number of the end of each loop is set. If the Loop button is set to LoopOn then whenever the playhead is in between any selected loop then that section will loop continuously until the Loop button is set to LoopOff.

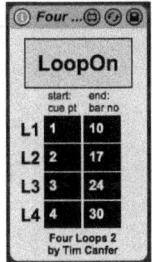

Figure 6. User interface of the Four Loops device.

## 5. Practical Use

Use of the Reactive Backing system has proved encouraging. The system is designed specifically for the use of the author and reacts as hoped, although there was a significant period of training to get used to using the system smoothly. Several successful live performances have demonstrated the suitability of the system to a live Popular Music environment and it will be particularly interesting to test the system with other musicians.

An interesting and unexpected use of the Relative Tap Tempo (Wii_OSC) device is for real-time performance timing analysis in practice. The panel behind the tempo display flashes a colour dependent on how much of a timing change is triggered by each foot tap. The colour goes from bright green at the limit of an early tap, to yellow on the beat and then to red at the limit of a late tap. Using this, the musician can see immediately how they are deviating from the tempo and can use this to correct unwanted tempo fluctuations in performance.

## 6. Conclusion

The toolkit of devices discussed here demonstrates a system of Reactive Backing intended to augment live Popular Music performance. Previous work in this field shows that the main element of tempo syncing to live music is a complex problem with no one simple solution.

This system of Reactive Backing bypasses the traditional method of interpreting the tempo from either Audio or MIDI information from played music in favour of Foot Tapping data; a method that aims to provide both a more direct and discrete alternative means to control tempo. Previous work in the related field of Synchronisation shows a solid theoretical basis for this approach. Also, the development of Dannenberg's basic foot tapping system, as well as the author's use of the Relative Tap Tempo (Wii_OSC), Dynamic Control and Four Loops devices is highly encouraging.

The author's use of the system so far demonstrates that while this approach works, it does currently suffer from similar drawbacks of both B-Keeper and InTime, in that it requires much rehearsal and a compromise needs to be found to balance a fast system response against an unpleasant tempo slew.

Future plans are to test the system thoroughly with other musicians and to continue refining and developing the devices.

## 7. References

[1] Tagg, P. Analysing Popular Music: Theory, Method and Practice, Popular Music, Vol. 2, pp. 37–67, (1982)
[2] Cont, A. ANTESCOFO: Anticipatory Synchronization and Control of Interactive Parameters in Computer Music, Proceedings of the International Computer Music Conference (2008)
[3] Ritter, M., Hamel, K and Pritchard, B. Integrated multimodal score-following environment, Proceedings of the International Computer Music Conference (2013)
[4] Ingo, V. Circular Logic InTime, Real-time Tempo Tracking Software [Mac/PC]. Accessed March 2015 from http://www.soundonsound.com/sos/jun05/articles/intime.htm
[5] Robertson, A. and Plumbley, M. D. Synchronizing Sequencing Software to a Live Drummer, Comput. Music J., Vol. 37, No. 2, pp. 46–60, (2013)
[6] Dannenberg, R. B., Gold, N. E., Liang, D. and Xia, G. Methods and Prospects for Human–Computer Performance of Popular Music. Comput. Music J., Vol. 38, No. 2, pp. 36–50, (2014)

[7] Davies, M. E and Plumbley, M.D. Context-Dependent Beat Tracking of Musical Audio, IEEE Trans. Audio, Speech, and Language Process., Vol. 15, No. 3, pp. 1009–1020, (2007)
[8] Repp, B. H. Sensorimotor synchronization: A review of the tapping literature, Psychon. Bull. Rev. Vol. 12, No. 6, pp. 969-992, (2005)
[9] Repp, B. H. Musical synchronization (Altenmüller, E., Wiesendanger, M and Kesselring, J. Editors) Music, Motor Control and the Brain. Oxford University Press, pp. 55–76, (2006)
[10] Fraisse, P., Voillaume, C and Repp, B. H. The subject's references in synchronization and pseudo-synchronization, Psychomusicology: Music, Mind and Brain, Vol. 20, No. 1-2, pp. 170-176, (2009)
[11] Aschersleben, G. Temporal Control of Movements in Sensorimotor Synchronization, Brain and Cognition, Vol. 48, No. 1, pp. 66–79, (2002)
[12] Wohlschläger, A and Koch, R. Synchronization error: An error in time perception (Desain, P and Windsor, L. Editors) Rhythm perception and production. Swets, Lisse, pp. 115–127, (2000)

# Exploring the sound quality dimensions of hyper-compression

Malachy Ronan[1], Nicholas Ward[2], Robert Sazdov[3]

Digital Media and Arts Research Centre, Department of Computer Science and Information Systems, University of Limerick, Ireland

[1]malachy.ronan@ul.ie

[2]nicholas.ward@ul.ie

[3]rsazdov@gmail.com

## Abstract

*This study explores the sound quality attributes and dimensions of hyper-compression. Four expert listeners took part in an elicitation experiment drawing on descriptive analysis methods for data elicitation and content analysis for data analysis. Participants were presented with unprocessed and hyper-compressed stimuli in an A-B comparison test and required to record any differences perceived. Axial coding of this text data resulted in a total of forty-three sound quality attributes. These attributes were abducted into four established sound quality dimensions: (1) Clearness/distinctness, (2) Feeling of space, (3) Fullness vs. thinness and (4) Brightness vs darkness. Proposed dimensions comprised: (1) Energy and (2) Instrument level changes (Ensemble balance) while 'no difference' was also perceived. This study represents a first step towards uncovering the sound quality attributes and representative sound quality dimensions associated with hyper-compression.*

## 1. Introduction

Hyper-compression is a term used to describe the over-use of compression in order to achieve a perceptually louder sound recording when auditioned via peak normalization [1, 2]. Several authors have proposed that hyper-compression has a negative effect on sound quality [1–3]. However, the method by which these conclusions were reached is unclear. Katz bases his opinion on listening experience, Milner on primary data incorporating interviews with experts, listening experience and waveform analysis, while Vickers utilizes secondary data. Early reports of sound quality issues included the presence of 'distortion' coupled with a 'crowded', 'unnatural' sound that loses 'impact' [4]. Others report a reduction of 'clarity', leading to a 'congested' sound lacking 'air' [5]. Associated artifacts involve the denigration of kick drums to a 'dull thud' and a lessening of the perception of 'snap' on snares [5]. Furthermore, hyper-compressed music is perceived as lacking 'detail', 'definition' and presenting a general musical 'clutter' [6].

Growing discontent with the effects of hyper-compression led to the implementation of loudness normalization standards. These standards removed the competitive advantage previously offered to hyper-compressed masters while addressing issues relating to listener comfort [7] and DAC distortion by 0dBFs+ signals [8–10]. This led to the assertion that the loudness wars were over [11, 12]. However, loudness normalization does not specifically address sound quality issues but rather is an end-user solution designed to reduce level differences between programs [7, 13–15]. Consequently, the practice of hyper-compression may prevail in this 'loudness normalized' music industry due to confusion concerning the perceived sound quality attributes of hyper-compressed music [16, 17].

Prior research into dynamic range compression (DRC) has focused on listener preference. Results indicate a general preference for moderate compression [18–20]. However, an ecologically valid experiment revealed no significant preference for original recordings vs. recordings re-mastered with reduced dynamic range [21]. In this instance, additional processing used during re-mastering was thought to account for the discrepancy. It should be noted that expected differences between stimuli are small due to the reported difficulty perceiving the effects of DRC [21]. In order to address this difficulty, studies have used a forced choice pairs methodology. This methodology minimizes disagreement between participants due to the absence of the option to select 'no preference' [22]. While forced-choice experiments ensure statistically relevant data, they do not indicate whether differences are audible for all levels of the stimuli. This reduces the experimental sensitivity and may result in a false-positive outcome. These preference judgments are affective measurements based on cognitive factors and importantly, on specific quality attributes of the sound [23]. In order to fully understand the factors leading to preference for DRC, clear identification of the attributes underlying this judgment is necessary. This study represents a first step towards uncovering the sound quality attributes and representative sound quality dimensions associated with hyper-compression.

## 2. Methods

A hybrid methodology, drawing on descriptive analysis methods for data elicitation and qualitative techniques for data analysis was used. Descriptive analysis is an approach derived from the food industry to determine specific sensory attributes of a single product or sensory differences between products [24]. It comprises various methodologies. The specific method adapted for this study is known as 'deviation from reference method' [24]. This method uses a reference sample to judge subsequent samples. It is useful when perceived differences are small or when the objective of the study is to compare the stimuli to a meaningful reference [24]. For the current study, an open-ended question was used to generate text data for analysis. Open-ended questions minimize the chance that audible attributes are overlooked [25].

Following the elicitation of text data, analysis was performed using a technique called content analysis. The purpose of content analysis is to facilitate specific inferences to be made from text concerning its context. This method may be conducted in both quantitative or qualitative modes [26]. Quantitative content analysis is described as a 'statistical technique for obtaining descriptive data on content variables' [27] and is used to test hypotheses. In contrast, qualitative content analysis is suitable for establishing hypothesis, which is the focus of this study. While both approaches utilize frequency data, qualitative studies are used to determine the presence or absence of content rather than the number of times the content appears [27].

In this study, content analysis involved three phases: in vivo coding, axial coding and a final abstraction (Figure 1). The 'in vivo' method records the exact language used to describe the differences between the stimuli by participants [28]. Phrases used by participants were analyzed and distilled into a number of categories whilst maintaining data integrity and ensuring no loss of detail. References to sound quality attributes were recorded as codes in brackets at the side of the page.

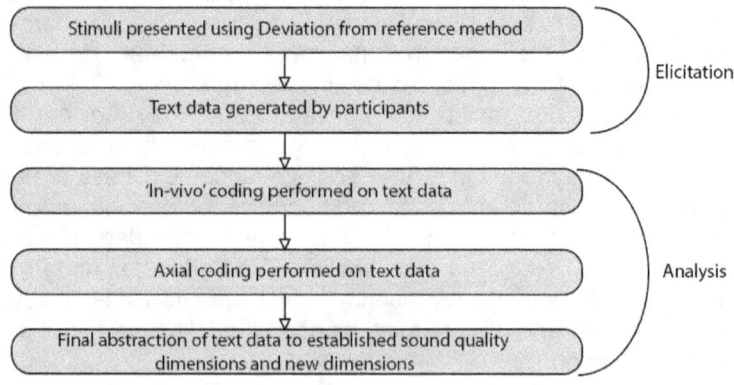

Figure 1. The methodology from elicitation to analysis

The axial coding stage is used to group similar data into higher-level categories in order to reduce the number of initial codes developed to a more manageable number [28]. The process involved re-visiting the data numerous times to determine the label that most accurately describes the sub-categories it contains.

This process requires the researcher to have in-depth knowledge of the subject area to ensure accurate categorization.

Following this, a final abstraction was used to abduct the revised categories into known sound quality dimensions using attribute descriptions provided in literature. This bridges the gap between colloquial attributes and established dimensions, allowing perceived differences to be described using a recognized lexicon. When an established sound quality dimension is inapplicable, a new dimension is developed. The resulting dimensions therefore rely on interpretations provided by the participant and researcher. This data is used to generate a hypothesis concerning what sound quality dimensions are affected by hyper-compression. These dimensions will be evaluated in a further experiment.

## 2.1. Sample

Four expert listeners aged between 29 and 41 ($M = 35$, $SD = 5.05$) took part in the elicitation experiment. All participants were informed the test concerned the perception of dynamics processing, were free of known hearing impairments and had used DRC in the past. The participants were graduate students enrolled in an audio production module delivered by the researcher, which included critical listening exercises in dynamics processing. While the ITU recommend that no less than 20 expert subjects should be used, Bech suggests this number can be reduced by a factor of up to seven if highly trained subjects are utilized [23]. Furthermore, the participants' varying backgrounds in terms of musical and engineering experience (rock, traditional, classical and electronic genres) provide a degree of diversity. This heightens the possibility of discovering the full complement of sound quality attributes [29]. It also ensures the population demographic of interest, in this case those involved in music production, is the focus of the study.

## 2.2. Stimuli

Two samples of 'rock' and 'classical' recordings derived from CDs were used as the basis for the stimuli, 'IGY' by Donald Fagan [30] and 'Concerto for violin and orchestra: I. Allegro molto' by David Chesky [31]. These are termed the unprocessed recordings. In order to develop hyper-compressed stimuli, it was essential to start with recordings comprising wide dynamic range and no digital limiting. Eight seconds of IGY was chosen due to its wide dynamic range, sharp transients, presence of vocals and the absence of digital limiting. A six second sample of Concerto for violin and orchestra: I. Allegro molto was selected due to the use of minimalist recording techniques typical of classical recordings. These techniques are reported to record spatial dimensions more accurately than multi-miked recordings in a reverberant space [3]. Applying digital limiting to these recordings resulted in hyper-compressed stimuli, given the goal to make the recording 'louder'.

The hyper-compressed stimuli were created by importing the unprocessed files to a 32bit floating point Pro Tools session to reduce quantization error resulting from subsequent processing. The chosen excerpts were peak normalized to -4dBFs and the threshold of the Massey L2007 digital limiter was varied in 4dB increments representing six conditions: uncompressed, -8dBFs, -12dBFs, -16dBFs, -20dBFs and -24dBFs with the output set to 0dBFS [19]. The mode was set to 'loud', release to 'normal' and all other settings were left in the default state as per previous research [19]. The Waves Loudness Meter [32] was inserted on the stereo bus in the default setting. The unprocessed recordings were measured using the loudness meter and the parameters recorded as seen in Table 1. Individual tracks were processed with the limiter threshold lowered to match the required condition. The channel fader gain was then reduced to match the long-term loudness of the unprocessed excerpts using the Waves Loudness Meter. This track was saved as a separate file, remaining in stereo playback format.

| Track name | Loudness (LT) | Momentary | True peak level | Fader Gain |
|---|---|---|---|---|
| **Fagan unprocessed** | -19.1 LUFS | -16.6 LUFS | -3.3dBTP | 0dB |
| Fagan -8dB | -19.1LUFS | -16.8 LUFS | -6.0dBTP | -7.9dB |
| Fagan -12dB | -19.1 LUFS | -17.0 LUFS | -9.5dBTP | -11.4 dB |
| Fagan -16dB | -19.1 LUFS | -17.6 LUFS | -11.4dBTP | -13.3dB |
| Fagan -20dB | -19.1 LUFS | -17.9 LUFS | -11.6dBTP | -13.6dB |
| Fagan -24dB | -19.1 LUFS | -17.8 LUFS | -11.6dBTP | -13.6dB |
| **Chesky unprocessed** | -18 LUFS | -13.6 LUFS | -4.0dBTP | 0dB |
| Chesky -8dB | -18 LUFS | -14.0 LUFS | -7.4dBTP | -7.6dB |
| Chesky -12dB | -18 LUFS | -15.1 LUFS | -10.2dBTP | -10.6dB |
| Chesky -16dB | -18 LUFS | -16.7 LUFS | -12.1dBTP | -12.6dB |
| Chesky -20dB | -18 LUFS | -16.9 LUFS | -12.0dBTP | -12.5dB |
| Chesky -24dB | -18 LUFS | -16.9 LUFS | -12.1dBTP | -12.6dB |

Table 1. Loudness normalization of stimuli

## 2.3. Experimental setup

Two ATC SCM20 ASL loudspeakers were set up on stands 150cm apart in a recording studio. This room was acoustically treated to function as a live recording room although it was characteristically damped. A MiniSPL microphone and NTi Acoustilyser were positioned at the apex of an equilateral triangle set to C weighting and slow. Each loudspeaker was fed from a Benchmark DAC-1HDR calibrated to 67dB SPL at -18dBFs using pink noise. Given the use of the ITU-R

BS 1770 loudness weighting to develop the stimuli, 70 dB SPL was chosen as the reference level. The ITU-R BS.1770 weighting was developed with broadcasting in mind and therefore the reference level is tied to preferred listening levels in a domestic environment, found to lie between 60.5dBA for television to 69dBA for home theatre applications [33]. The ITU-R BS.1770 weighting is known as the revised low-frequency B curve (RLB) and therefore, 70dBSPL, which represents B-weighting, was used to ensure no loudness differences between stimuli are perceived.

Four chairs were arranged in a square 2*2 with the apex of an equilateral triangle, derived from the loudspeaker locations, lying between the two rear chairs. In an effort to retain ecological validity in the data gathering exercise, all four subjects were tested together. Participants were asked to refrain from talking to each other and avoid using other forms of non-verbal language during the test. However, they were allowed to request additional repetitions of the stimuli controlled by the researcher. Asch suggests that when participants communicate during a session, biases can occur [34]. Indeed, communication can encompass any characteristic derived from the presence of others that causes distraction during the test [35]. Such characteristics include distracting noises or gestures, high status and unusual dress or mannerisms [35]. It should be noted that distractions triggered by the researcher are equally disturbing. However, given the participants were familiar with each other and the researcher, it was deemed acceptable.

## 2.4. Listening test method

The stimuli were presented as an A-B comparison. This method was chosen as it tends to draw attention to the most audible differences while deflecting listener attention away from the imperfections contained in both stimuli [36]. Uncovering the audible differences between stimuli is the focus of the study.

For each trial, the unprocessed recording was assigned to position A and a hyper-compressed stimuli, chosen at random, was assigned to position B. Participants were unaware the unprocessed recording was always the same. This was intended to help in focusing the task on describing the differences between the two stimuli presented. Given the difficulty hearing the effects of dynamic range compression reported in recent studies [21], this approach, which makes differences more audible, was considered most appropriate.

Participants were given answer sheets containing the question 'what has changed?' Stimuli pairs were initially presented five times, with a 500 millisecond delay between the unprocessed and hyper-compressed tracks. Following the A B presentation, participants wrote their responses on paper. No restrictions were set regarding how changes were to be described. Participants were also free to request additional playbacks as often as necessary, signifying this requirement verbally. Each compression threshold in both 'rock' and 'classical' conditions was presented once. The listening test took approximately 25 minutes.

## 3. Results

The resulting data was a mixture of single adjectives and sentences. Axial coding resulted in a total of 43 attributes, 33 elicited in the classical condition and 22 in the rock condition. The attributes coded in both conditions can be seen in Figure 3.

In order to refine the attributes into a format that more easily identifies findings, codes are placed into pre-set categories thereby creating sub-categories and new categories [37]. Careful scrutiny was required to correctly read the context of the answer given and group it accordingly. This process shifted the focus from categorizing common descriptive experiences, to the development of theoretical constructs which organize the current list of themes [38]. Given that hyper-compression occurs in sound reproduction, sound quality dimensions associated with sound reproducing systems were utilized as theoretical constructs. The attributes were categorized using Gabrielsson and Sjögren's sound quality dimensions [39]. The final abduction yielded seven dimensions as seen in Figure 4. Four were derived from Gabrielsson and Sjögren's established sound quality dimensions: (1) feeling of space, (2) Clearness/distinctness, (3) brightness vs darkness and (4) fullness vs thinness. Two were specific to hyper-compression: instrument level change and energy. The perception of 'no difference' occurred primarily in rock music suggesting hyper-compression is more audible in classical music, which adheres to the findings of similar research [19].

**Clearness/distinctness:** This dimension describes whether each instrument/voice can be clearly distinguished, is free of distortion, and onsets, transients and other details are easily perceived in the music [40]. It may also be perceived negatively as muddy, thick, diffuse, noisy, distorted, mushy and rough. Hyper-compression was primarily perceived as negative in terms of clearness/distinctness (Figure 5). Inability to perceive instruments separately was a source of negative attributes but the most prevalent attribute was 'distortion', occurring chiefly in the classical condition.

**Energy:** Hyper-compression was generally perceived as less energetic (Figure 5). Using elicited attributes, this dimension could be characterized in a bi-polar manner as static sounding vs an energetic/dynamic sound with punch and snap. Obvious alterations of the energy through pumping and lack of perceived animation in performance were considered negative changes while a punchier result was considered positive.

**Feeling of space:** stimulus sounds spacious, open, has width and depth, fills up the room and gives a feeling of presence [39]. This dimension embodied the perception of three-dimensional attributes such as depth and an increased perception of reverberation. The results show attributes elicited were perceived as negative more often than not (Figure 5) but the perception of width was enhanced in some conditions.

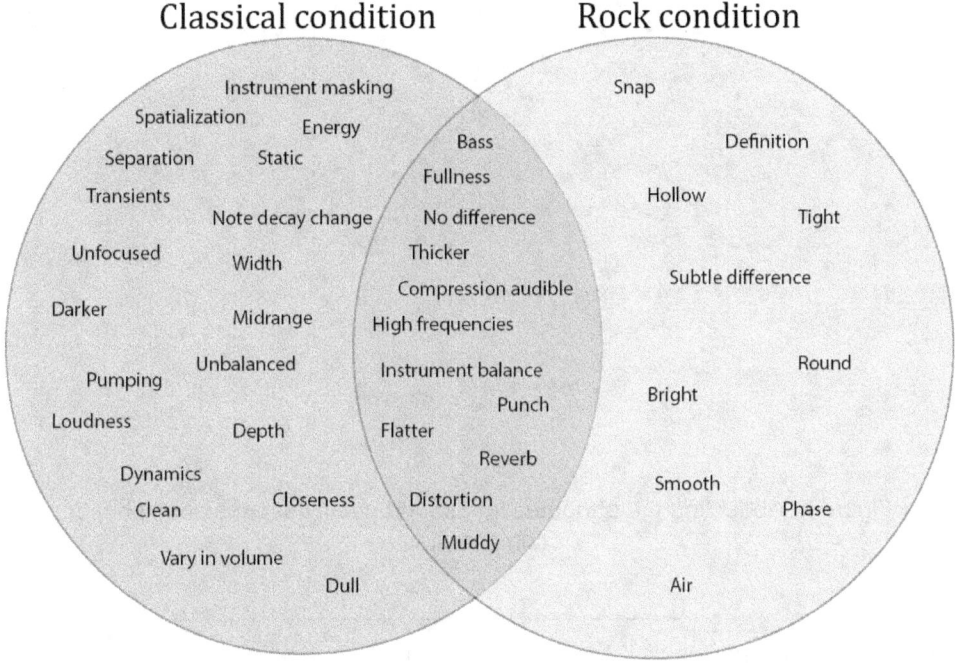

Figure 3. Attributes derived from axial coding

**Brightness versus darkness:** bright as opposed to a sound that is dull, dark or rumbling [39]. 'Brightness' indicates a frequency response rising towards the treble and a reduction of the high frequencies results in the perception of 'dark' [39]. The results indicate a general negative response to the reduction of high frequencies (Figure 5.).

**Fullness versus thinness:** perception of a change in the full spectrum particularly the bass frequencies [39]. It relates to whether the signal is considered full range (fullness) or band-limited (thinness).

**Instrument level change (Ensemble balance):** the alteration of instrument levels via the action of the compressor. This was primarily perceived in a negative manner and relates to the audibility of the compression action and the adjustment of ensemble balance. This bi-polar dimension is characterized as obvious balance changes vs. no perceived change.

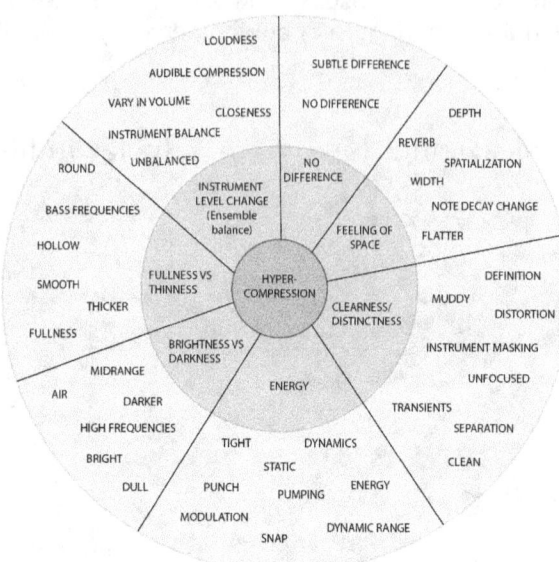

Figure 4. Abducting the attributes into sound quality dimensions of hyper-compression

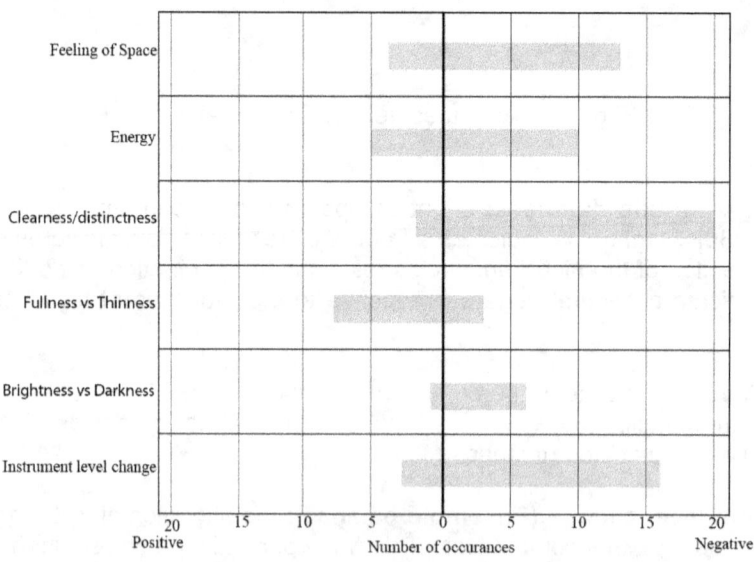

Figure 5. The number of positive and negative occurrences in each construct

## 4. Discussion

The results of this study suggest six sound quality dimensions are related to hyper-compression: feeling of space, energy, clearness/distinctness, fullness vs. thinness, brightness vs. darkness and instrument level change. Of the established dimensions, clearness/distinctness is most negatively affected by hyper-compression, while both dimensions specific to hyper-compression are also negatively polarized.

The emergence of clearness/distinctness as an important dimension finds agreement with anecdotal evidence. Artists such as Donald Fagan and Bob Dylan have reported this objection to hyper-compressed music. They perceive heavily compressed music as lacking detail, definition and presenting a general musical clutter [6]. This clutter is charged with smudging things together. Participants in this study concur, reporting a lack of definition and separation between instruments. Hyper-compression was also perceived as unfocused and muddy due to instrument masking. It is known that a more coherent result is a side effect of using DRC as the process fuses together individual sound sources [41]. This fusing together is caused by coherent amplitude changes [42]. When components of a scene are amplitude modulated in the same way, they become fused together into a single percept and they are listened to as a whole [42]. This can lead to difficulty perceiving individual sound sources within a complex signal. Difficulty perceiving individual sources is caused by the brain's use of the common modulation of sources as a means of grouping them together or, conversely, the lack of common modulation as a means of identifying them as individual sources [42]. When source segregation is interrupted by the compression of a group of sources, a common modulation envelope is applied to all of the instruments. This common modulation of signals makes extraction of information more difficult, thereby reducing intelligibility [41]. This phenomenon may explain the generally negative attributes conveyed by participants in this study and correlates well with anecdotal reports.

Energy was crafted as a new dimension for hyper-compression. This supports recent findings, which evaluated fifty-one extant documents and highlighted the use of analogue compression to alter the perceived energy of a source [43]. References to the effect of hyper-compression on perceived energy, both positive and negative, abound. Lars Ulrich, of Metallica, defended the hyper-compression of 'Death Magnetic' by describing the resulting sound as lively, loud, exciting and jumping out of the speakers [44]. Participants in this study used the terms punch, snap and tight to denote positive attributes related to perceived energy. This contrasts with negative reports suggesting hyper-compression flattens emotional peaks, such as choruses, thereby removing emotional impact [6]. Results in this study support this statement as perceived alterations to dynamics, dynamic range and energy were negatively polarized. Carroll proposes hyper-compressed music is initially perceived as exciting and attention-grabbing but subsequent listening results in an 'artificial punch' that leaves the listener with a "wearing, dull, flat sensation" [45]. This may be a factor influencing the elicitation of positive attributes by participants in this study. Furthermore, choruses written to sound bigger than verses owing to the addition of further instrumentation actually sound smaller due to the lack of available headroom [46] inferring an alteration of the perceived energy of the music.

The development of instrument level change (ensemble balance) as an independent dimension is unsurprising. A limiter works primarily on signal peaks and therefore level alterations between loud and soft instruments result. Mastering engineer Bob Olhsson states that peak limiting may change the position of a vocal in the mix [47] and Greg Calbi uses compression to change the position of instruments in mastering [48]. Participants in this study directly referred to instrument level changes in a predominantly negative manner though some reported positively valenced attributes suggesting this may be a salient factor in preference tests. Instrument levels may also be altered by compression added to FM broadcasts. Mixing engineer, Andy Wallace, uses mix bus compression to avoid balance alterations when the music is broadcast on the radio [49]. This suggests that listeners using radios as their primary listening device may prefer the instrument levels changes induced by this medium. Regarding the effect on musical performance, variations in rhythm, timbre, pitch and loudness are considered the primary means of generating excitement in music and holding one of these constant results in a musical piece that is perceived as monotonous [6]. In this study, holding loudness constant resulted in an audible performance alteration that was particularly noticeable by expert musicians.

The dimension, 'feeling of space', is similar in many respects to instrument level change in that limiters, through their functionality, alter the difference between loud and quiet instruments. The results of this experiment suggest that reverberation and depth were the two primary attributes affected. These attributes indicate that changes to spatial-attributes-of-space and spatial-attributes are audible. Rumsey states the former relates to qualities associated with a space such as reverberance, warmth and intimacy, while the latter concerns perceptual constructs related to the three-dimensional components of a spatial audio scene [50]. An enhanced perception of reverberation can be explained by analyzing the waveforms of the stimuli. It can be seen in Figure 6 that the space formerly allowed for quiet signals is replaced by increasing this low level signal through compression. The note decay is now relatively loud, heightening the perception of reverberation and reducing the sense of space between notes. Southall suggests that hyper-compression "sucks the space out of music" resulting in a sound that "loses its space, its dynamic, its vitality" [51]. It would seem this reference refers to the effect on the perceived instrument decay and its resulting alteration of listener perception of musical rests. These rests provide information concerning the space the instruments inhabit. The heightened perception of reverberation was generally perceived as negative in this study.

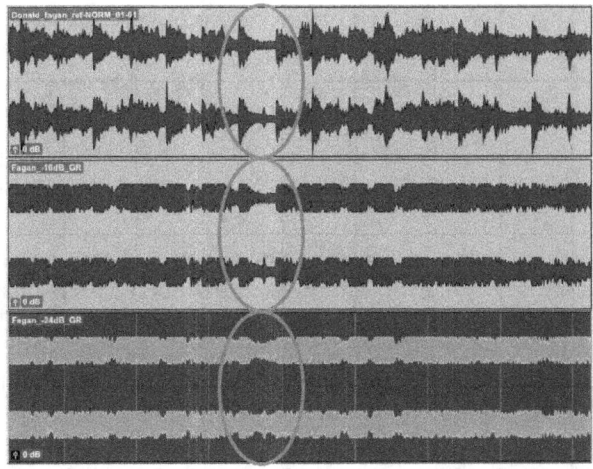

Figure 6. The effect of gain reduction on the perception of space. From top to bottom: reference, -16dB, -24dB

This study found depth to be both positively and negatively affected by hyper-compression. Rumsey defines depth as an exocentric construct concerning the sense of perspective created by the reproduced scene as a whole [50]. To further clarify depth, Rumsey refers to it as 'the ability to perceive a scene that recedes from the listener, as opposed to a flat sound image' [50]. Depth is primarily created through differences in intensity, early reflections, reverberation ratio and high frequency attenuation [52]. As hyper-compression simultaneously alters all of these attributes, it results in a confounding perception as found in this analysis. Furthermore, Ekman and Berg found depth to be a component in the overall perception of 'authenticity' [53] while a separate study manipulated the spatial depth of stereophonic material using additional early lateral reflections between the main stereo microphones and the spot microphones in an attempt to make the sound more 'natural' [54]. The use of the terms authentic and natural to describe depth would seem contrary to a hyper-compressed sound, which alters the note decay in a way that could be characterized as unnatural.

The occurrence of Fullness/thinness as a relevant dimension in hyper-compressed music reflects the necessity to reduce bass in order to make a track louder. Engineers at Motown used a steep HPF at 70Hz to facilitate louder masters but also boosted the second harmonic of the bass which re-introduced a perception of fullness [2]. As bass frequencies need more headroom to develop, they usually represent the highest peaks in a complex waveform and are therefore the first to be affected by limiters, which work primarily on peaks. However, the extent of the effect on fullness/thinness is dependent on the frequency spectrum of the signal. Similarly, brightness/darkness is affected by a reduction of low frequencies, resulting in an increased perception of higher frequencies. Circuits of some hardware compressors are known to alter the frequency spectrum of signals [43] and it has also been noted that certain digital limiters, such as the Waves L2, have a specific sound quality [48]. Therefore, dynamics processing in mastering may lead to a brighter or darker sound by virtue of the particular processor used.

## 5. Conclusion

The goal of this study was to uncover the sound quality attributes affected by hyper-compression. The resulting attributes were used to establish the proposed sound quality dimensions of hyper-compression. The research utilized a hybrid methodology adapting elements of descriptive analysis to elicit text data and content analysis to code the text into sound quality attributes and dimensions. Four expert listeners were presented with two stimuli; one unprocessed and one hyper-compressed, and asked to describe the changes perceived. The resulting answers were categorized into attributes using axial coding and further abstracted into four established sound quality dimensions and two new dimensions. Established sound quality dimensions found to be relevant to hyper-compression were: (1) Clearness/distinctness, (2) Feeling of space, (3) Fullness vs thinness and (4) Brightness vs darkness. New dimensions comprised: (1) Energy and (2) Instrument level change (ensemble balance) while 'no difference' was also perceived signifying the difficulty perceiving the effects of hyper-compression. This study provides the dimensions for a further quantitative experiment. The subsequent rating experiment will seek to uncover the most salient dimensions of hyper-compression.

## 6. References

[1] Milner, G.: Perfecting sound forever: an aural history of recorded music. Faber and Faber, New York (2010).
[2] Vickers, E.: The loudness war: Background, speculation, and recommendations. Audio Engineering Society Convention 129 (2010).
[3] Katz, B.: Mastering Audio: the art and the science. Focal Press, London (2007).
[4] Katz, B.: Integrated Approach to Metering, Monitoring, and Leveling Practices, Part 1: Two-Channel Metering. J Audio Eng Soc. 48, 800–809 (2000).
[5] White, P., Houghton, M.: Crafting loud mixes that sound great, (2012).
[6] Levine, R.: The Death of High Fidelity: In the age of MP3s, sound quality is worse than ever, (2007).
[7] Lund, T.: Control of Loudness in Digital TV. Proc. of the NAB-2006 Convention (2006).
[8] Nielsen, S.H., Lund, T.: 0 dB FS+ Levels in Digital Mastering. Audio Engineering Society Convention 109. Audio Engineering Society (2000).
[9] Lund, T.: Stop counting samples. Audio Engineering Society Convention 121. Audio Engineering Society (2006).

[10] Lund, T.: Level and Distortion in digital broadcasting. EBU Tech. Rev. (2007).
[11] Reierson, G.: The loudness war is over, http://mixonline.com/mixline/reierson_loudness_war_0802/, (2011).
[12] Robjohns, H.: The end of the loudness wars?, (2014).
[13] Association of radio industries and businesses: Operational guidelines for loudness of digital television programs. (2011).
[14] EBU-R128: Loudness normalisation and permitted maximum level of audio signals. European Broadcasting Union, Geneva (2011).
[15] ITU-R BS.1770-3: Algorithms to measure audio programme loudness and true-peak audio level., Geneva (2012).
[16] Ronan, M., Sazdov, R., Ward, N.: Loudness normalisation: paradigm shift or placebo for the use of hyper-compression in pop music? ICMC-SMC 2014., Athens (2014).
[17] Ronan, M., Sazdov, R., Ward, N.: Factors influencing listener preference for dynamic range compression. AES 137 Convention., Los Angeles (2014).
[18] Wagenaars, W.M., Houtsma, A.J., van Lieshout, R.A.: Subjective evaluation of dynamic compression in music. J. Audio Eng. Soc. 34, 10–18 (1986).
[19] Croghan, N.B.H., Arehart, K.H., Kates, J.M.: Quality and loudness judgments for music subjected to compression limiting. J. Acoust. Soc. Am. 132, 1177–1188 (2012).
[20] Taylor, R.W., Martens, W.L.: Hyper-Compression in Music Production: Listener Preferences on Dynamic Range Reduction. Audio Engineering Society Convention 136. Audio Engineering Society (2014).
[21] Hjortkjær, J., Walther-Hansen, M.: Perceptual Effects of Dynamic Range Compression in Popular Music Recordings. JAES. 62, 37–41 (2014).
[22] David, H.A.: The method of paired comparaisons. Griffin; Oxford university press, London; New York, N.Y. (1988).
[23] Bech, S., Zacharov, N.: Perceptual Audio Evaluation-Theory, Method and Application. John Wiley & Sons Ltd., Chichester, UK (2006).
[24] Lawless, H.T., Heymann, H.: Sensory evaluation of food principles and practices.
[25] Dillman, D.A.: Mail and internet surveys: the tailored design method. Wiley, Hoboken (2007).
[26] Krippendorff, K.: Content analysis: an introduction to its methodology. Sage Publications, Thousand Oaks; London; New Delhi (2004).
[27] Krippendorff, K., Bock, M.A.: The content analysis reader. Sage Publications, Thousand Oaks, Calif. (2009).
[28] Saldaña, J.: The coding manual for qualitative researchers. Sage, London; Thousand Oaks, Calif. (2009).
[29] Ritchie, J., Lewis, J., McNaughton Nicholls, C., Ormston, R.: Qualitative research practice: a guide for social science students and researchers. Sage, Los Angeles (2014).
[30] Fagan, D., Okun, M.: The nightfly. Cherry Lane Music, Port Chester, N.Y. (1983).
[31] Area 31. Chesky Records, [United States] (2005).
[32] Waves: Waves Loudness Meter. Waves (2015).

[33] Benjamin, E.: Comparison of Objective Measures of Loudness using Audio Program Material. Audio Engineering Society Convention 113 (2002).
[34] Asch, S..: Effects of Group Pressure upon the Modification and Distortion of Judgments. Soc. Psychol. 3, 113–124 (2003).
[35] Sanders, G.S., Baron, R.S., Moore, D.L.: Distraction and Social Comparison as Mediators of Social Facilitation Effects. J. Exp. Soc. Psychol. 14, 291–303 (1978).
[36] Toole, F.E.: Listening tests-turning opinion into fact. J. Audio Eng. Soc. 30, 431–445 (1982).
[37] Harding, J.: Qualitative data analysis from start to finish. SAGE, London; Thousand Oaks, Calif. (2013).
[38] Auerbach, C.F., Silverstein, L.B.: Qualitative data: an introduction to coding and analysis. New York University Press, New York (2003).
[39] Gabrielsson, A., Sjögren, H.: Perceived sound quality of sound-reproducing systems. J. Acoust. Soc. Am. 65, 1019 (1979).
[40] Gabrielsson, A., Lindström, B.: Perceived sound quality of high-fidelity loudspeakers. J. Audio Eng. Soc. 33, 33–53 (1985).
[41] Stone, M.A., Moore, B.C., Füllgrabe, C., Hinton, A.C.: Multichannel Fast-Acting Dynamic Range Compression Hinders Performance by Young, Normal-Hearing Listeners in a Two-Talker Separation Task. J. Audio Eng. Soc. 57, 532–546 (2009).
[42] Moore, B.C.J.: An introduction to the psychology of hearing. Emerald Group, Bingley (2008).
[43] Ronan, M., Ward, N., Sazdov, R.: An investigation into the sound quality lexicon of analogue compressors using category analysis. Presented at the Audio Engineering Society Convention 138, Warsaw May 7 (2015).
[44] Michaels, S.: Death Magnetic "loudness war" rages on, http://www.theguardian.com/music/2008/oct/01/metallica.popandrock, (2008).
[45] Carroll, J.: Stone deaf is the new loud, (2006).
[46] Blair, J.J.: Mo' Better Mastering: The Case Against Brickwall Limiting, (2007).
[47] Jones, S.: The Big Squeeze, (2005).
[48] Artists House Music: Mastering Engineer Greg Calbi Explains the Equipment Used in the Mastering Process. (2010).
[49] Barbiero, M.: Andy Wallace. Talking tech with the hottest mixer in rock, http://www.mixonline.com/news/profiles/andy-wallace/365554, (2005).
[50] Rumsey, F.: Spatial quality evaluation for reproduced sound: Terminology, meaning, and a scene-based paradigm. J. Audio Eng. Soc. 50, 651–666 (2002).
[51] Southall, N.: Imperfect sound forever, http://www.stylusmagazine.com/articles/weekly_article/imperfect-sound-forever.htm, (2006).
[52] Neher, T., Brookes, T., Rumsey, F.: Unidimensional Simulation of the Spatial Attribute "Ensemble Depth" for Training Purposes. Audio Engineering Society Conference: 24th International Conference: Multichannel Audio, The New Reality (2003).

[53] Ekman, H., Berg, J.: The three-dimensional acoustic environment as depth cue in sound recordings. Audio Engineering Society Convention 118 (2005).
[54] Wöhr, M., Theile, G., Goeres, H.-J., Persterer, A.: Room-related balancing technique: A method for optimizing recording quality. J. Audio Eng. Soc. 39, 623–631 (1991).

# Paradigms of Music Software Interface Design and Musical Creativity

Mark Marrington

York St John University, Lord Mayor's Walk, York, UK
m.marrington@yorksj.ac.uk

## Abstract

*Building on previous studies I have undertaken in the educational context, this paper offers observations arising from my ongoing research into attitudes and approaches towards music creation engendered by digital tools. The primary focus is on evaluating paradigms of software interface design (with a particular focus on the Digital Audio Workstation [DAW] and attendant third party plugins), ranging from the virtual environment scenario in which hardware tools are painstakingly modeled to imitate the real world of studio production, to interfaces which are rather more abstract in their visual structures, often encouraging the musician to think in terms low level computer process. The user's capacity to negotiate the constraints of the tool and assimilate its particular language is of importance in either case, whether engaging with visual metaphors for familiar technologies in terms of their real-world practical application or learning system-specific languages which constitute the building blocks of musical processes that are highly determined. A question concerning the extent to which software interfaces shapes aspects of musical detail, structure and style is at the heart of this discussion and is considered with reference to established theories of creativity (especially Csikszentmihalyi's 'systems' theory).*

## 1. Introduction

During the last decade the Digital Audio Workstation (DAW) has established itself as the predominant technology for music creation and production. Indeed there is little contemporary popular music being produced today that has not at some point come into contact with a DAW, whether as a casual scratchpad for initial musical ideas or a powerful tool for the creation of fully produced and engineered recordings for distribution to the marketplace. In certain areas of popular music practice, such as songwriting, it has even supplanted the more traditional guitar and piano. This paper has two objectives. The first is to provide an overview of current perspectives on the nature of the DAW as a tool for music creation with reference to particular frameworks that can assist us in characterizing its effect. The second is to offer ideas on how we might begin to appreciate the role that the DAW has played in re-configuring of the *domain* of popular music practice over the last two decades. The word *domain* here originates from Csikszentmihalyi's *systems theory*, which in recent years has been widely used to frame discussions of musical creativity in a number of contexts [1]. Summarised broadly, Csikszentmihalyi considers creativity relative to the particular environment within which the individual operates. He uses the term *domain* to refer to an existing context of practice from which one assimilates patterns of creative approach (the rules of the game as it were) and *field* to refer to the social factors — namely people and institutions — which determine those creative contributions that are most likely to be accepted into the domain. Participation within the domain necessitates being conversant with what Csikszentmihalyi calls its 'memes and systems of notation', in other words the specific symbol systems that one engages with in order to assimilate and communicate creative ideas. These are — to varying degrees — bound up with the nature of the medium employed, that is to say, the particular tools we use to create the music, whether pen and paper, the turntable or the piano. Where the DAW is concerned, its impact is responsible for engendering new ways of creating music – or in Csikszentmihalyi's terms, the DAW has introduced 'variations' into the domain which have been 'instrumental in revising and the enlarging' it [1].

## 2. An Overview of Current Research into the DAW Interface

The DAW is primarily a visual environment represented graphically on a computer screen. Graphical interfaces have been a fundamental part of software design since the 1980s, and are intended to enable the most intuitive and unencumbered means of accessing required functionality. The essential functionality of a DAW, when reduced to its simplest terms, is to allow for the manipulation of two main forms of information: MIDI data and digital audio. The manner in which this takes place depends upon the design of the DAW interface in question and its visual structures and aesthetic connotations, which have particular consequences for creative decision-making and work flow.

It should be pointed out that a range of software platforms qualify as DAWs for the purposes of this discussion, each with its own paradigm for the representation of MIDI and audio information. By way of classifying these various forms of DAW and the various modes of interaction they engender, Duignan et al [2] have contributed a useful 'taxonomy of sequencer user-interfaces', informed by theories derived from the field of Human Computer Interaction (HCI). They posit four basic types – 'textual language music tools', 'music visual programming tools', 'sample and loop triggers' and 'linear sequencers'. The first two refer to interaction at the level of software coding whether in terms of textual or object-oriented programming languages. For example, this would include programs such as MaxMSP and Pure Data. It is the third and fourth types which are closest to what most people understand to be DAW functionality, and significantly, bear the closest relationship to technologies and practices previously associated with the hardware domain. Sample and loop trigger models, for example, refer to earlier hardware such as the Roland drum machine or the MPC sampler (most obviously referenced in programs like Reason and Ableton Live) while linear sequencers refer to the multi-track studio environment (Logic, Cubase and Pro-Tools amongst others).

The design trend focused around the visual emulation of past technologies has been a predominant factor in DAW development since the release of Propellerhead's Rebirth in 1996. This phenomenon, which is sometimes referred to as skeuomorphism [3], has arguably flourished most in the area of third-party plugin design, as seen for example in the products developed by the Waves company including emulations of the SSL desk, the Eddie Kramer Master Tape and the Abbey Road plugins collection. Duignan et al [4] have employed *conceptual metaphor theory*, as suggested by Lakoff and Johnson (1980), to evaluate this aspect of DAW design. They specifically discuss this in reference to Propellerhead's Reason and Ableton's Live, with a consideration of the extent to which the software design objective is concerned with 'leveraging people's real world knowledge'. In discussing Reason, for example, they highlight the metaphors of the *rack*, the physical hardware *device* and the *cable*. A range of conventional metaphors common to DAWs are found in Ableton Live, such as the mixer (in *Session* view), multi-track recorder (in *Arrange* view), and the oscilloscope (the waveform delay), although as the author's note, Live's approach to representation is on the whole more abstract than Reason's. With Live the authors also hit on a key point of interest relating to the conflation of contrasting approaches to dealing with musical material in a DAW. This is reflected in the tension between the sample and loop trigger possibilities of *session* view with the sequencer timeline approach suggested by the *arrange* view.

While it is clear that graphical, rather than textual interfaces offer the most immediacy of interaction (in HCI terms, *direct manipulation*), commentators have pointed out that metaphors for past technologies do not necessarily map effectively to the software domain. For example, there is a question as to the prudence of modelling more cumbersome aspects of real-world hardware (such as Reason's requiring the user to route multiple cables by hand), when it is within the power of software environments to offer more efficient and elegant solutions. Barlindhaug, however, has made the point that the use of real-world metaphors in the design of DAW owes to the appeal of specific tools in reference to the aesthetic characteristics of the music they were originally used to create [5]. The primary concern of a software package like Reason is thus not with user-efficiency, rather it is about tapping into the user's desire to commune with simulations of often inaccessible iconic technology of yesteryear. It follows from this statement that metaphors found in the DAW are tied to the notions users have about the particular kinds of music they wish to create with the software. On that basis we might, for example, generalize that Reason is meant to appeal to Hip Hop artists, Live is made for DJs, Pro-Tools is designed for the serious recording artist and Sibelius is meant to appeal to classical musicians. The medium in this sense essentially constitutes the creative process itself, in that one could only make *this* kind of music, using *this* kind of technology. It is doing more than simply functioning as a vehicle for the articulation of previously formulated musical ideas. Duignan et al [2] refer to this in terms of 'the underlying assumptions and structures that favours one form of musical structuring over all others.' [2, p. 3] Essentially we are dealing with the notion of technological determinism, which has frequently informed discussions of computer-based music-making. Brown [6], for example, echoing Marshall McLuhan's famous 'medium is the message' slogan, suggests that the computer,

> ' ... like any other medium, effects the information (sound of music) that is stored in it or passes through it. The medium is not neutral; it has an effect on the music. When we are aware of this transforming nature of a medium, we can either compensate or utilize it. Only when we ignore it, or deny it, we risk the transformational change taking us by surprise or undermining our true intention.' [6, p. 9]

Mooney [7] has proposed a 'frameworks and affordances' model, for interrogating the effects of a given medium on the music it is used to create:

> 'A framework for music is any entity, construct, system or paradigm that contributes in some way to the composition or performance of music. [...] An affordance is something that a framework allows one to do.' [7, p. 144]

Of particular interest are Mooney's thoughts on the restrictions a given medium places on what is possible, or 'the relative ease or difficulty with which a given affordance can be actioned within a given framework' [7, p. 145]. To elaborate, frameworks afford a range of musical possibilities, which require varying degrees of skill to actualize depending on what is demanded in the use of the framework. To take a traditional musical instrument as an example, there are easy and difficult pieces that can be written for that instrument, all of which fall within the bounds that the framework permits. Pushed to its limits however, certain tasks become challenging and ultimately impossible to achieve within that framework – thus a solo flute will not allow for a faithful rendering of a Chopin piano piece, for example. This raises the interesting question of the extent to which a particular medium can be bent to accommodate another affordance, an idea which is explored by Zagorski-Thomas in his recent book, *The Musicology of Record Production* [8]. Here the discussion is couched in terms of *ergonomics*, with particular reference to the ways in which equipment designed for one particular kind of use becomes re-configured through user experimentation to another. Zagorski-Thomas uses the expressions 'centripetal forces of conformity' on the one hand to describe the user's adherence to what the technology was designed for, compared to 'centrifugal forces of rebellion' to indicate manipulation of the technology in the service of 'creative abuse'.

The question of what the medium *encourages* the user to do relative to what can be achieved in reality has also been a central premise of my own research which has focused on case studies of individual DAW users in an educational context [9]. The main conclusion that emerged from this investigation was that particular DAW frameworks do indeed modify the way in which users approach creating music. I noted, for example, the ways in which instrument-based approaches to composing were dramatically re-configured by the rationalized programming-style activities that were typically undertaken in DAW environments. On the other hand, it was also particularly revealing to observe the disregard that students often had for the implied conventions of a given DAW environment when unencumbered by preconceptions about what metaphors the DAW in question might have been designed to suggest. Take the Sibelius interface, for example. Its design is virtual manuscript paper, whose rules the classical musician follows, even though this effectively hides a MIDI sequencer. The user composes onto realistic looking pages of music (which can even be given a parchment like texture), inputting MIDI controller information which masquerades as score-specific performance instructions (indications for dynamics, articulation, expression etc). Armed with this awareness of what goes on under the hood, it becomes possible the push the tool further than its metaphor might permit, or in the words of Duignan et al [3], one can 'circumvent the metaphorical means of achieving tasks' [3, p. 113].

## 3. DAW-Specific Literacies

Returning to Csikszentmihalyi's aforementioned notion of 'memes and systems of notation' that one engages with in order to assimilate and communicate creative ideas, we can usefully begin to assemble an inventory of such elements where the DAW is concerned. The visual language of the typical *arrange* window in a DAW, for example, might be regarded as a DAW-specific literacy which encourages particular attitudes to handling the materials of a composition. Zagorski-Thomas has remarked on the strong effect of the visual 'block diagram' aspects of the sequencer-based DAW which 'would seem to encourage the user to think in terms of sound as an object rather than a stream' and that the 'choice of visuals, of what is represented — when and how — is a very powerful influence on the user' [8, pp. 134-5]. I have similarly suggested that the capacity to zoom out of the arrange window deconstructs the established notion of the composition as a design made apparent through unfolding in time and emphasizes the composition as object in visual space [9] — in other words, the piece is essentially a block to be sculpted. Zagorski-Thomas also adds that ' "cut and paste" methods of desktop systems have encouraged composers to work in a modular fashion' [8, pp. 147-8] as opposed, to say an organically evolving one. Mark Hansen [10] perhaps offers the most apt summation of these points in his comment that 'digital audio recording workstations ... confer the capacity to word process with sound.' [10, p. 121]

DAW-based artists themselves have also frequently remarked upon this particular visual aspect of the DAW. For example, in a 2003 *Sound on Sound* interview [11] discussing the making of his album, *Rounds*, Kieran Hebden (aka Four Tet), remarks that:

> 'People who make music on computers don't realise how powerful the visual element is. Whether you like it or not, your mind starts to think in

terms of patterns, because it's a natural human way to do things, and you start seeing the way drums are lining up on the screen, and it becomes completely instinctive to line them up in a certain way.'

He also adds the caution that 'It's important just to close your eyes and use your ears, and trust what's coming out of the speakers more than anything' [11].

The following comment from Dubstep artist, Burial, in a 2007 interview for *Wire* [12], implies a specific literacy built around the visual properties of waveforms:

'I've seen people using sequencers and I've tried hard to use them but it's blocks in different colours and I'm only used to just seeing the waves. I don't need to listen much to the drums because I know they look nice, like a fishbone, rigged up to be kind of skitty ... '

More recently, the singer-songwriter James Blake, in a 2011 *Guardian* interview [13], made the following remarks on the importance of the DAW's visual structures (here referring to Logic Pro) in facilitating the creation of his music:

'I could record them and look at them, almost physically – graphically – and just chop up what I did like and I didn't like ... It didn't have to be all in one take, it could be something I designed from the ground up, visually. That process completely solved that problem for me.'

Duignan et al [2] have also drawn attention to the particular attitudes towards *linearisation* engendered by DAWs — that is, the extent to which they encourage the organization of material on a timeline and how much flexibility there is for experimenting with alternative configurations. Mooney has commented (in reference to Steinberg's Cubase) that the timeline aspect of the DAW interface suggests to the user that the 'music should be built additively by appending one item after another until the desired duration is achieved', adding that the 'grid' encourages a 'default state of affairs' for the creation of 'rhythmical music in 4/4 time at 120 beats per minute.' [2, p. 147] Sequencer based linearisation of material certainly appears to encourage what Mark Spicer has referred to as *accumulative* forms of composition, in which elements of a composition are built up by the addition of smaller formal units until the piece appears as a completed jigsaw puzzle [14]. This is one aspect of the DAW that has become entrenched in writing approaches using it, which was why Ableton's move to Session View, for example, appeared to be such a game-changer in the early 2000s.

Sample-loop techniques — as exemplified by Kieran Hebden's work, and numerous other DAW-based users — have, since the early 2000s, arguably become the most prevalent compositional approach engendered by the DAW. The naturalization of this way of creating music is supported by the fact that nearly all DAWs come pre-loaded with large libraries of musical phrases ready for incorporating into a track, and there is a lucrative market for third party-materials (created by companies such as Loopmasters for example). This has particular implications for the question of what defines the domain of creativity in contemporary popular music because here the DAW itself is providing the essential building blocks of the composition for the user. So-called *loops* such as these are often of such high quality that it is preferable to use them rather than invent musical material from scratch. It is therefore not surprising that such loops should have ended up in released music, including some that have been globally successful- Rihanna's 'Umbrella', for example, which was famously built from a Garageband drum-loop [15]. Bennett, in a recent discussion of the prevalence of computers in songwriting, has even suggested that the proliferation of loop-based thinking as a result of the DAW has caused the technique to 'jump species' from computer-based genres back to band-based genres [16]. For Väkevä [17], sample-based music-making is a form of 'digital artistry' specific to the DAW, which has transformed the idea of the original popular music artwork. Pre-conceived musical materials (including whole songs), used as the basis for musical compositions, she suggests, are akin to the *ready-made* — Marcel DuChamp's term to describe mass-produced artefacts taken from the environment and re-contextualized as art. This has taken us a long way from the songwriter model of the earlier folk, pop and rock traditions, in which originality and authenticity of utterance were foregrounded. As well as radically altering approaches to building songs, the sampling aesthetic thus also reconfigures the domain from the perspective of the ethics of musical creation.

## 4. Traditions of Popular Music Practice and the DAW

One way to gain insight into the effects of the DAW on popular music practice is to look at situations in which clearly delineated modes of practice, such as songwriting, have come into contact with and been re-configured by computer-based approaches. The practice of songwriting was largely driven by the guitar and piano for much of the twentieth century, and these instruments determined both the musical content of the song and mode of its performance. The songwriter's engagement with technology beyond this point was when he/she took their rough demo to a recording studio, where responsibility for the sonic elaboration of the music was usually passed to other personnel (until songwriters began to assume more control of the studio environment). In the era of the laptop, this practice has of course continued, with songwriters now employing the DAW in terms of its recording studio metaphor — in other words, it is used as a virtual tape recorder to capture the completed song's performance for the purposes of arranging, mixing and mastering. The personal DAW has some obvious practical benefits over the traditional studio in this regard, for example: the ability to recall multiple past states of creativity, the capacity to quickly comp together multiple takes into a single performance and the ability to build up complex arrangements using virtual instruments.

It is the DAW's potential to impact musical creativity beyond such conventional notions of its use that are of greater interest to the current paper. Even in the context of employing the DAW as a production engine for a traditionally conceived song, the user's relationship with it will ultimately be determined by the attitude he/she takes towards using the tools the software offers. For example, while one has the option of using the various signal processing plugins with the DAW in terms of accepted practice, this requires a certain competency with the functioning of the hardware equivalents upon which they are modelled. The vast majority of songwriters are not necessarily professionally trained engineers and therefore would not naturally engage with the technology in these terms — instead they may be more likely to resort to *dabbling* with the tools. This quasi-incompetence where such specialist skills are concerned is, as artists such as Brian Eno have illustrated, actually advantageous in discovering new creative possibilities. To this effect, it is interesting to note that the rhetoric of current marketing strategies for the DAW is concerned with making DAW tools appeal in term of their alleged creative properties. Take, for example, the use of the word *creative* in the following statement found in the online promotional literature for Logic Pro X [18]:

> 'Shift, shape, or completely warp the sound of any track using a wide variety of creative effects. Add texture using realistic reverbs that simulate hundreds of acoustic spaces. Build creative, complex delays or emulations of vintage tape echoes. Introduce harmonic saturation and sparkle with vintage tube modeling. Dial in fuzz and warmth with overdrive. Or capture that retro 8-bit arcade style with bit crushing. Use effects like phaser, chorus, flanger, and ring modulator to add subtle shimmer or glassy overtones. Create warm, pulsating sweeps or icy, morphing shifts using a variety of vintage and modern filter effects. You'll never run out of ways to mutate and twist your sounds.'

An exploratory approach towards employing the DAW's tools supports the aforementioned concepts of 'circumvention' and Zagorski-Thomas's notion of 'creative abuse' within DAW operation. Hugill [19] would even go so far as to suggest that this is the definition of the digital musician:

> 'A classical pianist giving a recital on a digital piano is not really a digital musician, nor is a composer using a notation software package to write a string quartet. These are musicians using digital tools to facilitate an outcome that is not conceived in digital terms. However, if that pianist or composer were to become intrigued by some possibility made available by the technology they are using, so much so that it starts to change the way they think about what they are doing, at that point they might start to move towards becoming a digital musician.' [19, p. 3]

There have been examples in recent popular music history of artists who have approached using computer technology in this manner of being 'intrigued by some possibility'. For example it is well documented that DAWs (specifically ProTools,

Cubase and Logic) were used by Radiohead as a means of breaking out of the post-rock rut they found themselves in after *Ok Computer* in 1997. For the two albums which followed — *Kid A* (2000) and *Amnesiac* (2001) — the group purposefully avoided the paradigm of multi-track band recording and instead concentrated on using computers to sculpt new sounds from scratch (in Simon Reynolds' words, 'concocting sonic fictions [20]'), which would then be the subject of a programming process. The move to computers was to an extent driven by the band's awareness of how certain ways of working with instruments had contributed to their prior, now unsatisfactory, musical trajectory. In the documentary, *Reflections on Kid-A*, Thom Yorke, for example, describes how he substituted the guitar for the piano during the making of *Kid A*, as a means of breaking the former's stranglehold on his *sound* [20]. Being a 'terrible' piano player was not a problem because 'the less you know about an instrument the more excited you get about it'. Computer-based methods, according to Yorke functioned as an antidote to the romanticism of 1990s post rock:

> '... what I find interesting about taking on the electronic sort of things, like taking on programming, editing and that, sampling is that it stops you trying to emote. There's something I find incredibly exciting about just leaving something to run and stand there.'

The results of this electronic-music focused approach were particularly remarkable where the use of the voice was concerned. In an interview with Simon Reynolds [21], Yorke stated that he wanted to *instrumentalise* his lead vocal, turning it via various forms of digital transformation (vocodering, autotuning etc) into a 'grammar of noises' — engendering a kind of reduction (or *de-territorialization*) of the voice which causes it to appear as accompanying sound.

In effect, what took place in this instance was a re-configuring the rock band model as a result of its combination with an electronic music aesthetic (derived predominantly from Yorke's interest in the Warp catalogue), which the DAW, then in its relative infancy, facilitated. While Radiohead present an interesting and prescient example of genre-transitioning via computers from one domain of practice to another, what is notable about the post-2000s generation who have developed their creative approach entirely within computer software is that the DAW constitutes an instrument in its own terms — in other words it is a starting point for the creative process rather than an endgame. Kieran Hebden, in the aforementioned *Sound on Sound* interview, states that:

> '... the idea is very much that the computer's the instrument. If I wanted a guitar line or something, I'd never pick up a guitar and write a guitar melody to go on it. I might record some guitar into the computer, then start working on a track, and if I decide I need some guitar, I'd go to that recording, break it up into pieces, and then compose the melody using that sound. To get the sound I want and do what I want to do, it's all about using the computer as the instrument, and the most interesting stuff I've

done has been all about that kind of idea.'

This is a significant observation which indicates that with the DAW we have essentially approached an era of simulation where references to past modes of practice are concerned. For Hebden it is the *effect* of a guitar performance that is achieved by using sampled guitar timbres as the material basis for more extensive ideas constructed entirely within the DAW itself. Ultimately the paradigms foregrounded by the software environment will determine how that particular material is manipulated and transformed. It is also worth remarking, incidentally, that Hebden is credited with single-handedly inventing Folktronica, a genre which relies heavily on sample-based techniques and owes its existence primarily to the advanced audio processing possibilities of the DAW [22].

## 5. Conclusion

The DAW is perhaps best understood as a repository of virtual tools that refer, metaphorically or otherwise, to both the pre- and post-digital hardware traditions of music technology. It is an environment in which loop-trigger and sequencer paradigms — each with particular tendencies for organizing musical material — rub shoulders with sound design and sample editing tools, as well as virtual recreations of traditional musical instruments and notation systems. The DAW allows, in one location, for the conflation of a range of creative practices which hitherto might have remained separate from one another. For example, the user has available a number of tools which previously had been the exclusive province of electronic and computer-based music. The significant difference is that these tools are now available to anyone of any musical persuasion to be harnessed in any musical context desired. In addition we have the specific kinds of literacies that the DAW is lending to techniques of composition in that environment which are unique to the software architecture. Perhaps the most noticeable effect of the DAW's widespread use in the creation of contemporary music is that the boundaries between older instrument based approaches to creating music (traditional songwriting for example) and more recent methods derived from the electronic domain are beginning to be blurred, as illustrated for example by the fusion of Dubstep and singer-songwriter aesthetics in the recent work of James Blake. In other cases the DAW has spawned its own independent musical genres — built from the ground up within the DAW environment — as evidenced by the (now relatively *long-in-the-tooth*) examples of Folktronica and Dubstep. The existence of these genres indicate that the DAW's capabilities extend well beyond the recording studio metaphor which is still nonetheless used to market such software today. Perhaps the most telling indication that DAWs have established a niche as creative tools in their own right is the presence of extensive communities of practice associated with them — the vibrant user forums on websites for all major DAWs, for example, and the proliferation of trade periodicals such as the UK's *Music Tech* magazine and *Computer Music*, which provide an easily accessible knowledge-base of current DAW-specific creative approaches. It remains to be seen whether DAW design will change radically in response to plethora of alternative creative approaches that are becoming associated with its users but the DAW's longevity as tool for music creation would appear to be increasingly connected with the responsiveness of its designers to these developments.

## 6. References

[1] Csikszentmihalyi, M.: Society, Culture, and Person: A Systems View of Creativity. In: The Systems Model of Creativity. pp. 47–61. Springer Netherlands (2014).
[2] Duignan, M., Duignan, M., Noble, J., Biddle, R.: A Taxonomy of Sequencer User-Interfaces. Proceedings of the International Computer Music Conference. 725–728 (2005).
[3] Duignan, M., Noble, J., Barr, P., Biddle, R.: Metaphors for Electronic Music Production in Reason and Live. In: Masoodian, M., Jones, S., and Rogers, B. (eds.) Computer Human Interaction. pp. 111–120. Springer Berlin Heidelberg (2004).
[4] Bell, A., Hein, E., Ratcliffe, J.: Beyond Skeuomorphism: The Evolution of Music Production Software User Interface Metaphors. Journal on the Art of Record Production. 9, (2015).
[5] Barlindhaug, G.: Analog Sound in the Age of Digital Tools: The Story of the Failure of digital Technology. In: Skare, R., Windfeld Lund, N., and Vårheim, A. (eds.) A Document (Re)turn. Contributions from a Research Field in Transition. pp. 73–93. Peter Lang Publishing Group, Franfurt am Main (2007).
[6] Brown, A.R.: Computers in music education: Amplifying musicality. Routledge, New York (2007).
[7] Mooney, J.: Frameworks and affordances: Understanding the tools of music-making. Journal of Music, Technology and Education. 3, 141–154 (2011).
[8] Zagorski-Thomas, S.: The musicology of record production. Cambridge University Press, Cambridge (2014).
[9] Marrington, M.: Experiencing musical composition in the DAW: the software interface as mediator of the musical idea. Journal on the Art of Record Production. 5, (2011).
[10] Hansen, M.B.N.: Deforming Rock: Radiohead's Plunge into the Sonic Continuum. In: The Music and Art of Radiohead. pp. 118–38. Ashgate, Aldershot (2005).
[11] Sound on Sound: Four Tet. Accessed May 2015 from http://www.soundonsound.com/sos/jul03/articles/fourtet.asp, (2003).
[12] Mark Fisher: Burial: Unedited Transcript. Accessed May 2015 from http://www.thewire.co.uk/in-writing/interviews/burial_unedited-transcript, (2012).
[13] Alex Needham: James Blake: "I didn't make this record for Chris Moyles, I'm in the dubstep scene." Accessed June 2015 from http://www.theguardian.com/music/2011/jan/22/james-blake-dubstep-scene.

[14] Spicer, M.: (Ac)cumulative Form in Pop-Rock Music. Twentieth-Century Music. 1, 29–64 (2004).
[15] Webb, A.: Is GarageBand top of the pops? Accessed June 2015 from http://www.theguardian.com/technology/2007/oct/18/news.apple.
[16] Bennett, J.: Collaborative songwriting – the ontology of negotiated creativity in popular music studio practice. Journal on the Art of Record Production. 5, (2011).
[17] Väkevä, L.: Garage band or GarageBand®? Remixing musical futures. British Journal of Music Education. 27, 59–70 (2010).
[18] Apple (United Kingdom) - Logic Pro X - Plug-ins and Sounds, https://www.apple.com/uk/logic-pro/plugins-and-sounds/.
[19] Hugill, A.: The Digital Musician: Creating Music with Digital Technology. Routledge, New York (2007).
[20] Hodselmans, R.: Reflections on Kid-A. VPro (2000).
[21] Reynolds, S.: Walking on Thin Ice. Accessed July 2015 from http://www.followmearound.com/presscuttings.php?year=2001&cutting=131, (2001).
[22] Smyth, D.: Electrifying Folk: Folktronica, new folk, fuzzy folk - call it what you will. Laptops are replacing lutes to create a whole new sound. Accessed July 2015 from http://www.standard.co.uk/goingout/music/futuristic-folk-7284965.html, (2004).

# Loompianola: A Contemporary Hybrid Instrument

Esthir Leml[1], Collin McRae[2], Reed Esslinger[2]

[1]School of Music, Theater and Dance, University of Michigan, USA
lemi@esthir.info

[2]Stamps School of Art and Design, University of Michigan USA

## Abstract

Loompianola is an instrument emerging out of the combination of two distinct objects: a Cranbrook rug loom and a 100 year old Grinnell Brothers piano. The goal of this hand-made interactive collaboration between the authors was to construct a haptic sound object utilizing the natural forms of percussion and strings endemic to both. The result was exhibited for 7 days at the Duderstadt Gallery at the University of Michigan, May 2014. The installation's experimental performances resulted in further research of technology (jacquard punch cards, player piano scrolls, sensor technologies etc), the poetic connection of music and visual art, as well as each object's connection to regional history. The path of two significant Michigan industries, Grinnell Brothers Piano Company and Cranbrook looms, intertwined in unexpectedly fruitful ways. This paper is a short description of parallel worlds re-connecting the gaps of loss and finding ways to reconstruct a vision of a possible future.

## 1. Introduction

Loompianola is an ongoing project exploring the shared lineage of a loom, a piano and early computers. The goal of the first version of Loompanola was to examine the basic mechanics of a Countermarche loom, hammers of piano keys and to form a relationship grounded in the physics of string vibration. Modifying an existing loom and player piano provided a musical soundscape out of the compromised and amplified functions of each but also drew on the provenance of the individual objects. The Cranbrook Loom and Grinnell Brothers Player Piano each form a strong link to the ingenuity and industry of southeast Michigan.

The first iteration explored "hybridity" by constructing a soundscape with the loom and piano as pillars anchoring their respective ends of their shared strings. Loompianola exerts the notion that "play" and "work" may be in concert, in conversation, even conflated. As sculpture, the utilitarian levers and fulcrums are stretched and inflated, abstracting but not obscuring the depiction of a loom and a piano. Ten foot long treadles are pressed to raise hefty harnesses whose sinewy threads explode across the room before they bend and dive into the soundboard of a hundred year old music box. The dichotomy of play and work is as much in question as the independence of loom and piano: The strings conduct vibrations, communicating both the actions of weaver and musician. The distinction of actions causing sound versus textile production is blurred as the tapestry grows across the space; percussive surfaces are tucked into the weft along with colors and shapes that are then read as a graphic score for guest performers.

Drawing on the tradition of chamber music, "a musical conversation among friends in the home", Loompianola fosters dialogue between not only distinct objects but three artists of various backgrounds: Reed Esslinger, a performance artist and weaver; Collin McRae, an experimental musician and animator; and Esthir Lemi, a composer, musical theorist and new media artist. Like any organic conversation among friends, the language of Loompianola emerges organically from its operators.

## 2. History

Even though the Grinnell Brothers Piano factory was located in Holly, Michigan, the pianos are stamped with the word 'Detroit,' where they were distributed through 35 different stores. The company was founded in Ann Arbor, Michigan, and eventually moved to Holly, a city named after the red berries that surround the area [1]. In 1955 the business was sold to WKC Inc. and in the mid-60s faced a serious decline, as the consumers' interest shifted to electronic keyboards. This lack of need for traditional pianos put the company to bankruptcy in 1981 [2].

The Cranbrook Loom, as it is known in the industry, is a Countermarche loom of Scandinavian design that was developed by Swedish immigrants Marie and John P. Bexell. John P. Bexell, a woodworker, was initially employed to construct crates for the sculptures shipped in and out of what had become an academy of arts and science, but soon developed a loom according to his wife's specifications in order to weave the textiles to grace the new Cranbrook buildings [3].

There is plenty photographic material from Grinnell Brothers Music House in Bay City from the early years in the beginning of the 20th century depicting a view of Woodward Avenues showroom with employees, its brass instruments and guitars in glass display cases, the floral arrangements on counters, the balconies decorated with garlands. This reproduction of photograph from the Burton Historical Collection stamped on front: "The Manning Studio, 96 Broadway, Detroit" (handwritten on back: Grinnel Bros, new store, 1515 Woodward) is the remains and documentation that we have of the year 1908, in the first floor a ticket office on left and a tuning department were taking place. Then, general offices, cashiers, executive offices and bookkeeping band instruments and angled pianos. Grinnell built their first pianos in 1902, starting with traditional upright and baby pianos, 'introduced a line of spinet, console and apartment size baby grand pianos during the 1930's and 1940's and continued to flourish until the early 60's. In the 1990's the Grinnell name was revived in a limited number of pianos built by Samick International, a large Korean musical instrument manufacturing firm' [2].

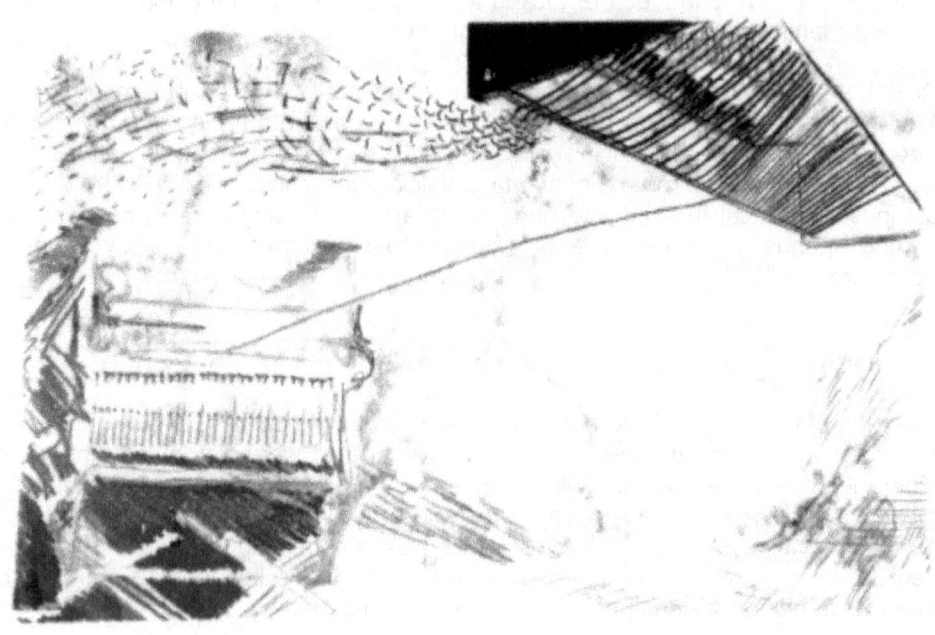

Figure 1. Reed Esslinger, The Loompianola (Trace Monotype on Paper, 2014)

The Cranbrook campus designed in 1925 [4]. The common thread that we have found between the two industries is Cranbrook essential role in promoting cross-fertilization between twentieth century industrial design and studio craft and the way piano evolved while changes in technology that have evolved musical aesthetics.

Looks like the Cranbrook expertise with weaving may have actually come over form Europe. In 1925 the Finnish-born architect Eliel Saarinen (1873-1950) was commissioned to design the campus for what would later be called the Cranbrook Educational Community including various educational institutions [5]. The patrons were newspaper magnate George Gough Booth and his wife Ellen Scripps Booth, well-known promoters of the American Arts and Crafts Movement. The Booths bought land outside Detroit city and lived there since 1908, forming their own estate and a village community. Bauhaus aesthetic approaches the United States under the influence of weaving technique:

'Swedish weavers who arrived in the United States in the early 20th century before World War I found hand weaving a dying art in the United States, but their own skills were valued. American textile mills produced inexpensive and vast quantities of fabrics, but there was also growing interest in reviving the lost arts and crafts of the Colonial and pioneer areas. Influence from the European Arts and Crafts movement and the Bauhaus design philosophy was growing in modern America. These factors created new opportunities for a revival of hand weaving' [6].

Transdisciplinarity originates in experimentation. It resembles an exploration of diverse techniques and modular schemata, recalling the shift "off-loom" of fiber artists (such as Lenore Tawney in the 1960s) where architecture and the human body entered the conversation with the medium [7]. The transcendence of form metaphorically and viscerally redefines the threads' function that can be seen at Figure 1 and one of the first sketches of Loompianola by R. Esslinger. Hand knotting techniques as well as enlargement of scale (beyond the limitations of the loom) empowered the threads with the ability to sculpt spatial contours and thus relationship with the viewer. Cranbrook influenced the global textile design [8]. A description of how Cranbrook influenced music follows.

## 3. The Music Loom

The goal of the hand-made interactive collaboration between the authors was to construct a haptic sound object utilizing the natural forms of percussion and strings endemic to both but based on the loom as a percussive, string instrument. Loompianola as a hybrid object, has taut strings pluck at each other's original function and meaning. When activated by performers, the loom's warp and a piano's array of strings create music that is altered as the tapestry accumulates. Sensory technology embedded in the object activates a synergy of sonic, laborious and playful movement. The knowledge of how a loom functions is crucial for this endeavor.

Although there is a monumental evolution of weaving technology contributing to the industrialization of textile manufacture, the Cranbrook Loom maintains recognition as the finest Countermache loom available for hand weaving today. A Countermarche loom is a balanced system of rising and sinking shafts which we augmented in height and length in order to accommodate the distance between the weaving mechanism and the accumulation of weft starting 15 feet away at the soundboard of the piano. In a conventional Cranbrook loom there are two sets of lamms, an upper suspended lamm and a lower pivoting lamm. Each shaft works independently, its operation not affecting that of the other shafts. The front, rear, and knee beams of powder-coated tubular steel give the loom added rigidity, while affording a better protection for the warp. The solid octagonal warp and cloth beams are 16 ½ " in circumference. The Cranbrook can be expanded from four to six or eight shafts at any time. The locking treadles are especially helpful for rug and tapestry weaving. Solid bronze ratchet gears, pawls, and beater hanger racks are featured on all Cranbrook Looms. The warp beam ratchet gear is released by a foot pedal. This evidence of solid structural design are already a valuable attribute when weaving a wide rug, but essential when spanning the length of the gallery.

The more we get to know this loom, the more we appreciate the Cranbrook's unique design and the advantages of Countermarche weaving. Our modifications, decidedly do not improve the productivity of the weaving process, however they allow the essential Countermarche mechanics to interface with the piano's soundboard. We extended the frame of the loom to increase the "shed" (depth of space between the raised and lowered warp threads) by 15". We engineered additional weights to either instrument and planks spanning the floor between the piano and loom in order to maintain the high tension needed in order to establish playable strings at this distance. This not only makes treadling easier when using high tension, it allows more room inside the frame to throw the weft across the width of the tapestry. This particular model of Cranbrook loom permits a 60" woven surface and therefore commands a comparable "presence" as it's conversation partner: the Grinnell Brothers Player Piano. This Scandinavian-style loom has mortise-and-tenon construction so any additions to the looms structure reflected this construction technique.

The goal of this hand-made interactive collaboration between the authors was to construct a haptic sound object utilizing the natural forms of percussion and strings endemic to both and emerging their "dialog", as depicted in Figure 2. The result was exhibited for 5 days at the Duderstadt Gallery at the University of Michigan. A description of the first draft follows.

Figure 2: Loompianola's first performance at Duderstadt Gallery May 10<sup>th</sup> 2014. Performers: Esthir Lemi, Reed Esslinger, Collin McRae and Sile O'Modhrain

## 4. Loompianola's Predecessors and First Draft Technology

The installation's experimental performances resulted in further research of technology (jacquard punch cards, player piano scrolls, sensor technologies etc), the connection of music and visual art, as well as each object's connection to regional history.

In 1801 Joseph Marie Jacquard demonstrated his updated version of a mechanical loom that simplified (and therefore sped up) the weaving process of such complex patterns as brocade, damask and matelasse. Building on a series of earlier inventions by the Frenchmen Basile Bouchon (1725), Jean Baptiste Falcon (1728) and Jacques Vaucanson (1740), Jacquard's loom included a mechanism that controlled a "chain" of punched cards which in turn indicated the specific continuous sequence of heddles that needed to be lifted for each weft, resulting in the "programmed" design [9]. Chains, like the much later paper tape allowed sequences of any length to be constructed, not limited by the size of a card.

The mechanism that controlled this sequence of cards is known as the "Jacquard head" and, because it used replaceable punched cards to control a sequence of operations, is considered an important step in the history of computing hardware: a tabulating machine to input data for the 1890 U.S. Census; Charles Babbage's use of cards in storing programs in his Analytical engine; the IBM 1401 Solid State Data Processing Unit- the first fully transistorized computer- released October 1959- received its input program instructions from an IBM 1402 punch card reader, capable of reading 800 IBM punched-cards per minute. Punch card technology consequently resulted in numerous applications in computing up until the mid 1980s [10].

The second edition of the Loompianola will consider controlling woven and sonic "pattern" through a form of punch-card technology. One option may be where the project becomes a self-feeding loop: a "score" of music translated onto a series of punch cards which then informs the loom how to weave, which in turn contributes to the soundscape which then gets inscribed into the following fabrication of cards. As punch card technology is an antiquated computing system, as could be argued the haptic knowledge of hand weaving or a piano's hammer and string vibrations, we aim to explore the nuances of this relationship: information, its interpretation, more information drawn from generation of new material, etc. Essentially the exchange is a looping dialogue, evidencing a relationship of direct cause and effect, while still producing vestiges of chance and convergence.

Because the ability to change a pattern of the loom's weave by simply changing cards was an important conceptual precursor to the development of computer programming and data entry we are interested in the concepts of sequence, accumulation, "data" and the way in which each object instructs and obeys the instructions of the other machine. At what point do the two machines' functions merge to become one system? Is it a closed loop or do the occasional circumstances of chance create an evolving system?

Figure 3: Loompianola The May Album Cover (2014)

For the first draft of the Loompianola we set two different kind of sensors:

1. We used the Makey Makey Invention Kit by adding alligator clips to the strings connecting the loom with the piano and using a real time mixer on computer while amplifying varia sound filters. Makey Makey is technology at least 10 years in progress by Jay Silver and Eric Rosenbaum based on their research at the MIT Media Lab [11]. The circuit was designed in collaboration with Sparkfun. We used Makey Makey to amplify and filter different parts of the Loompianola, focusing on the loom and the common string part. The best results were achieved with the spindles (holding a bobbin of weft thread) and the external string which also was performed with bowing and plucking, pizzicati techniques.

2. For the back of the piano we have used Eric Sheffield's Metal Mirror (2014). Metal Mirror can also been used as a musical instrument per se [12]. For the Loompianola's purpose we set the sensor on the downside part of piano's harp in order to exploit its resonant properties by adding a metallic delicate distortion effect when needed. Via real-time controller we had precise control of amplitude and subtle tuning adjustment over a set of pitches chosen in advance.

## 5. Recordings and Performances

During Loompianola's demonstration at the gallery space we had the chance to research further the instrument via three performances and studio recordings. The first performance took place the 10th of May 2 2014 we examined mostly the Loompianola as a percussive instrument in a traditional form using also a bow for the two external strings of the loom. Additionally we added amplified pitch to the external string via Makey Makey. For the second performance the 14th of May we used the Loompianola as a duo with a solo violin (performed by the local legend "The Violin Monster") accompanied by silent films and for the last performance we added the Metal Mirror. Collin mastered a cd selection of these recordings and for the next three months we focused on evaluating the results as music. The CD is on line entitled The May Album and for its cover we used Loompianola's Logo, depicted in Figure 3 [13]. This five track collection of approximately 25 minutes of music is a documentation of all creative work we did in the gallery and its results.

Figure 4: Loompianola's final tapestry

1. Meet the Loom, Meet the Strings 01:36
2. Improvisation No.1, Rhythm 01:49
3. Simon Alexander-Adams, Strands in Descent 05:14
4. Esthir Lemi, Eterna for Loompianola 13:08
5. Weaving is at Once 03:00

The first track entitled "Meet the Loom, Meet the Strings" manifests our first recordings and familiarization with the sounds produced. These first sounds being basically percussive lead the research to a future path in research in recording parameters. "Improvisation No.1" is an effort to create music with rhythmic potentials that can form access to a pop culture of dance experimental music in the 90's. Simon Alexander-Adams' "Strands in Descent" uses specific percussive noises as leitmotivs and builds an atmospheric 5 minute narration based in the treadle movement that makes the harness' chain make a creaky sound. This creaky sound transposed in two different accords creating a haunting loop that with additional filters and constant variations create a cubistic compositional model. "Eterna", E. Lemi's work, is a cartography of the whole procedure (with the Metal Mirror added) whose score is based on the final tapestry created through the seven day's procedure of Loompianola's demonstration depicted in Figure 4. The fifth track entitled "Weaving is at once" is a text read by Reed Esslinger (audio sampled and mastered by Collin McRae) concerning the aesthetics of weaving as a soloist in the process of Loompianola performance, since the weaver always remains a soloist.

## 6. Conclusions

This paper has been an exploration of parallel worlds of history and creativity. It has been created in hope of continuing to revive the history of mechanics and redesigning structures around musical creativity, namely inquiring into the relationships of automata, musical expression, embodied cognition, and play. Using the Loompianola as a collaborative instrument creates a venue for further research on perception, teamwork, and education, as well as discovery of musical improvisation in a new collaborative and playful manner.

## 7. Acknowledgments

Kathi Reister, Jack Esslinger, Violin Monster, Eric and Adam, Aprillianto "Lilik" Sundandyo, Patricia Anderson, Shawn O'Grady, Henry Pollack, Sile O'Modhrain. The publication of this article has been made with the financial support of the Scholars Association of A.S. Onassis Foundation.

## 8. References

[1] Holly Historical Society, Accessed April 2015 from www.hsmichigan.org/holly/
[2] Antique Piano Shop, Accessed March from http://antiquepianoshop.com/online-museum/grinnel/
[3] Patrick J. The legacy of the Cranbrook Loom, HANDWOVEN, September/October 2002, pp. 64-66, (2002)

[4] Gile, M.A. and Marzolf M.T, Fascination with fiber: Michigan's handweaving heritage, University of Michigan Press, (2006)
[5] Cranbrook Educational Community, Accessed May 2015 from http://www.cranbrook.edu
[6] Marzolf M.T., The Swedish presence in 20$^{th}$-Century American weaving fascination with fiber: Michigan's handweaving heritage, Textile Society of America Symposium, John P Bexell Co., The Handicrafter, Handweaver and Craftsman, Shuttle, Soubdke abd Dyepot and Handwoven, Heritage Woodcrafts, Proceedings Textile Society of America, University of Michigan Press, (2006)
[7] Constantine M. and Larsen J. L., Beyond craft: Art fabric, Van Nostrand Reinhold Company, (1973)
[8] Zollinger W. S., Advancing textile craft through innovation: The influence and legacy of Jack Lenor Larsen, Craft Research, Volume 5, Number 1, pp.97-109 (2014)
[9] Newton W., Newton's London Journal of Arts and Sciences; A record of the progress of invention as applied to the arts. New Series Vol XXIII, pp.333-335 (1820)
[10] Essinger J., Jacquard's web. How a hand-loom led to the birth of the information age, Oxford University Press, (2007)
[11] Shaw D. Beginner's Mind Collective, Makey Makey: improvising tangible and nature-based user interfaces, TEI'12 Proceedings of the Sixth International Conference on Tangible, Embedded and Embodied Interaction, pp.367-370 (2012)
[12] Sheffield E. Metal Mirror, Accessed May 2015 from cycling74.com/project/metal-mirror/
[13] McRae C., The May Album, Accessed Feb 2015 from http://loompianola.bandcamp.com/reseases

# Gestalt Theory and Mixing Audio

Matthew Shelvock

Don Wright Faculty of Music, The University of Western Ontario, Canada
mshelvoc@uwo.ca

**Abstract**

*This paper uses Gestalt theory as a perceptual model to discuss the practice of mixing audio for recorded music. While Gestalt design principles have been naturalized into the study of other design-based arts including music theory (Lerdahl 1985; Tenney 1986), visual arts (Wagemans 2012), GUI design (Chang, Dooley, Tuovinen 2002), and sound design for non-musical applications such as operating systems (Hereford and Winn 1994); I offer the perspective that Gestalt theorization is equally applicable to the discussion of mixing practice. The Gestalt perceptual model is based on the concept of 'prägnanz,' or the tendency of the mind to organize objects into simple and meaningful constructions. The law of prägnanz explains how individuals form perception of diverse sensory stimuli, and accordant sub-laws of similarity, common fate, disjoint allocation, continuation, and figure-ground phenomena are particularly instructive as design guidelines within the sound ecology of a mix.*

## 1. Introduction

This paper discusses Gestalt theory as a possible method for theorizing, analyzing and categorizing mixing practices within record production. Gestalt principles have been successfully absorbed into a variety of design-based fields including visual arts, graphic user interface design, audio interface design (ex. sonification and audification), and music composition [22]. The design processes involved in each of these endeavours have benefited from Gestalt laws that describe a person's psychophysical engagement with a given audio or visual design arrangement, such that the aesthetic impact of a design can be described via its perceptual qualities. When applied this way, Gestalt psychophysical principles can be used to predict how an individual might respond to the design features of a given aesthetic stimulus. The practice of mixing audio can also benefit from analyses and discussions based upon Gestalt laws. Roey Izhaki (2013) comments on the creative nature of the mixing process by offering the following perspective:

'A mix is a sonic portrait of the music. The same way different portraits of a person can each project a unique impression, different mixes can convey the essence of the music in extremely different ways. We are mixing engineers, but more importantly: we are mixing artists.' (p. xiii) [1]

Izhaki's analogy likens mixing audio to painting portraits, and borrows the language of visual arts in order to explain the mix as an aesthetic event. As in other artistic fields, Gestalt theory can aid audio educators and amateur practitioners in categorizing available sound-designing techniques. Additionally, available Gestalt research provides a number of studies that demonstrate psychophysical tendencies of human hearing. Few resources exist to specifically aid mix engineers and recordists in understanding the psychoacoustic consequences of their work. An exception, however, is Jay Hodgson's *Representing Sound* which describes mixing as "painting on the canvas of psychophysiology, as it were" [11]

This paper uses Hodgson's research as a methodological starting point, and will build on available literature by categorizing some basic mix practices within a Gestalt perceptual framework. I offer the discussion to follow as a pedagogical aid for those learning the practice of mixing, as well as a potential vehicle for inspiration for more advanced practitioners of the craft.

## 2. Background and Related Work

Gestalt, as a perceptual concept, was first introduced to psychology by Christian von Ehrenfels in a paper entitled "On Gestalt qualities" in 1890 [4]. Von Ehrenfels' paper discusses the transpositional properties of musical melodies, noting that a melody can be transposed to a key that shares none of the same notes, and listeners can still recognize the melody. He suggests that a *Gestalt quality* informs the perceptual reception of these notes, such that a sonic relationship can be repeated using different pitches. The perceived *whole object*, or *melody* in this case, is dependent on a number of constituent pitch relationships, rather than on the specific notes used.

Two later developments in Gestalt theory in the 1920s are particularly influential to the field: the concept of *psychophysical isomorphism*, and the formation of Gestalt laws as we know them today. Wolfgang Köhler introduces the concept of psychophysical isomorphism as a correspondence between a given stimulus and the brain's general state while perceiving that stimulus [5]. In a general sense, this principle works under the notion that properties of consciousness result from accordant electrochemical processes within the brain [6].

In 1923 Wertheimer elucidates a number of fundamental laws of Gestalt theory. Here, the most general Gestalt law — the law of *Prägnanz* — is introduced [23]. This law, sometimes referred to as the law of pithiness, states that both the perceptual field and objects inside of it take on the most simple structure available within a given context. A number of more specific laws are also established in Wertheimer's paper such as the laws of proximity, similarity, closure and good continuation [23]. These laws, in addition to others, form the basis of the majority of Gestalt research and will be examined in relation to mixing practice in the following sections.

There currently exists a wealth of contemporary research that engages in artistic and empirical investigations of Gestalt principles. These concepts find application, for example, in James Tenney's *Meta (+) Hodos* (1964) and *META Meta (+) Hodos* (1977). Tenney's research addresses the ineptitude of standard musical analytic tools for discussing innovative 20th century compositional conventions (4). Tenney contends that 20th century music, when compared to previous Western Art Musics, employs a number of new *musical materials*, and thus requires new tools for analysis (1964: 4-5). Of these new musical materials, Tenney delineates timbre, intensity and density as three important musical parameters that were previously considered to be of secondary importance to music analysts [3]. Tenney's application of Gestalt theory encourages a more complete description of the new musical materials of the 20th century, and accomplishes this by facilitating an analysis of the psychophysical impressions caused by sound parameters such as timbre or intensity within a composition. Of course, of the musical parameters newly considered by Tenney, timbre is perhaps most important to both mixing and mastering engineers [1][2][14]. Tenney's clever application of Gestalt theory to the theorization of timbre for the purpose of compositional analysis serves as the inspiration for this paper. I aim to borrow Tenney's general approach in applying psychophysical concepts to the analysis of timbre. Unlike Tenney, however, I will instead direct this discussion towards musical recordings rather than musical scores and compositional design.

In addition to music theory and composition, audio interface designers have utilized Gestalt theory for the purpose of improving interface usability. A paper written in 1994 by Winn and Hereford explains, for example, guidelines for applying Gestalt theory to the creation of Earcons [15]. Earcons are most easily understood as a form of auditory icon, and exist to aid users in human-computer interaction. Earcons are also used in data analysis for the purposes of sonification and audification. These two methods are used to express data as sound in such a way that users can delineate salient trends within a given data set. In order to design an intelligible signal, the sound design process for earcons often considers Gestalt perceptual laws. The precedence for the use of Gestalt theory in sound design makes plausible its application for mixing audio, which also includes a number of sound-designing activities within its procedural scope.

Despite diverse usage and acceptance, Gestalt theory does receive criticism within some fields for being largely descriptive in nature rather than explanatory [8]. These criticisms emanate from cognitive psychology and computational neuroscience for the most part, where a descriptive system may be less useful for the generation of new empirical research. This fact has not caused research on Gestalt theory to cease, however, as, for example, the other fields mentioned in this paper routinely use Gestalt-based descriptions of perceptual systems in order to improve design intelligibility. Another consideration for contemporary researchers is that no alternative model has fully supplanted Gestalt theory within the research community [22].

## 3. Gestalt Laws and Mixing: Audio Streams

Perhaps the most discussed aspect of audio cognition as it relates to Gestalt theory is the tendency for humans to separate sounds into distinct auditory streams [10, 16, 17, 18, 20]. When listening to an arrangement of sounds in sequence — whether musical or ecological — these sounds can be perceived to emanate from a single source or multiple sources [10]. This tendency is demonstrated in a lab experiment by van Noorden in 1971 [20]. A tone labelled "A" was played, followed by tone labelled "B", and played in the sequence ABABAB. The sequence was played again with every second "B" eliminated as follows: ABA_ABA_ABA_. Depending on the frequency gap between tones A and B, the sequence may be perceived to demonstrate 1 or 2 distinct audio streams. For the experimental condition with a smaller frequency gap, a single stream with a *gallop*-like effect is heard. In the instance with the larger frequency gap, on the other hand, causes listeners to separate stream A from stream B as two distinct alternating sound sources [20].

In a broad methodological sense, the perceptual illusion of stream segregation is important when mixing audio. I use the term illusion, because, ontologically, music recordings can only exist as a single auditory stream. Although there may be a left and right component, as in stereo recording, the two components are summed to be perceived as a single sound source [11]. Mix engineers, whether knowingly or unknowingly, take advantage of human perceptual illusions in order to cause one component of a mix to sound separate *from*, or cohesive *with*, another component within a mix. Much of the literature that seeks to empirically demonstrate Gestalt laws in auditory perception also focuses on this issue of stream separation and stream segregation [10, 16, 17, 18, 20].

### 3.1. Rule of Similarity

Gestalt theorists describe a rule for similarity within human perception. Viewers tend to group similar visual elements, for example, such as shapes (Figure 1). When applied to audio, the Gestalt rule for similarity suggests that sonic elements are grouped if they are similar in a general sense [10, 16, 17, 18, 20]. Humans separate sounds based on differences in fundamental frequencies (F0), differences in timbre over time, and differences in perceived location [10].

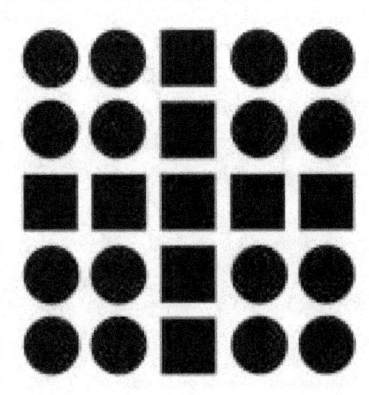

Figure 1. Visual representation of the Law of Similarity. [25] Humans tend to group similar visual and audile objects.

Each of these causes for stream segregation are easily controlled throughout the production and mixing process. Perceived location of a sound, for instance, is easily affected via panning, which moves a sound component within the stereo field. Reverb also adds a sense of spatial depth to a recording [14], and may be combined with the technique of panning within the stereo field in order to aid stream segregation or coherence for listeners, depending on the approach taken. If an entire stereo mix is panned to the left, for example, and the stereo bus is drenched in cavernous reverb, listeners will face difficulty in separating the available sonic components within the mix. On the other hand, the judicious use of both reverb and the stereo field will aid the listener in separating sonic components by creating the illusion that two or more sounds originate from different physical spaces. Of course, strategies will vary genre to genre, and song to song, but the Gestalt law of similarity may provide a pedagogical entry point for discussing how different generic and artistic mixing procedures may be received by listeners.

### 3.2. Rule of Common Fate

The Gestalt rule for Common Fate states that perceptual stimuli are grouped when they express similar changes, or implied changes, over time (Figure 2) [10]. When this law is applied to audio, it describes the tendency for the spectral image of a sound to mutate predictably throughout time. Frequency components emanating from a sound source tend to exhibit coherent temporal variances . For instance, a sound's component parts often start and finish, change in intensity, and in frequency together [10]. The Law of Common Fate, then, is thought to be a result of impressions caused by ecological hearing [10]. If two or more components in a complex sound — such as a mix composite— undergo similar changes at the same time, then they are grouped by listeners and perceived as part of the same source. Additionally, the onset of sounds is an important factor for stream coherence or segregation. Sounds that start and stop synchronously are perceived to be a result of the same sound source, and about 30 ms is a sufficient amount of time for humans to perceive a sound as a new source depending on its complexity [10].

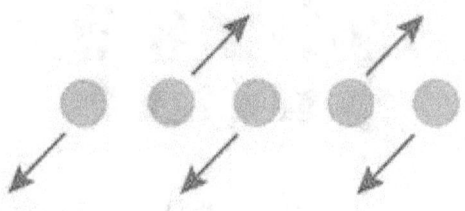

Figure 2. Visual representation of the Law of Common Fate [26]. Viewers place the outer circles and the middle circle together, and the remaining inner circles fall in a separate group. The arrows imply directionality, which causes the viewer to group circles moving together, or with a *common fate*.

In mixing, the practice of bus-processing conforms to the law of Common Fate. Often mix engineers group similar instruments, such as drums for example, into a drum-bus for signal processing purposes. One advantage of this method is that it allows easier control of the overall level of several related instruments. More important to the law of Common Fate, however, is the ability to process the signals fed into the bus in a uniform way. For example, a compressor can be applied to a drum-bus such that all of the compressor's topological nuances effect every sound within that drum-bus in a similar way. In so doing, one establishes a general coherency within the drums via a unified compression algorithm, and also aids the listener in retaining perceptual fusion amongst the available drum parts within a song. One might, for instance, apply a Fairchild 670 (or software clone) to the *side* signal of a drum bus, leaving the *middle* signal less compressed. The kick and snare should retain transient detail while extra compression on the *side* signals may increase the audibility of room noise with this strategy [9]. Additionally, by processing a variety of drum tracks using the same general algorithm and programme, changes made to the spectral and dynamic characteristics of the drums (and accordant room noise) will occur uniformly within the drum bus. Bus processing in this way occurs frequently [1], and the prevalence of this technique may be explained by the perceptual law of Common Fate.

A second aspect of the law of Common Fate deals with the onset of sounds. Listeners tend to perceptually group sounds based on when they occur over a duration of time. The exploitation of the Haas effect in mixing, for instance, provides an example of this aspect of the law of Common Fate. The Haas effect refers to the tendency of humans to fuse auditory stimuli that are separated by a sufficiently short time delay [24]. Within the practice of mixing, the Haas effect is used to add an illusory sense of depth to a track by splitting a signal between left and right components in the stereo field and adding a time delay to either signal. Depending on the type and complexity of the signal, if the delay time is too long then the second signal will form an echo sound for listeners.

### 3.3. Rule of Disjoint Allocation

Another Gestalt law that may be useful for explaining fundamental mixing techniques is the law of Disjoint Allocation. This law states that sounds tend to emerge from one source at a time, and once an object forms a single auditory stream, it cannot also form an additional auditory stream [10]. This law is demonstrated in an experiment conducted in 1975 by Bregman and Rudnicky [19]. In their study tones "A" and "B" are presented alone, and it is easy for listeners to distinguish their order. In the presence of two short distractor tones, however, labelled "x," which occur immediately before "A" and immediately after "B," it is more difficult to distinguish the order of tone "A" and tone "B." The final condition, however, uses a longer series of distractor tones, and once again subjects were able to distinguish tone "A" from tone "B." It was suggested that, given a longer distractor sequence, the distraction tones are perceived to combine into a single perceptual stream; and can thus allow tones "A" and "B" to sound distinct in comparison. A shorter distractor sequence, however, causes the "x" streams to separate for listeners, and it is more difficult for tones "A" and "B" to exhibit distinguishable characteristics within this experimental condition [19].

The human perceptual tendency to group similar sounds, as described by the law of disjoint allocation, may also explain the prevalence of the technique of layering within mix practice. Layering refers to the practice of reinforcing a track with some type of duplicate auditory information. This often occurs in the form of additional takes, where a single musical passage might be recorded or duplicated several times and then added back into the mix composite [1][7]. For example, a kick lacking in high-mid and high frequency information can be made to sound more exciting through the technique known as layering. One way to accomplish this is to take the original kick signal and duplicate it with an added Gate. The gate on this duplicated kick can be programmed with a fast attack time in order to engage an audible "click" sound. By changing the attack and threshold of this gate, different timbral instantiations of the click can be added to the original kick without the application of additional EQ. If hold and release settings are also set to a short time period, then the click will will be predominately heard on the gated track. At this point, the click-kick and the regular kick can be mixed together, and the resultant sound should feature the "power" of the first kick, blended with harsher transient click on the second track [1].

### 3.4. Rule of Good Continuation

Another Gestalt law that may be pertinent to mix design is the law of Good Continuation. The law of Good Continuation states that audible changes in frequency, intensity, spectrum, and location tend to be smooth and continuous [10]. Abrupt changes in any of these parameters may cause stream segregation in listeners. Darwin and Bethell-Fox (1977), for instance, demonstrate this tendency in a lab experiment using synthesized spectral patterns that move between two vowel sounds [21]. When F0 is constant, the speech sounds are heard to emerge from a single source. When F0 moves stepwise to other pitches, a separate stream was perceived to emerge [22]. The law of Good Gestalt, then, is strongly related to how humans interact with sound in an ecological sense [10].

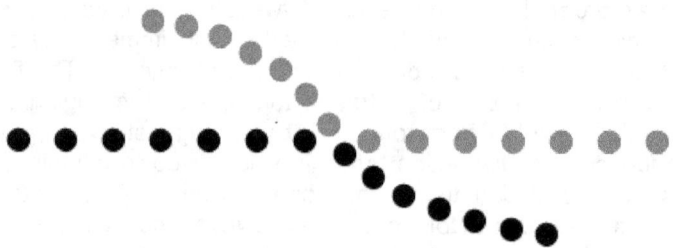

Figure 3. Visual representation of the Law of Good Continuation. We perceive this image as a straight line and a curved line criss-crossed, rather than two nearly touching misshapen lines. [27]

The law of good gestalt, or good continuation, is one area that receives criticism from empirical researchers who typically ask, 'what is meant by *good* continuation?' (Bruce, Green, Georgeson 1996). When applying the idea of "good continuation" to audio, researchers typically define *good* as *ecological* [10]. In other words: a good continuation should simulate some aspects of real world sound. Mixes, however, are aesthetic events and sometimes benefit from a non-ecological approach to sound design. As William Moylan (2007) offers,

'The person controlling, or creating, these sound qualities (the recordist) is functioning as a creative artist. This person is a musician of sorts — 'conducting' by encouraging and ensuring quality performances, "performing" recording, mixing and processing devices, and 'composing' the mix.' (pp. xxii)[14]

As an inherently creative act, the process of mixing ay require one to work against natural perceptual tendencies in listeners. An understanding of how available mix techniques work *with* or *against* these perceptual descriptions, such as the law of Good Gestalt, may provide some clues to how one can craft or enhance a song's artistic programme to best express its content.

A number of EDM mix techniques, for example, work contrary to the law of Good Gestalt. A ubiquitous technique across numerous EDM genres is the technique of automating a high pass filter to sweep towards higher frequencies before introducing some type of *drop* or b-section, for example. Typically, when used in this fashion, a low pass filter placed on the stereo bus slowly adds back in high-end frequency content over 2-4 bars by sweeping upwards through the frequency spectrum. Once the maneuver has finished, a new section within the song's structure typically emerges. The reintroduction of frequency content at this point breaks the law of Good Gestalt by causing abrupt unnatural-sounding spectral changes. As in visual arts, occasionally a discourteous aesthetic component is necessary to create a desired emotional effect, and Gestalt theory may provide some clues or inspiration for how and when to depart from a so-called good continuation.

### 3.5. The Figure-Ground Phenomenon

The final Gestalt law I'd like to discuss is the figure-ground phenomenon. This law states that, when listening to complex audio sources, we attend to one "stream" at a time. Even though we feel like we should be able to attend several streams, or perhaps all available audio streams, this simply doesn't seem to be the case [10]. An attended stream will stand out in comparison to an unattended stream, which will seem to be less prominent for the listener. This phenomenon is also referred to as the "cocktail party effect," or the tendency of our perceptual systems to bring to the foreground whatever conversation we happen to be focused on. A second aspect of the cocktail party effect is that individuals can also switch between available conversations, or streams, fairly easily. As a result, individuals may experience recordings differently based on their experience and attention set.

Figure 4. Visual representation of the Figure-Ground Phenomenon. The image is perceived as either two faces or a chalice depending on whether the viewer places the dark space or the light space in the foreground. [28]

Craig Golding and Russ Hepworth Sawyer describe the importance of this focus-switching phenomenon for those who produce and engineer music in their book *What is Music Production*. They prescribe a way of listening to recordings that considers both macro and micro foci, building on previous work by Bob Katz who delineates both an active and a passive listening state [12, 13]. Macro listening simply refers to a broader imaginary vantage point for engineers to reflect on a given mix, where all available sonic material is considered to reflect a cohesive whole. To borrow the analogy used by these authors, macro listening is akin to viewing and appreciating a city landscape from a distance. Micro listening, on the other hand, refers to the act of perceptually attending to the details present within a mix composite, and is akin to zooming in on a particular street within a town landscape [12].

Golding and Hepworth-Sawyer also recommend a number of ways of developing these skills, and provide appendices for further skill development. One way to do this, according to their text, is to practice switching between listening foci on a track with robust instrumentation. Individuals can focus in on a single instrument before switching his or her listening focus back to the entire tune, for example [12].

The authors synthesize this idea with the work of William Moylan to create a structured analytic framework for evaluative listening [14]. Their system proposes that individuals first assess a track's rhythmic components (time signature, groove, syncopation, bassline); then a track's arrangement, chord structure, and backing (instrumentation, structure, emotional architecture, dynamics and interplay); before finally examining a tracks overall sound quality (width, depth, height, balance) [12].

Audile technique guides by Katz, Moylan, Golding, and Hepworth-Sawyer indirectly acknowledge the figure-ground phenomenon by suggesting that effective sound engineers must possess the ability to switch between diverse listening foci within a mix composite. For educators, Gestalt theory could provide a way of concretizing in students the need for such perceptual mastery as identified by these influential recordist-authors.

## 4. Conclusion

This paper has discussed several Gestalt laws of auditory perception, and how certain mixing techniques conform to these laws in a general sense. Future papers will cover both mixing techniques and Gestalt perceptual descriptions in more detail. Through categorizing fundamental mix techniques via Gestalt concepts, as this paper begins to do, we can develop a model for teaching the art of mixing that first considers the perceptual implications of available sound-shaping techniques.

Mixing has been described by Jay Hodgson as 'painting on the canvas of psychophysiology [11].' An audio engineer's awareness of the perceptual implications of mixing, or lack of thereof, does not change this basic ontological truth. For this reason I believe that psychophysiological laws should be further discussed within audio texts and classrooms. Gestalt theory, with a successful record for application in a number of design-based endeavours, may prove to be a useful pedagogical tool for audio educators and beginner-to-intermediate mix practitioners. Another reason for adopting these laws within audio education is that they represent a *lingua franca* across many design-based arts, and may provide an easier point of access for many individuals seeking to develop artistry and skill in mixing.

## 5. References

[1] Izhaki, Roey. Mixing audio: concepts, practices and tools. Focal Press, (2013).
[2] Cousins, M. and Hepworth-Sawyer, R. Practical Mastering. Focal Press, (2013)
[3] Polansky, L. 'The Early Works of James Tenney.' Soundings. no 13. ed Garland, P. (1983). Accessed July 31st, 2015 from http://eamusic.dartmouth.edu/~larry/published_articles/tenney_monograph_soundings/index.html
[4] Von Ehrenfels, Christian. 'On "gestalt qualities.'. B. Smith (Ed. & Trans.), Foundations of Gestalt theory. pp. 82-117, (1988)
[5] Köhler, Wolfgang. 'Physical Gestalten.' APA Psycnet, (1938).
[6] Lehar, S. Gestalt isomorphism and the quantification of spatial perception. Gestalt theory, 21. pp. 122-139, (1999).
[7] Shelvock, M. 'The Progressive Heavy Metal Guitarist's Signal Chain: Contemporary Analogue and Digital Strategies.' Innovation in Music 2013. Future Technology Press, (2014).
[8] Bruce, V., Green, P. & Georgeson, M. Visual perception: Physiology, psychology and ecology (3rd ed.). LEA, p. 110, (1996).
[9] White, P. "Classic Compressors" Sound on Sound. September issue, (2009). Accessed July 31st, 2015 from https://www.soundonsound.com/sos/sep09/articles/classiccompressors.htm
[10] Moore, Brian CJ. An introduction to the psychology of hearing. Brill, pp. 303-313, (2012).
[11] Hodgson, Jay, and Steve MacLeod. Notes on the Ontology of Recorded Musical Communications. Wilfrid Laurier University Press, pp. 1-123, (2013).
[12] Golding, C. and Hepworth-Sawyer, R. What is Music Production? Focal press, (2011).
[13] Katz, B. Mastering Audio: The Art and the Science. Focal press, (2013).
[14] Moylan, William. Understanding and crafting the mix: The art of recording. Focal Press, pp. xxii-87, (2007).
[15] Hereford, James, and William Winn. "Non-speech sound in human-computer interaction: A review and design guidelines." *Journal of Educational Computing Research* 11.3, pp. 211-233, (1994)
[16] Miller, G. A., and Heise, G. A. The trill threshold. J. Acoust Soc. Am., 22, pp. 637--638, (1950).
[17] Bregman, A. S., and Campbell, J. Primary auditory stream segregation and perception of order in rapid sequences of tones. ). Exp. Psychol., 89, pp. 244-249, (1971).
[18] Bregman, A. S. Auditory Scene Analysis: The Perceptual Organization of Sound.Cambridge, MA: Bradford Books, MIT Press, (1990).
[19] Bregman, A. S., and Rudnicky, A. Auditory segregation: stream or streams? J. Exp. Psychol.: Human Percept. Perf., I, pp. 263-267, (1975).
[20] van Noorden, L. P. A. S. Temporal coherence in the perception of tone sequences. Ph.D. Thesis, Eindhoven University of Technology, Eindhoven, (1975).

[21] Darwin, C. J., and Bethell-Fox, C. E. Pitch continuity and speech source attribution. J. Exp. Psychol.: Hum. Perc. Perf., 3, pp. 665-672, (1977).
[22] Wagemans, J., Elder, J. H., Kubovy, M., Palmer, S. E., Peterson, M. A., Singh, M., & von der Heydt, R. (2012). A century of Gestalt psychology in visual perception: I. Perceptual grouping and figure–ground organization. *Psychological bulletin*, *138*(6), 1172.
[23] Wertheimer, M. Laws of organization in perceptual forms. APA Psycnet. (1938).
[24] Haas, H. The influence of a single echo on the audibility of speech. *Journal of the Audio Engineering Society*, *20*(2). pp. 146-159, (1972).
[25] Reproduced from http://wairimusensationndperception.weebly.com/gestalts-laws-of-perceptual-organization.html
[26] Reproduced from http://wairimusensationndperception.weebly.com/gestalts-laws-of-perceptual-organization.html
[27] Reproduced from http://media.mediatemple.netdna-cdn.com/wp-content/uploads/2013/05/08-continuation.png
[28] Reproduced from http://www.tau.ac.il/~tsurxx/FigureGround/goblet.jpg

# Formless Form as Forma Efformans

Chang Seok Choi

Department of Music, University of York, Heslington, York, UK
hesaias2000@hotmail.com

## Abstract

*The unique concept of Formless Form as Forma Efformans is a formal innovation in acoustic composition that regards a musical form as a constant process of transformation, rather than as a fixed shape in a conventional sense. This concept serves as an important thrust of a structural transformation that a microstructure becomes a macrostructure. This treatise consists of three sections. The first section explains backgrounds and questions of why and how poetry and the structure of water influenced the formal innovation in creating the idea of Formless Form. The second section discusses the compositional process in realising this ideal into reality, e.g. bonding agents including pitch, rhythm and time, as well as Sigimsae (Embellishments in traditional Korean music) and Talea (Isorhythm) in an orchestral work Eolgae (Structure) for Symphony Orchestra [1]. The last section includes the outcome of this praxis that creates flowing characters and a forward-moving directionality through a constant transformation in the music.*

## 1. Introduction

What is form? More specifically, what is a musical form? Obviously, you can hear and feel musical sounds, but you cannot see them regardless of whatever the shape they may have. How about water? Water is transparent and has a clear structure in a micro level, but you cannot see this micro structure of water with the naked eye. According to Rossing, Moore and Wheeler's *The Science of Sound*, sound can be described as two things: 'an auditory sensation in the ear and the disturbance in a medium that can cause this sensation.' [2, p. 3] In terms of auditory perception, it says, 'Sound waves travel in a solid, liquid, or gas…As the wave travels through the air, the air pressure changes by a slight amount, and it is this slight change in pressure that allows our ears (or a microphone) to detect the sound.' In his *Water*, Felix Franks writes, 'Water is the only inorganic liquid that occurs naturally on earth…It is also the only chemical compound in all three physical states: solid, liquid and vapour.' [3, p. 1] There is something between sound and a micro structure of water, i.e. the invisibility of the existence. They are invisible with the naked eye, but they do exist. There must be some agents to make their existence possible and meaningful. However, this is not a scientific research, but an artistic research, so this treatise is about transferring the characteristic of water to a musical composition, particularly about flexibility, one of the distinctive qualities water has. Felix writes, 'A liquid, on the other hand, is characterised by the random diffusion (Brownian motion) of molecules and by the absence of periodic order. In other words, the liquid state cannot be described by a set of molecular coordinates.' [3, p. 41] In general, the visible shape of water in a macroscopic sense depends on its surroundings rather than itself. In other words, a microstructure of water can transform into a macrostructure without losing its original quality. This characteristic of water became a main focus on a formal innovation in my music, and also a question of how I can apply this flexibility of water into a compositional process as an underlying concept of a musical form in order to build a larger structure which has a seamless flow. In this vein, the understanding of form as a force that refers to Forma Efformans (living form) through a constant transformation is an essential and necessary tool to see a musical form differently. Therefore, Forma Efformans as a living form becomes the important element to create the distinctive concept of Formless Form that yields the fluidity in the music like that in water. The aim of this research is to have a creative approach to a musical form not only that can provide me with a new compositional method to realise the ideal into reality, but also that can inspire creative minds to explore the uncharted territory in music as well as other disciplines.

## 2. Background

Back in 2013, reading T. S. Eliot's *The Waste Land* [4, p. 6], I was fascinated by the fact that the poem does not have any defined form, but instead is full of citations, even quoting from Wagner's opera *Tristan and Isolde*.

| Frisch weht der wind | Fresh blows the wind |
| Der Heimat zu | To the homeland |
| Mein Irisch kind, | My Irish Child |
| Wo weilest du? | Where do you wait? |

Despite the ambiguity of form in Eliot's *The Waste Land*, this unusual, collage-like, shapeless form that rejects the established tradition, has nurtured creative thinking on form that does not have to be seen in the way Angela Leighton describes it, 'Form is a shaping activity rather than a visual shape' [5, p. 7]. Eliot's unique perspective on a poetic form was a starting point for looking at a musical form differently. Seeing form as a force rather than a shape opened the door to a new musical form. Angela Leighton writes, 'Form is not a matter of correct techniques; it is a force of creativity generally" [5, p. 23]. She emphasises Coleridge's argument about the difference between the living and the dead form; form as proceeding and shape as superinduced. Coleridge writes, 'All form as body, i.e. as shape, & not as forma efformans, is dead' [6, p. 124]. This invisible force as form can be compared to powerful forces of deep ocean water currents, which shape water itself as well as its surroundings. Form in music is inarguably related to time rather than a physical shape like other genres of arts because sounds can be only audible as time passes. In a melodic, harmonic, and rhythmic development, time acts as a catalyst to bond these disparate musical materials together respectively or simultaneously, and transform them into something different, creating relationships between them. These relationships soon become function that seems to produce musical phenomena. This critical thinking process became a basis for a fresh and creative approach to a musical form. Form can be completely decomposed, then aggregated randomly. Ideas of Collage, cross-cutting, and mosaic texture have also influenced the idea of separating complex textures into small parts or fragments and arranging them orderly or randomly. This flexible and open approach led to a way to the concept of formlessness in a musical form.

## 3. Formless Form

### 3.1. Formless Form as Forma Efformans

Formless Form is the concept of a form in a micro level, which converts to a different form in a macro level, not only transforming itself constantly according to its surroundings, but also influencing them. Thus, by the application of this concept to the compositional process, a microstructure in pitch and rhythm can transform into a macrostructure without losing its originality, creating fluidity in the music. This idea was inspired by the structure of water that has a certain formula ($H_2O$) on a micro level while it has no regular shape on a macro level. Due to its shapelessness on a macroorganism, water can be spring, stream, river, or sea. Also it can be transformed into different substances such as ice, liquid, or water vapour. Whatever shape water has, it is still water! When I conceived this flexibility of water as a musical idea for a large orchestral work *Eolgae (Structure) for Symphony Orchestra* [1], I imagined continuous flow and changes of musical materials in a shapeless form based on fragments that construct a micro structure and become a macro structure as they evolve. My *Eolgae* is built on this concept of Formless Form, which creates flowing characters with a forward-moving directionality through a constant transformation. Formless Form is a procedural concept, i.e. a concept of transformation process, rather than a fixed shape (form). Angela Leighton regards form as a force rather than a shape, supporting Coleridge's interesting term Forma Efformans. Forma Efformans is Latin, and means forming form (living), rather than formed form (dead). This idea enhances the concept of Formless Form that understands form as a force, which refers to a living form through a constant transformation rather than a dead form (formed form). This view highlights the distinctive characteristic of Formless Form that yields the fluidity in the music analogous to that in water. In *The Musical Idea and the Logic, Technique, and Art of Its Presentation*, Schoenberg defines music as 'a musical poet's or thinker's presentation of musical ideas' [7, p. 1], and in *Fundamentals of Musical Composition*, he also describes form as 'the organisation of intelligible musical ideas, logically articulated' [8, p. 213]. In this sense, for me, a musical idea, imagination, or vision is a key element of my music and musical form. A musical fragment based on a musical idea is a starting point of my music, and evolves into a larger structure that expresses musical ideas fully in a musical form, but this form only serves as a medium to realise my artistic vision into a musical composition.

## 3.2. Eolgae (Structure) for Symphony Orchestra (2014)

*Eolgae (Structure) for Symphony Orchestra* is based on this musical and formal innovation in the concept of Formless Form as Forma Efformans that achieves simplicity with flowing characters and a forward-moving directionality. *Eolgae* combines Sigimsae with Talea, adopting Sijo, a three line short Korean poetic form that has a twist (or a surprise) in it, as an underlying structure. The structure of the music is built by constant transformation of Sigimsae and Talea through time, and dynamic modification with the use of Man-Jung-Sak, a gradual change of tempo in traditional Korean music that becomes faster as the music develops. A dense canonic structure serves as a melting-pot of transformation, blurring and interweaving multiple musical parameters, and fusing and turning them into something different which has a unique characteristic without losing its identity. There are three constructing stages of structures. Firstly, Sigimsae and Talea serve as a microstructure, and secondly, canon serves as a main vehicle to construct and develop this microstructure to a larger structure. Finally, Sijo serves as a macro structure for the whole piece. These processes serve as clear inner structures in order to realise constant changes and seamless flow of the music in a formless form that emanates blurring and amorphous effects to some extent.

Sigimsae is a musical term for embellishments in traditional Korean music, based on the manipulation of pitch that gives character, shape, and direction to a melodic line through different gestures at various levels, including bending, lifting, pulling down, and undulating pitch. It consists of four types of embellishments including Nonghyeon (or Yoseong), Jeonseong, Toiseong and Chooseong as shown in Table 1. These are not just ordinary ornaments, but the essence of the unique melodic development of traditional Korean music, because, unlike in western music, the concept of harmony is alien to traditional Korean music. Traditional Korean music is based on heterophony. In a narrow sense, Nonghyeon is a performance technique used on Korean string instruments such as Geomungo and Gayageum. Executed by the left hand, it is a technique of decorating tones with different gestures such as undulation, bend, etc., often accompanied with microtones. It largely depends on performers' capability to execute this technique which shapes the unique characteristic of music. This technique in performance has become the determinant of the genre of music. Moreover, Sigimsae is often associated with a main-tone technique. Main-tone technique deeply rooted in Korean court music, was established by Isang Yun, a Korean-German composer who introduced this original style to western music for the first time. In general, this technique is a linear approach to melodic development, derived from a main-tone embellished by other pitches during the development process. The main-tone serves as a centre of the melodic line in an atonal context. In my *Initium* [9], for example, individual lines, drawn from the three note collection C - E - G♯, develop independently as shown in Figure 1. As it develops, each horizontal line becomes a harmony of C - E - G♯ vertically. When this technique coincides with canon, it is possible to build multiple-voiced layers, creating dense textures, for instance a triple canon in *Psalm 37*. Canon used in my *Psalm 37* [10] only follows the order of the pitches, not the rhythms. The rectilinearity, created by the independent development of melodic lines, brings into the music a polivocality that results in a linear harmony. This yields vague and static effects in the work.

| Classification | Definition | Example | Remarks |
|---|---|---|---|
| Nonghyeon (or Yoseong) | Vibrato: Undulation Narrow ↔ Wide | | Court music: Narrow Folk music: Wide |
| Jeonseong | Appoggiatura (or acciaccatura): Short embellishment | | |
| Toiseong | Downward glissando (Downward portamento) | | |
| Chooseong | Upward glissando (Upward portamento) | | |

Table 1. Classification of Sigimsae

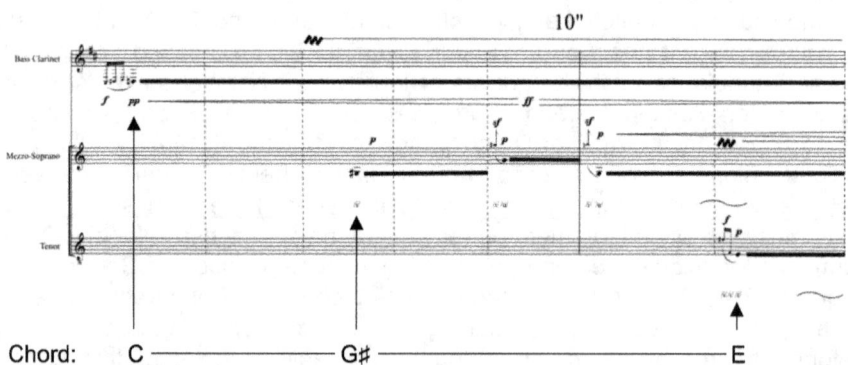

Figure 1. Chang Seok Choi, *Initium*, seconds 6 - 12

## 4. Bonding Agents

As I mentioned earlier, the idea of 'Formless Form' was inspired by the structure of water. What interests me about water is its microorganism that can turn itself into the macroorganism through the constant transformation. At the micro level, water has a certain chemical formula, but at the macro level, it is shapeless because it can be any shape according to its surroundings. Covalent bonds are the key force that connects atoms of water together, forming a larger structure than itself. Interestingly, this basic concept led me to the idea of 'Formless Form' in music, looking at the elements that can bond, develop, and transform musical materials into a much bigger structure without losing its originality. Angela Leighton regards form as a shaping activity [5, p. 7], supporting Coleridge's view of form that 'form is its self-witnessing, and self-effected sphere of agency' [6, p. 131]. She asserts that 'form is not a body but an agent' [5, p. 7] 'Form is not a fixed shape to be seen, but the shape of a choice to be made.' [5, p. 16] In her writings, she sees form as a communicated liveness, referring to the subject of Susan Wolfson's book, *Formal Charges* (1997), which defines form as a force, an energy, a subtle *j'accuse* [5, p. 23]. In *Eolgae*, this idea is realised by combining Sigimsae and Talea through canon. Canon is a main vehicle of blending the melodic and rhythmic fragments, and serves to build layers at the same and different speeds, obscuring the regular pulses as well as melodic contours. There is a clear melodic and rhythmic cell as Talea, often associated with Sigimsae in a micro level. As it develops through canon and ametrical rhythm, the texture, superposed by melodic and rhythmic lines, becomes intermingled, blurring the shape of the music. This gives formlessness to the music.

### 4.1. Pitch

The pitch organisation of the music was inspired by the structure of water which has one oxygen and two hydrogen atoms, joined together by covalent bonds as shown in Figure 2. Covalent bonds share two electrons in order to bond two hydrogen atoms. This idea led me to think about the idea of bonding agents in musical materials, specifically in intervals and rhythms, and then whether this critical understanding of chemical reactions can be applied to the compositional process as well as the music. Another element in my pitch organisation was the shape of a snowflake, which has hexagonal symmetry. These two ideas are combined to generate a six note collection which has symmetry by a tritone. This six note collection creates two motifs (Motif A and Motif B) in which a tritone acts as a bonding agent in a symmetrical structure (see Figure 3). These two motifs are basically the same, but with a different order of pitches, and produce their variants. These fragments from the pitch organisation become a larger structure as the music develops, interacting with Talea which is designed proportionally, as well as sometimes utilising elements of Sigimsae and a main-tone intermittently.

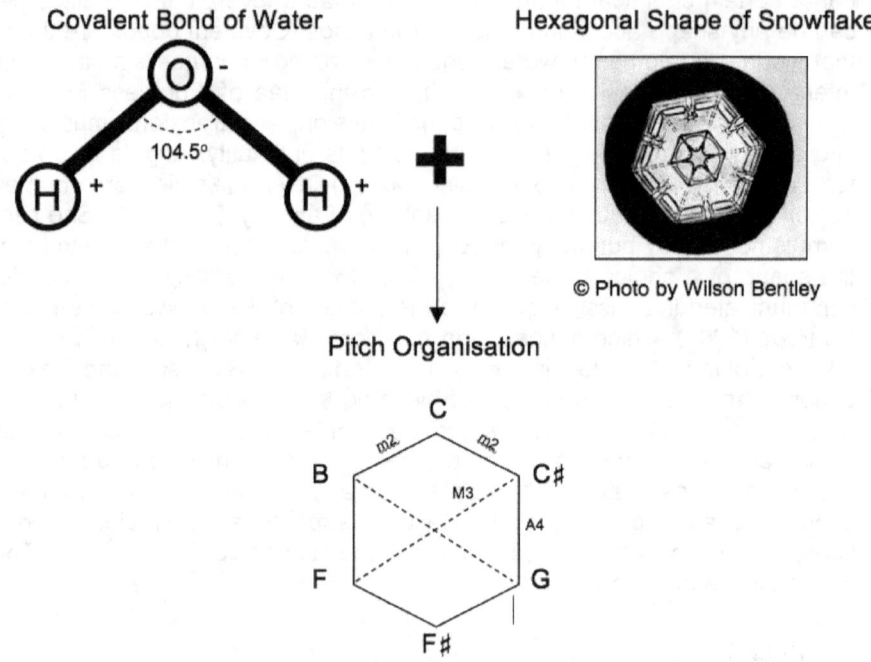

Figure 2. Pitch Organisation Inspired by the Structure of Water

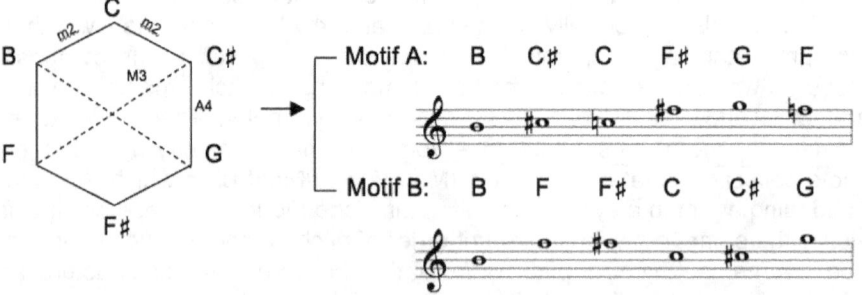

Figure 3. Motif A and Motif B Derived from the Six Note Collection in *Eolgae*

## 4.2. Rhythm: Talea

As for the rhythm, Taleas are constructed proportionally at the beginning of the planning stage, so they already have mathematical relationships among them. Thus, the stratification and the juxtaposition of these self-similar rhythmic patterns offers active motions to the music, creating tension and relaxation repeatedly. By using both intervals and rhythms simultaneously or successively, the constant directional quality is yielded. The rhythmic plan in *Eolgae* is inspired by fractals in mathematics. As shown in Figure 4, Talea ① is built on a symmetrical structure that is proportional and palindromic. This basic structure yields Talea ④ through retrograde. With the same method, Talea ② and ③ are generated. (see Figure 4) All four sets of Talea create four subsets of each respectively, except Talea ① that has five subsets, by multiplying and diminishing the note value proportionally (see Figure 5).

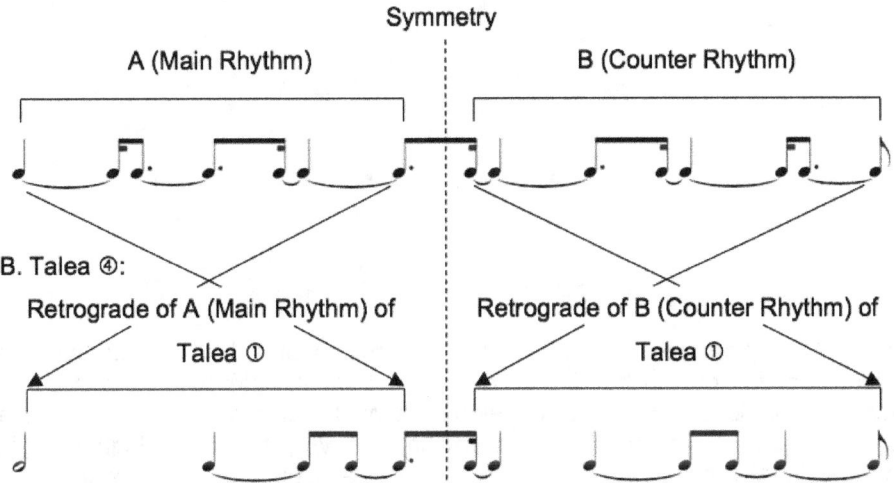

Figure 4. Structure of Talea

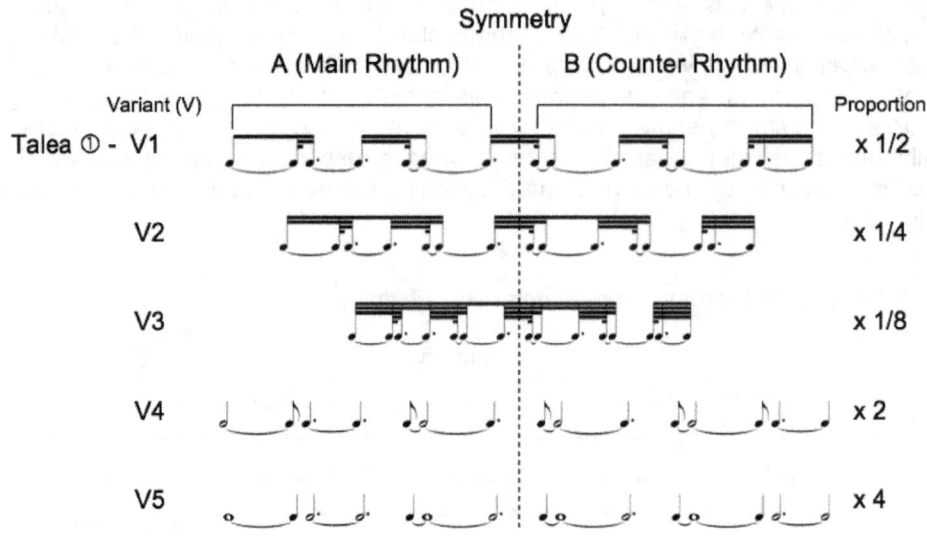

Figure 5. Variants of Talea ①

This mathematical treatment of the original rhythm of Talea ① contributes to a rhythmic coherence which is innate in the Talea itself. Talea ① and ④ are mostly used in melodic and rhythmic development on lower register instruments, and Talea ② and ③ in melodic and rhythmic development on higher register instruments. Multiple layers, fabricated by the stratification and the juxtaposition of canonic procedures at different time, serve to blur boundaries between melodic and rhythmic materials, creating a forward-moving directionality with fluid and shapeless movement. In this process, relationships between original sets and subsets of Talea become a bonding agent of musical materials, and an essential element to development.

### 4.3. Spatialisation of Time

My understanding of space and time simply began with the spatialisation of musical events through stratification and juxtaposition in time. From this process, I started to see time as space in my music (e.g. *Spacetime* [11]). The term spatialisation of time is largely based on the distribution of musical materials as a whole or a fragment at the same or different time in my musical compositions, using a canonic approach. There are two ways of realising this; one is vertical, using stratification, and the other horizontal one, using juxtaposition. Both are closely related to the point of departure, and evolve respectively or simultaneously. The former, for example, appears in cello and double bass sections at the beginning of *Eolgae* at the same speed, but at different starting points by the value of the crotchet, and Motif B in the parts, e.g. in the cello 1, has a palindromic structure in pitch and rhythm [12]. There are three categories for the latter. The repetition of Talea ① - V3 and its fragments at different time intervals on trumpets in bars 126 - 135 is the first example. The second example is the motif on the first violin 1 that juxtaposes Talea ② and its variants. The linking of Taleas and their variants through juxtaposition creates the linear projection of proportional rhythms at different speeds. The third example is based on a fractal relationship. The smaller variant of Talea ① - V2 exists in the bigger variant of Talea ① - V5 on viola, cello, and double bass sections. The best example of the combination of the vertical and horizontal approaches appears on pizzicati of the second violin, viola, and cello at bars 82 - 86. The vertical and horizontal treatment of Talea ① - V1 appears simultaneously, creating intervals of time which imply imaginary space of time.

## 5. Structural Transformation

A structural transformation, i.e. a microstructure that becomes a macrostructure, uses a Korean poetic structure in addition to pitch, rhythm and time as a bonding agent. *Eolgae* is based on the structure of Sijo which consists of three lines with an average of 14 - 16 syllables per line as shown in Table 2.

| Line (Korean Term) | Syllables | Logical Order |
|---|---|---|
| 1 (Chojang) | 3  4  4  4 | Introduction |
| 2 (Jungjang) | 3  4  4  4 | Development |
| 3 (Jongjang) | 3  5  4  3<br>↑<br>Twist or Surprise | Conclusion |

Table 2. Structure of a Regular Sijo

The first half of the third line of Sijo always includes a twist. This twist is expressed in *Eolgae* by a sudden forte attack in brass, percussion, harp and lower strings (bar 32). The three line structure of Sijo is the basic structure of *Eolgae* which becomes a larger structure of three sections with three sub-sections, apart from the second section which has six sub-sections. (see Figure 6) In general, this self-similar structure adopts the concept of Man-Jung-Sak in tempo as well as in dynamics. Man-Jung-Sak is a concept of speed (tempo) in traditional Korean music; Man is slow, Jung is moderate, and Sak is fast. This gradual change of tempo and dynamics is at the very heart of *Eolgae*, expressing a constant flow of musical materials. The symmetrical design of pitch and rhythm further develops a structural symmetry by stratification. The motif (F G F♯ C C♯ B) with the rhythmic pattern of Talea ② which is also a palindrome is introduced on the second violin in bars 17 to

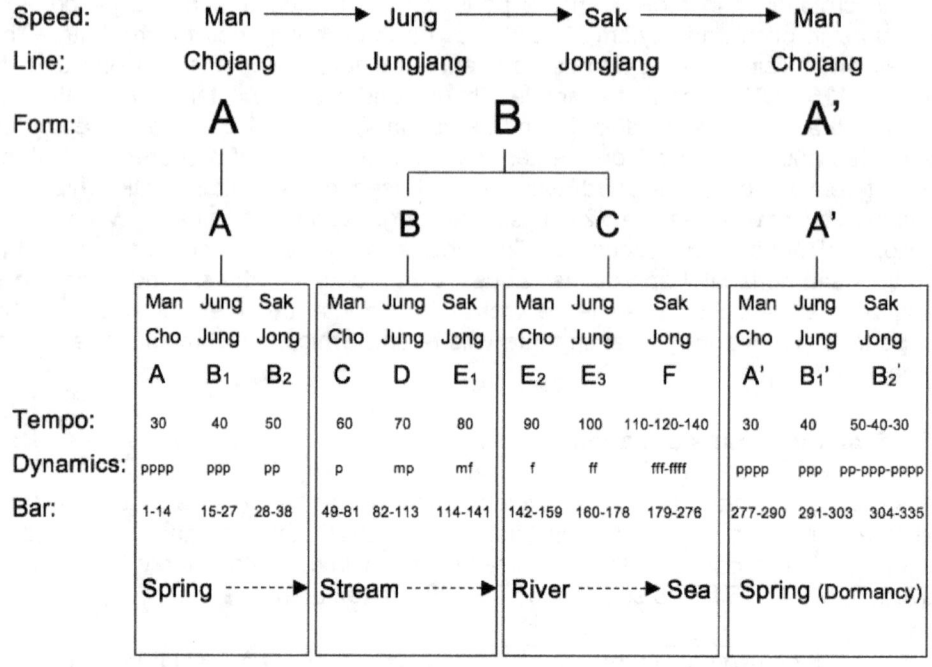

Figure 6. Structure of *Eolgae*

21, employing Jeonseong, Toiseong and Chooseong from Sigimsae, and is distributed successively through a canonic procedure. (see Figure 7) The feature of a palindrome recurs in a different format, for example, on the second violin and viola in bars 25 - 30 as shown in Figure 8. One of the significant changes during the compositional process is the transformation of Sigimsae and Talea. For instance, Talea ① - V3 on violins, viola and cello in bars 138 - 139 becomes Sigimsae, embellishing main-tones around them. This also means that Sigimsae itself becomes Talea, swapping its role with Talea. (see Figure 9) In this process, Sigimsae has become transformed, retaining its original characteristic within an atonal context. At the same time, Talea keeps its originality in the process of interplay with Sigimsae. This transformation process becomes one of factors that contribute to formlessness in the music, blurring its overall shape. Despite the dense, complex textural approach, the music sounds simple. Interdependence between Sigimsae and Talea creates a powerful effect, repeating divergence and convergence that decentralise and centralise a musical structure.

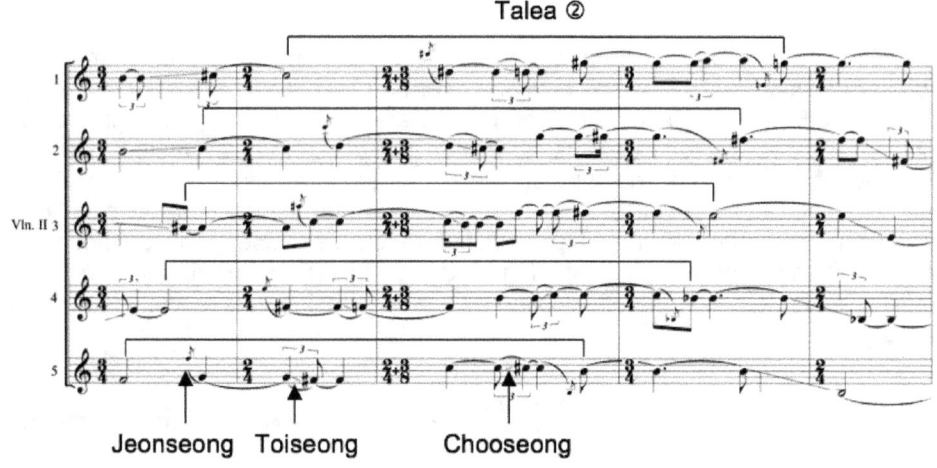

Figure 7. Chang Seok Choi, *Eolgae*, bars 17 – 21

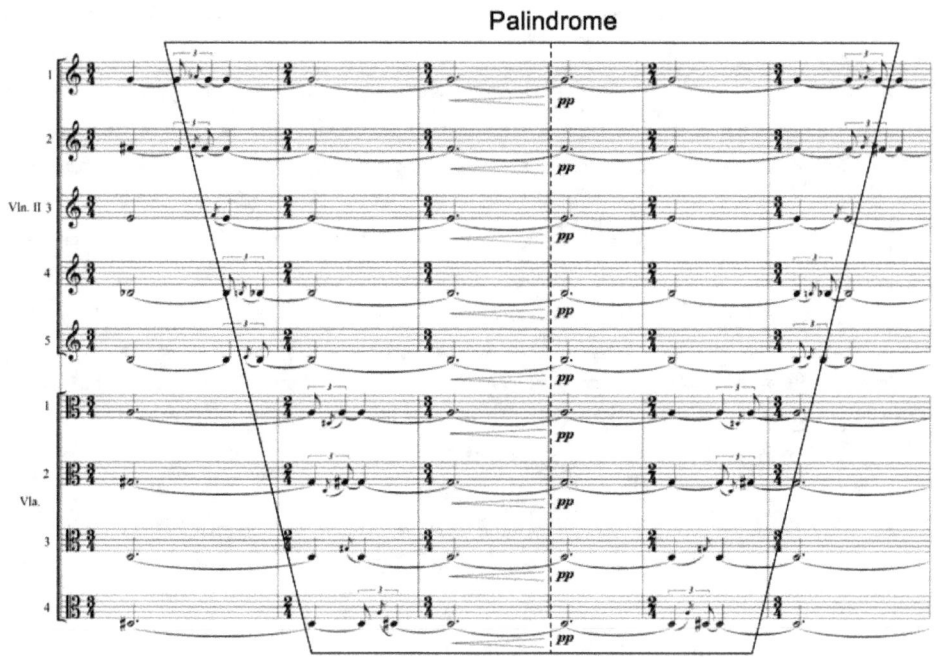

Figure 8. Palindrome in the Second Violin and the Viola
Chang Seok Choi, *Eolgae*, bars 25 - 30

## 6. Results

This whole process of becoming a large structure from a fragment through the constant transformation of self-similar patterns is similar to the effect of Chaos Theory (or Butterfly Effect). Small drops of water, formed from molecules of one oxygen and two hydrogen atoms, give birth to spring, form a small stream, and then become river and sea topologically. This transformation is the skeleton of *Eolgae*. The interlocking system of a canon intermixes these two different materials, i.e. Sigimsae and Talea, building layers of melodic and rhythmic lines through stratification and juxtaposition, and then transforms them into one unique entity that creates powerful effects with a constant moving quality analogous to that of water.

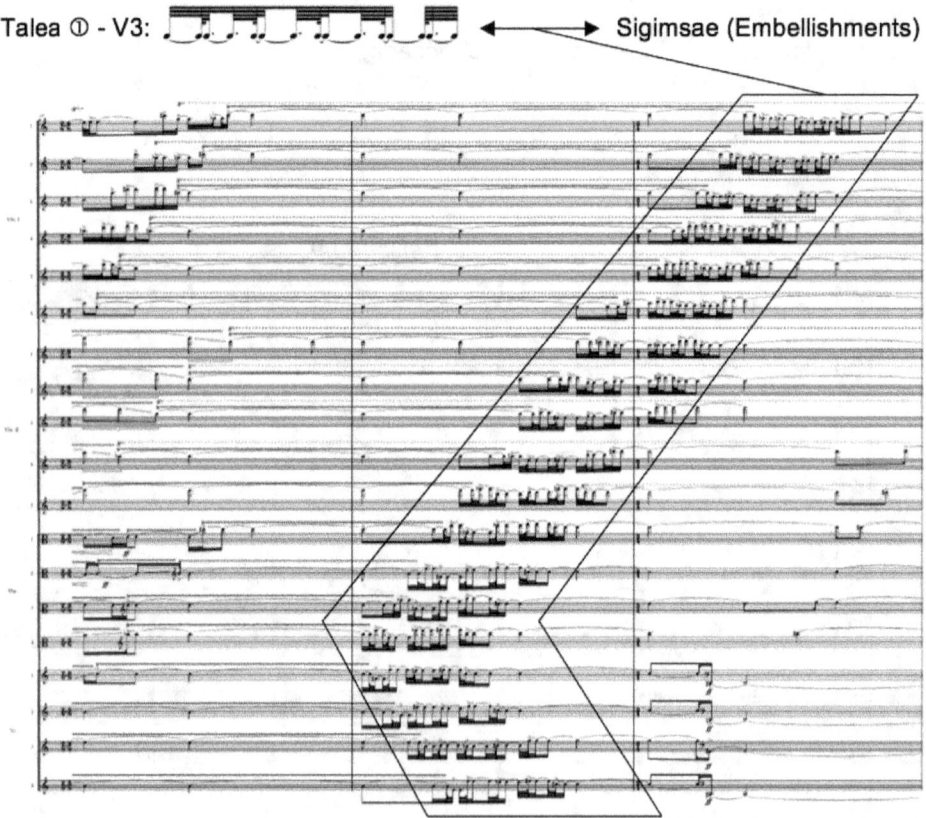

Figure 9. Transformation of Sigimsae and Talea
Chang Seok Choi, *Eolgae*, bars 137 - 139

The entire piece is constructed by stratifying and juxtaposing Taleas simultaneously and successively, so that the structure of the music becomes a cobweb-like texture which is alternately interlocked together, changing rhythms and pitches constantly. This continuous transformation of rhythms and pitches creates formlessness in my music that has the fluidity with a forward-moving directionality. The visual representation of the score in a smaller scale somewhat exhibits this quality as shown in Figure 10.

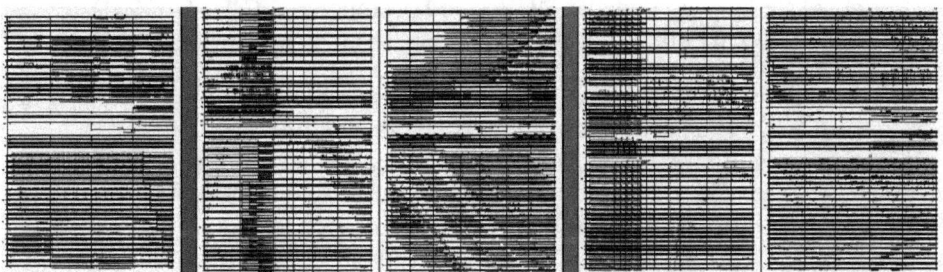

Figure 10. Visual Representation of Forward-moving Directionality in the Score in a Smaller Scale. Chang Seok Choi, *Eolgae*, bars 154 - 190

## 7. Conclusion

The fundamental of Formless Form as Forma Efformans is the flexibility of water, and this principle permeates every part of the music, shaping it as a whole as well as evolving into a complete entity of the music itself. A formal innovation based on the idea of Formless Form as Forma Efformans through a constant transformation creates flowing characters with a forward-moving directionality. This is a new viewpoint on a musical form by looking at it not as a fixed shape, but as a procedural concept, i.e. a concept of transformation process. During this critical thinking process, I have developed an ability to envision new ideas, and to invent a relevant compositional tool to realise this vision into a musical composition, at the same time developing a facility to reduce the complex musical materials to the minimum. This ability has become a great strength for me as a composer to realise the artistic vision into a work of art, i.e. a musical composition. It was the moment of the revelation through the artistic reorientation. The constant transformation of Sigimsae and Talea with the idea of Formless Form as Forma Efformans has enabled me to realise the musical idea that I first conceived into a musical composition that exhibits the continuous flow of music and time.

## 8. References

[1] Choi, C. S. Eolgae (Structure) for Symphony Orchestra, (2014)
[2] Rossing, T. D., Moore, F. R. and Wheeler, P. A. The Science of Sound. $3^{rd}$ ed. San Francisco: Addison Wesley, pp. 3-4, (2002)
[3] Franks, F. Water: $2^{nd}$ Edition A Matrix of Life. Cambridge: RSC Paperbacks., pp. 1 and 41, (2000)
[4] Eliot, T. S. The Waste Land: Authoritative Text, Contexts, Criticism, ed. Michael North. New York: W. W. Norton & Company, INC., p. 6, (2001)
[5] Leighton, A. On Form: Poetry, Aestheticism, and the Legacy of a Word. Oxford: Oxford University Press, pp. 7, 16 and 23, (2007)
[6] Coleridge, S. T. Coleridge's Notebook: A Selection, ed. Perry, S. Oxford: Oxford University Press, pp. 124 and 131, (2002)
[7] Schoenberg, A. The Musical Idea and the Logic, Technique, and Art of Its Presentation. Ed. Patricia Carpenter and Severine Neff. New York: Columbia University Press, p. 1, (1995)
[8] Schoenberg, A. Fundamentals of Musical Composition. Ed. Gerald Strang with the collaboration of Leonard Stein. London: Faber and Faber Ltd, p. 213, (1967)
[9] Choi, C. S. Initium for Mezzo-Soprano, Tenor, Bass Clarinet and Electroacoustics with Video, (2011)
[10] Choi, C. S. Psalm 37 for Narrator, Tenor, Woodwind and Percussion, (2013)
[11] Choi, C. S. Spacetime for Flute, Clarinet, Trumpet, Trombone, Percussion, Harp, Piano, Violin and Cello, (2014)
[12] www.changseokchoi.com

# New Acoustic Technology for Indoor Live Music Events

Niels Adelman-Larsen

Flex Acoustics, 1760 Copenhagen, Denmark
nwl@flexac.com

**Abstract**

*Research shows that too much low frequency reverberation is the primary source for an unpleasant sonic experience as perceived by musicians as well as audiences at amplified music concerts. The author has researched which acoustics are suitable in halls for amplified music, from medium sized venues to the biggest arenas. These results show that it is essential to provide means for additional low frequency absorption in most venues. Typical temporary solutions involve installation of several layers of fabric material at various distances from reflecting surfaces. However, this method provides a relatively modest absorption coefficient in the important 63 and 125 Hz octave bands, while damping well the high frequencies, which are already absorbed substantially by the audience.*

*A new mobile technology of inflated, ultra thin plastic membranes seems to solve this challenge of low-frequency control and is suitable for halls and arenas that occasionally present amplified music and need to be treated for single events. The same technology, permanently installed, applies to multipurpose halls that need to adjust their acoustics, to accommodate various musical styles, at the push of a button. This paper presents the authors' research as well as the technology showing applications in differently sized venues, including before and after measurements of reverberation time versus frequency.*

## 1. Introduction

Professional musicians survive playing their music under almost any condition. And they can do it well. That does not imply however, that they necessarily enjoy it. It is simply more pleasurable when the acoustics of the hall supports the music. An anonymous survey [1] among Danish pop and rock musicians showed, that at least 35% refrain from returning to venues with acoustics they deem unsatisfactory and that the acoustics in general is "very important" for them. A similar trend probably applies for musicians of classical music.

The acoustics play such a big part: does the hall treat the performed music in a way that allows the musician to get his/her musical message through? Can they play all tempos effortlessly? Do they feel connected with their instrument and with their colleagues? With the audience? Sound engineers tend to agree: acoustics is an important factor second maybe only to the musician and his/her sound, in the long chain of parts that play a role in the overall sound quality of an amplified concert. They too survive anything but in many cases inadequate acoustics lead to dissatisfactory sound quality and an undesirable mix.

Good acoustics is not an absolute notion, but depend on which type of music is to be played. A rock band does not sound good in a symphonic music hall while classical music is not suitable in most rock venues. Still all kinds of music is being performed in many halls which is why there is a need for varying the acoustics to suit a given type of music also most notably for the sake of the audience.

In the first ever scientifically based investigation of recommendable acoustics for amplified music [1] it was statistically proven, based on questionnaire responses correlated with objective acoustic measurements in relevant halls, that what acoustically distinguishes the best from the less well-liked halls for amplified music is *a shorter reverberation time (RT) in the 63, 125 and 250 Hz octave bands*. This is not surprising partly referring to the fact that a pop or rock concert is as loud and rhythmically active in the 63 Hz to 250 Hz bands as at higher frequencies which was also pointed out in [8,9]. The Reverberation Time is the time it takes for sound to decay by 60 dB in a given room.

The *critical distance*, $r_{cr}$, in meters is defined as the distance from the loudspeaker in a room, at which the undefined reverberant sound is as loud as the direct sound. The formula was further developed by Anders Gade in [7] and given by Equation (1):

$$r, cr = \sqrt{\frac{QV}{100 \pi T (1 - \alpha') N}}$$
Equation (1)

where $Q$ is the directivity of the sound source at a given frequency, $V$ is the volume of the room in m$^3$, $T$ is the reverberation time in seconds of the room at a given frequency, $\alpha'$ is the average absorption coefficient of the room at a given frequency and $N$ is number of discrete loudspeaker clusters. At a given frequency band, further away from the speakers than this distance, the sound level of the reverberant sound is louder than the direct sound. It is inherent from the equation that since $Q$ is low, for instance 1 to 3, at low frequencies a big share of audiences will suffer from reverberant, undefined low frequency sound if not the reverberation time here is tamed. The directivity at higher frequencies can easily be 10 and it is unlikely that the reverberation time of a room is a factor of 3 to 10 higher at high frequencies than at low.

Seen in that light, it is at least plausible, that the reverberation time in an empty room for amplified music can be accepted longer at high frequencies than at low and that the critical distance will still be shortest in the bass domain. Further, an audience absorbs 4-6 times more mid-high frequency sound than bass [1]. If the loudspeakers are correctly aimed towards the audience the combined effect of a higher $Q$ and a lower reverberation time due to audience absorption, by itself will advantageously control the critical distance at mid-high frequencies. In [1] the recommended reverberation time as a function of hall volume was set forward for these genres, directly deducted as well from the questionnaire results. Further, studies by the author lead to proposed acceptable tolerances of recommendable *RT* as a function of frequency in [3].

Due to the punchy, boomy nature of the 125 Hz band and to the fact that our hearing does not roll off as fast in this band with the decay of sound as in the 63 Hz band due to a lower threshold of hearing, the 125 Hz band is probably the single most important octave band to control. This is in agreement with what the author and his colleagues have encountered at concerts. It seems that reverberant 125 Hz octave band sound unfortunately is a good and dominant masker of the direct sound.

Also in [1] it was found that there was a tendency, that sound engineers preferred an overall very short *RT*, but musicians preferred a somewhat longer reverberation time. One reason for this is probably that musicians enjoy a sensation of being *enveloped* in sound and of "*togetherness*" with each other and the audience while sound engineers in a quite dead room often enjoy the higher degree of control over their effects including artificial reverberation tools.

It is believed, but not proven, that the audience also has a desire for a sense of *envelopment* since they are not attending live concerts to experience solely a high fidelity sound quality adventure, but rather a good sounding social event. Such a preference has been encountered for classical music by researchers such as Mike Barron [10]. To achieve this, a certain level of reverberant sound at live pop and rock concerts is required, but evidently according to the above, *not* at low frequencies. Hence a design goal for pop and rock halls can be to allow for an amount of higher pitched reflections for a sensation of envelopment. In very big spaces such as the largest sports arenas, this may not be true due to the very big distances the sound is traveling [4, 6]. Therefore extremely precise speaker coverage for all audiences is here needed.

From our knowledge that a low *RT* at low frequencies is required for amplified music while the need for "warmth" at classical music demands a higher value of low frequency *RT*, attaining a high absorption coefficient over a broad spectrum including most importantly lower frequencies was one aim in the development of a new variable and mobile sound absorber.

## 2. Inflatable Sound Absorber Technology

The basic technology of *inflated plastic membranes* as means for lowering the reverberation time in venues was presented in [2]. The absorption features of such an inflated absorber are given by its dimensions, shape, material-weight per area, material damping properties and the pressure which to some degree determines, among other things, the stiffness of the membrane.

Since the plastic developed for the practical embodiment of the technology is extremely thin and light, absorbers are mobile, and can be installed temporarily in any venue to lower the reverberation time in the most crucial frequency bands. The plastic is flame retardant and complies with required safety standards in Europe, the USA etc.: B,s1,d0, US NFPA 701, ASTM E 84, and therefor no special permission is needed to use the absorbers publically at concerts. It is a specially engineered plastic with a high degree of inner damping.

## 2.1. Permanently Installed On/Off System

The first measurements on an embodiment of the patented technology were presented in [3]. The technology enables a practical way to achieve enough absorption variability when installed in the ceiling of a hall to make it possible, for example, to present both symphonic music and rock concerts in the same venue both with favorable acoustics. The product is installed permanently direct onto the ceiling for ON/OFF use as seen in Figure 1 and 2. The figures implicate how any number of rows can be activated to reach a desired reverberation time.

Figure 1. A number of absorber-rows are mounted in the ceiling. For symphonic music and choir *no* absorbers are inflated.

Figure 2. At pop and rock concerts all absorbers are activated by pushing an *All On* button.

In the OFF position the product has close to no effect on the reverberation time of the venue (Figure 3).

The absorbers are 1.2 m of height and are attached to tracks since they contract some 10% when inflated. All absorbers may be connected to a common fan installed in the hall or in another room. It takes approx. 5 min. before the absorbers are fully inflated after a push of an ON/OFF switch. A control unit automatically surveys the air pressure on the system, to ensure maximum absorption at all times. A lowered acoustically transparent ceiling can be mounted underneath the absorbers for aesthetic or utility purposes and may include attachment of lighting, fire sprinklers etc. Low- and mid-frequency sound energy is absorbed by this new technology with an absorption coefficient of some 0.5 over the entire ceiling area (Figure 3) with a spacing of baffles of 75 cm center-to-center. With a spacing of some 130 cm the absorption coefficient difference between inflated and deflated state becomes approximately 0.35 as proven in a certified real case measurement (Figure 4) where an app. 40% reduction of RT was encountered.

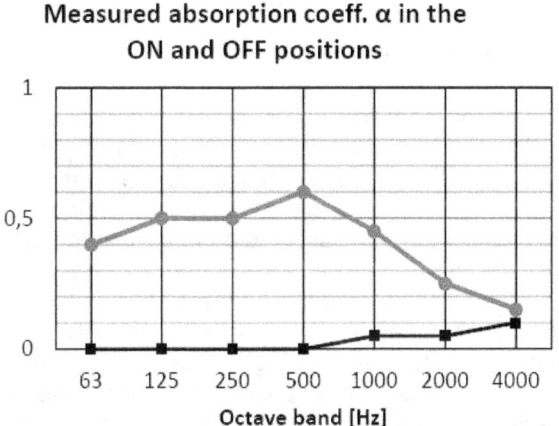

Figure 3. The author's best estimate of highest achievable absorption coefficient (upper line), based on certified measurements in reverb chamber and real-case measurements. Spacing between absorbers center-to-center: 75 cm, mounted direct on ceiling.

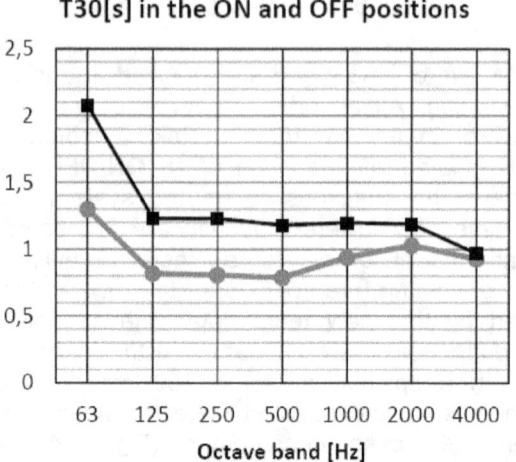

Figure 4. Certified measurements of RT in a Danish music conservatory. System in ON and OFF positions, one absorber row per app.130 cm. corresponding to a difference of alpha of app. 0.35 applied over the entire ceiling area.

## 2.2. Temporarily Placed Mobile Absorbers

Since the plastic used for the patented absorbers is extremely thin and light, they are mobile, easily handled and may be installed temporarily in any venue to lower the reverberation time in the fundamental, and therefor most crucial, frequency bands of musical instruments: 63-1k Hz. This mobile version weighs less than 1.3 kg/meter length and has a much larger diameter of app. 1.5 m when inflated compared to the smaller permanently installed baffles. The reasons for this bigger size are numerous and include a lowering of resonance frequency and a wider half power bandwidth whereby the tubes are less dependable on being placed in immediate proximity to a sound-reflecting surface for LF efficiency. A greater absorption coefficient can also be expected [2]. Since the sound pressure is greater close to reflecting surfaces a higher alpha is still obtained here though. These bigger dimensions also ensure that larger areas can be covered reasonably fast, and that packaging after use is easier handled. To some extend certain "unwanted" sections of a hall or arena can be sonically detached from the rest of the venue placing the tubes close together somewhat lowering hall volume and thereby the reverberation time in the part of the hall where the concert takes place. Also, a certain effect of scattering of the sound field is achieved helping to reduce RT further. Each tube can be either pre-inflated or have a dedicated, demountable micro fan attached. The latter ensures that tubes can´t deflate. One central fan may also supply all tubes interconnected with hoses. Absorbers are mounted vertically with simple straps to trusses or horizontally i.e. to wires and may thereafter be self-inflating as mentioned. 3 cases of use of this new technology, w.

absorption properties estimated in Figure 5, in sound reinforcement applications are mentioned in the following. The alpha shown in Figure 5 is estimated from the formulas for membrane absorbers in [2] together with the certified measurements on the technology for permanent placement discussed in the previous section.

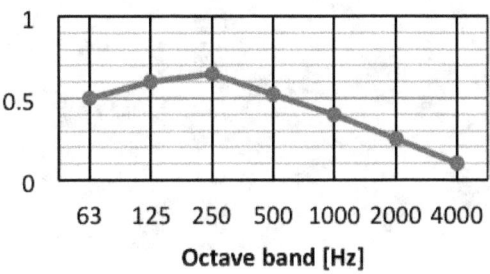

Figure 5. Absorption coefficient, alpha, of mobile technology mounted as close as possible. Estimated. Absorption effect only.

### Case 1

Some 7.000 m$^2$ of these patented, mobile sound absorbers were used in a 700.000 m$^3$ former shipyard for the Eurovision Song Contest 2014 both horizontally and vertically mounted (Figure 6 and 7). The empty space had a reverberation time of 9 -13 sec in the 63-250 Hz interval. This was reduced to less than 4 s, even before the audience arrived (Figure 8). Double layer molton fabric was used over vast areas on walls too. It could not be determined what precise effect the inflated membranes had but the acoustic consultant, Eddy Bøgh Brixen, was very pleased and got a better result than calculated, using an alpha value of 0.5 at low frequencies on the tubes. The reason is probably due to scattering and the partially isolation of a portion of the space. There was an app. 60-80 cm air-gap between the inflated tubes. The 7.000 m$^2$ projected area, used at the ESC 2014 were fitted into 20 large flight cases when deflated after use.

Figure 6. Horizontal tubes, 50 m, ESC 2014

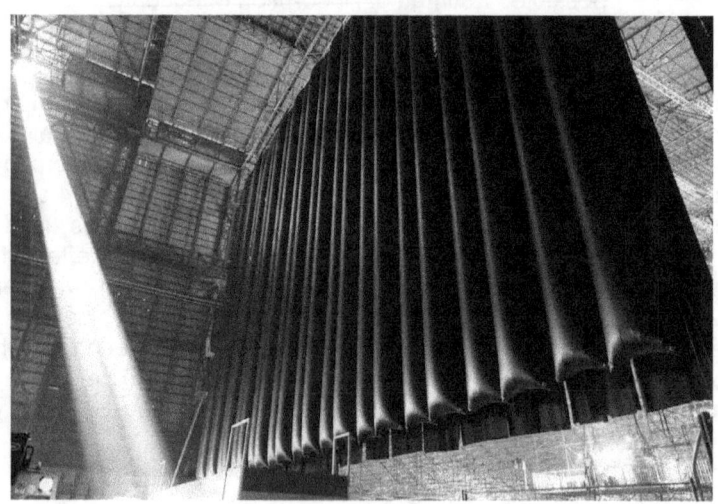

Figure 7. Vertically mounted 35 m tubes, ESC 2014

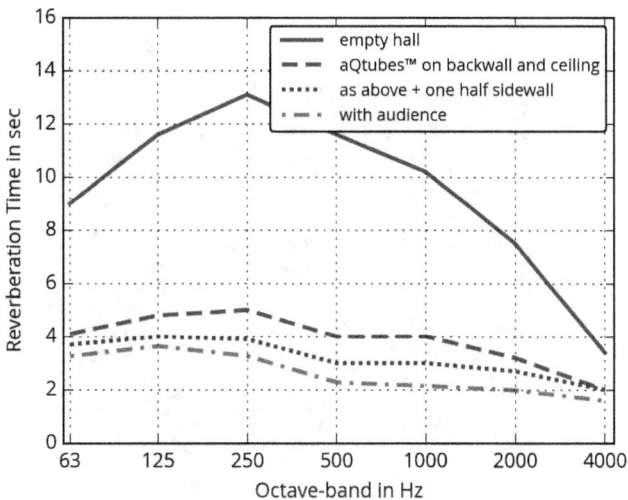

Figure 8. Eurovision Song Contest 2014, Upper line indicates RT in empty space. Middle and lower line: tubes included in hall.

## Case 2

One of the most successful bands these days is British/Irish boy-band One Direction. They had 55.000 audiences attending each of two concerts at Amsterdam Arena in June 2014. This arena was one of the first to be designed with the possibility of opening a (glass) roof. Due to noise problems the roof had to be closed at the concerts in June leading to reverberation times of considerable length also at low frequencies.

Acoustic consultant assigned to the job, P. van der Geer, took the approach of using the tubes as a combined absorber/diffusor/insulator with regards to the large volume between the glass-roof and the tubes. Only half of the open surface towards the roof (furthest away from stage) was treated as seen on Figure 9.

Further, at Amsterdam Arena, van der Geer took the same approach regarding the large empty volume behind stage (Figure 10). Even when using cardioid sub speaker arrays a lot of bass sound still propagates rear of the speakers. The total projected surface area of tubes was app. 3300 m$^2$. Calculating what impact this amount of tubes would have in an enormous volume like Amsterdam Arena, one gets to a quite little number. But as for ESC 2014 much higher absorption coefficients were encountered reducing RT by some 25% (Figure 11) probably due to the combined effect of not only absorption, but also diffusion and an effect of sound isolation. It must be noted that the measurement positions of RT in the treated hall took place on the floor below the tubes, rear in the hall at the sound engineers position.

Figure 9. Horizontally mounted 35 m tubes, One Direction concerts, Amsterdam Arena 2014

Figure 10. Vertically mounted 25 m tubes de-couples the space behind the stage, One Direction concerts, Amsterdam Arena 2014

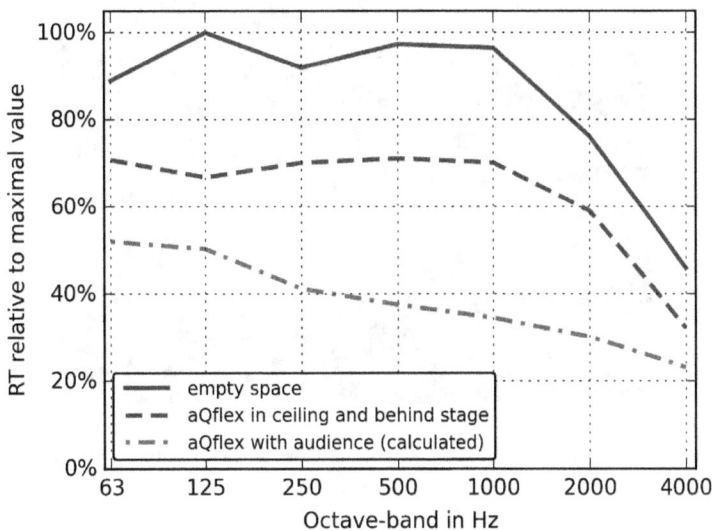

Figure 11. Amsterdam Arena 2014. Upper line indicates RT in empty space. In % due to discretion. Middle and lower line: tubes included.

## Case 3

Legendary German electronic band, Kraftwerk, played 8 shows in January this year in the just as iconic Neue Nationalgalerie by famous Mies van der Rohe. (1968). Production manager Winfried Blank had measured the acoustics in the beautiful 50x50x8 $m^3$ space on beforehand and had found a quite long RT also at lower frequencies (Figure 14). He and acoustician, professor, Dr. Ing. Anselm Goertz took the decision to utilize 22 7 m high mobile tubes all along the back wall opposite stage (Figure 12). And also to place 3 35 m horizontal tubes in the high sound-pressure zone junctions between ceiling and wall. All absorbers were placed in immediate proximity to sound reflecting surfaces and there is therefor no effect in this case of space-isolation. One layer of molton curtain was placed in front of back-wall tubes. Achieved reduction of $RT_{63-250}$: 30-50% (Figure 13) - a very acceptable result indeed.

Figure 12. Vertically mounted 7 m tubes, Kraftwerk concerts, Neue Nationalgalerie, Berlin 2015

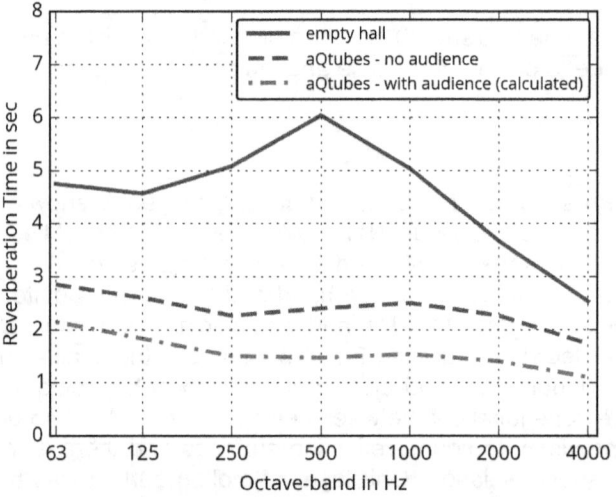

Figure 13. Upper line indicates RT in empty space. Middle line: tubes included in hall. Lower line: calculated RT w. tubes and audience. Kraftwerk concerts, Neue Nationalgalerie, Berlin 2015

## 3. Conclusions

The inventor of the technology and author of this paper is proud to be able to conclude, after more than 10 years of development, research, fund raising, trial and error etc. that now there is a technology that can variably or temporarily fix the most common and crucial acoustic problem at amplified music concerts: a too long low frequency reverberation. If the will is there, there is now a solution. The technology has proven even more efficient than expected, is reasonably easy to mount and takes up little space for transportation and storage.

An absorption coefficient in the region of approximately 0.5 at low and mid frequencies can be expected using the embodiments of the invention in their densest configuration. Cases have proven a reduction of reverberation time of some 40 % for the permanently installed technology and up to 70 % employing the mobile technology.

Several multipurpose halls are now adapting the ON/OFF system for permanent installation, and planned live events in the coming months are being equipped with the mobile technology even for just single events. The technology is patented [5]. Further, recommendations that ensure the best possible acoustics and thereby sound for amplified music concerts have been set forth [6]. To the best of his ability, the author has tried to create a foundation for enhancing sound quality at reinforced music concerts.

## 4. References

[1] N. W. Adelman-Larsen, E. R. Thompson, A. C. Gade: Suitable Reverberation Times for Halls for Rock and Pop Music. J. Acoust. Soc. Am. 127 (2010) 247–255.
[2] N. W. Adelman-Larsen, E. R. Thompson, A. C. Gade: Variable Low-Frequency Absorber for Multi-Purpose Concert Halls. Acoustical Society of America, Vancouver (2005).
[3] N. W. Adelman-Larsen, E. R. Thompson, J.J. Dammerud: On a new, variable broadband absorption product and acceptable tolerances for RT in halls for amplified music. Acoustical Society of America, San Diego (2011).
[4] N. W. Adelman-Larsen, J.J. Dammerud: A survey of reverberation times in 50 European halls presenting pop and rock music. Presented at Forum Acusticum, Aalborg (2011)
[5] N. W. Larsen: US patent # 7905323, EP 1779375, JP 2008510408, etc.; Method, device and system for altering the reverberation time of a room.
[6] N.W. Adelman-Larsen: "Rock and Pop Venues, Acoustic and Architectural Design", Springer Verlag, 2014.
[7] A. C. Gade: Tentative lecture notes for Course 31240, chapters 7 and 8, Technical University of Denmark, April 2003.
[8] Lautenbach and Vercammen, Peutz: Acoustics for large scale indoor pop events, ISRA, Seville (2007).
[9] Delta, Sense Lab, Denmark, "Live concert sound quality. Measurements and assessments of eight concert venues", Report, (2013).
[10] Mike Barron, Auditorium Acoustics and Architectural Design, second edition, Spon Press.

# Interactive Algorithmic Composition

Edward Averell[1], Don Knox[2]

[1]Glasgow Caledonian University, Cowcaddens Road, Glasgow, G4 0BA, UK
eavere200@caledonian.ac.uk

[2]Glasgow Caledonian University, Cowcaddens Road, Glasgow, G4 0BA, UK
d.knox@gcu.ac.uk

## Abstract

The research described in this paper gathers insights from music cognition research and applies them to the creation of a software-based performance and compositional tool which has the ability to improvise a musical sequence in accompaniment to user input. The software was developed using Cycling 74's Max, with incorporation into Ableton Live through the 'Max for Live' platform. The program employs a compositional algorithm which follows models of melodic expectation to react and adapt to musical input, creating melodic accompaniment in real-time. A rule set of four features is employed, controlling the selection of notes in relation to harmonic compliance, metric salience, post-skip reversal and intervallic distance incorporating late phrase declination. The system also allows the user to identify 'favourite' musical passages created by the system. From this input, a Hidden Markov Model (HMM) approach is used to generate new sequences based on the preferences of the musician. This paper describes the design and operation of the interactive algorithmic system in detail. Objective analysis of the system has shown it to consistently output phrases which correspond with models of melodic expectation, generating a suitable and consistent musical accompaniment which adapts to user input.

## 1. Introduction

Technology now plays a significant role in music recording and composition. Software tools of increasing complexity are available to the musician and composer in the form of Digital Audio Workstations, software instrument plug-ins and effects. It is common for a modern musician to work alone with an audio workstation, composing music without the input of additional performers. This method of composition can mean musicians lack the creative input of others. This paper examines whether technology can be designed to address this situation, and if tools can be developed to automatically produce realistic and meaningful musical accompaniment to the musician.

Algorithmic composition, the automatic creation of music via algorithms or sets of rules, has the potential to offer a solution. For example, it is possible to link 'live' musical input to the generation of algorithmic passages which respond and modify in relation to the current musical context, simulating the connection between musicians in a group performance. This sense of 'co-creation' found amongst human musical partners is currently lacking in the majority of algorithmic music systems. Any algorithmic system which aims to contribute to this shared creative musical context must be capable of reacting in a meaningful way to the musician's performance.

Research in the field of music cognition has shed light on human perception of musical structures. Knowledge gathered from this research can be applied to algorithmic composition processes, with the aim of creating musical output consistent with human expectations. Using this principle, this paper aims to bridge a gap in interactive music systems by designing an accessible musical accompaniment system which will react to user input and exhibit the ability to learn the musical preferences of the user. Ideally such a system should comply with the following criteria:

1. Produce musical output which is in keeping with expectations of the musician
2. React to musical input and adapt accordingly
3. Learn the musical preference of the user and modify its output to suit
4. Be accessible and provide a suitable interface for the technologically inexperienced user

## 2. Background and Related Work

### 2.1 Algorithmic Composition

Computer algorithms have been used in music composition since the mid-20th century. One of the earliest examples, 'The Illiac Suite', was created by Lejaren Hiller and Leonard Isaacson in 1956. The piece consists of four sections, each one demonstrating a different compositional algorithm [1]. Following the work of Hiller, Iannis Xenakis authored the 'Stochastic Music Program'. The Stochastic Music Program, originally developed to describe the behaviour of particles in gas, used probability distribution tables and random selection to generate a series of notes at its output [2]. The early methods employed in algorithmic composition by Hiller, Xenakis and their contemporaries displayed a contrast in approach, namely deterministic versus stochastic. Deterministic algorithms hold pre-defined input to output rules - the task performed by the algorithm, whilst possibly complex in nature, do not involve random selection [2]. By contrast, stochastic processes follow the principles of probability and random selection. The processes of stochastic algorithms make them a popular choice for interactive music systems [3] [4].

Modern algorithmic systems often utilise complex computer algorithms. The methods employed include *Grammars, Symbolic/knowledge based systems, Markov chains, Artificial Neural Networks, Evolutionary methods* and *Cellular Automata* [5]. Algorithmic composition has formed the backbone of interactive music and musical accompaniment systems; systems in which a user can influence or direct musical output. An interactive music system is one that can react and change its behaviour in accordance to a given input [6]. Whilst several authors have offered definitions of an interactive music system [6] [7], they may be broadly segmented into two main categories; score following and improvisational partners. A score following system aims to accompany a musician through a pre-set score, its musical output limited to play only its component part. In contrast, an improvisation system should be able to create music freely, with minimal constraints on the musical direction. Improvisation is of great importance in musical cultures and is inseparably tied to music composition [8]. It is the process of an artist drawing upon previous acquired musical knowledge, cultural influences, past associations and mental processes to create a piece of music spontaneously in real-time [9]. Algorithmic improvisation systems aim to recreate this experience, which is felt by many to be a highly inspiring environment [10]. The combined efforts of multiple performers create an interdependent musical relationship. These performance cues directly affect each musician's choice of notes and rhythmic patterns, allowing for spontaneity and 'creative risks' [11].

## 2.2 Music Cognition

Music cognition is a field of study which applies the methods of cognitive science to music. The aim is to gain insight into the human understanding of music through the exploration of human perception of music and examination of salient cognitive factors. The current research project aims to use lessons learned from this field as a basis for the design and development of the interactive music system.
Through exposure to music and culture, listeners form expectations of successive musical events [12]. Humans have an innate ability to understand the statistical properties of music, which brings a sense of satisfaction and pleasure when these expectations are realized [13]. Huron [13] [14] provides significant research which aims to define the statistical properties of melody. The findings are described over four categories:

- *Pitch Proximity* – Listeners expect small intervals between successive notes.
- *Post-Skip Reversal* – Listeners expect large intervals to be followed by a change in melodic direction.
- *Step Inertia* – Listeners expect small intervals to be followed by another small interval in the same direction.
- *Late-Phrase Declination* – Listeners expect the contour of a melody to descend in the latter half of the phrase.

Narmour [15] endeavoured to formally model melodic expectations through the development of the Implication-Realisation Model (IR). The model suggests that each successive tone implies the realisation of a further note, or the closing of a musical phrase. The principles outlined by Narmour have been tested in empirical studies [16] [17], with general agreement found for intervallic distance (smaller intervals preferred) and registral return (a change of direction after a large interval). Further examination and testing of the model [18] [19] has shown that it can be simplified to two governing principles without any effect on the predictive power of the model. Firstly, *pitch proximity*, which states that smaller intervals are expected over larger ones. Secondly, *post skip reversal*, a rule which states that if a large interval is heard, a change in melodic direction is expected [13].

Certain notes hold stronger harmonic relationships to certain chords. For example, operating within the key of C, the chord of C major holds the strongest relationship to the notes of its chord; the tonic, median and dominant scale degrees. The relationship between the melody and chord is termed *harmonic compliance*, and describes how well a given note harmonises with its supporting chord [20].

Melodies also contain temporal information. The time signature denotes the number of beats to the bar, but also contains lower level information. The metric structure of western music operates on a factor of two, with each lower level containing double the number of events than that of the level above. Each of the different levels of division (4th, 8th, $16^{th}$...) differ in their perceived metrical strengths. This is termed *metrical salience* [21]; the lower the number, the lower the salience. Western music places prominence on beat 1 and beat 3; commonly thought of as the downbeat and snare drum hit [22]. These positions in the bar hold the strongest metrical positions, with all other metric positions occupying varying levels of importance. The strongest metrical positions are the most common placement of note onsets [13], are often accented and can be viewed as a point of temporal expectation [23]. Prince and Schmuckler [24] performed statistical analysis on a corpus of classical music to ascertain if there was a relationship between points of strong metrical salience and notes of high tonal stability. Music from Beethoven, Mozart, Chopin and Bach was examined for the occurrence of each pitch class at all metrical positions within the bar. The results provided strong evidence that all composers exhibited a strong tendency to place notes of higher stability at positions of higher metric salience, particularly on the first beat of each bar.

## 3. System Design

To generate the initial melodic phrases, an algorithm was developed to implement key aspects of melodic construction from the music cognition research. The algorithm treats each note as a transitional step, considers several factors, and outputs the note considered the 'best choice' given the criteria set. Input from the user is examined, data is extracted and then passed onto the compositional algorithm. The input data consists of mode, chord, octave, velocity, density (note regularity) and duration (average note duration). Melodies can be thought of as containing two core pieces of information; the notes and the rhythmic pattern these notes are played out upon. Following this principle, the notes and rhythmic pattern are generated separately.

## 3.1 Rhythmic Pattern Generation

The rhythmic pattern is generated first, acting as a framework for all melodic passages created subsequently. Separating temporal and pitch information allows the rhythmic pattern to be reused with a different set of notes; a common component of melody construction [25]. Toussaint [26] describes an algorithm that, when applied in a musical context, can distribute a series of notes across a bar as evenly as possible. The patterns are termed *Euclidean Rhythms*. The rhythms created often correspond to the points of high metric salience within the bar. The creation of these patterns can recreate the most popular rhythmic patterns in African, western, and contemporary music. User input is analysed and used to set the event density of a Euclidean Rhythm generator [27]. The system examines the regularity of note occurrences and decides a suitable amount of notes to compliment the users' playing. Once decided, the desired amount of notes is distributed along a 32-step sequence, generating the rhythmic pattern. At this point, key information is collected – The number of notes required and their level of metric salience.

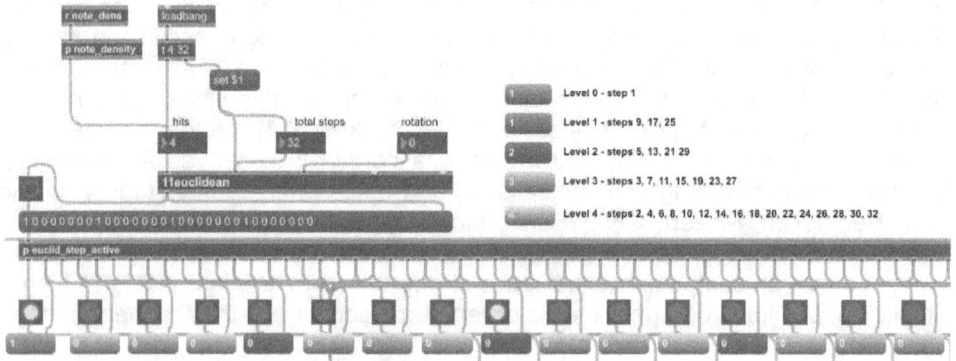

Figure 1. Rhythmic Pattern Generator Output

## 3.2 Note Generation

The note generation algorithm is a loop which repeats until the required amount of notes to fill the rhythmic pattern have been generated. Each note is generated in accordance with models of melodic expectation. The notes are generated by assigning each pitch class a weighting score derived from the features described below. After all features have been considered, the highest scoring note is selected as the next note in the melody. Once the desired amount of notes have been generated, the list of notes is interlaced with the rhythmic pattern, placing each note in its corresponding position within the sequencer.

## Harmonic Compliance

Harmonic compliance is determined from which chord is being played by the user. The chord input is assigned a number. From this, the system selects one of five weighted tables, one for each basic triad in the key of C major; *C, Dmin, Emin, F, G* and *Amin*. Each table is weighted to favour notes which hold strong stability to the current chord [20]. A small element of fluctuation is applied to the weighting score. This process aims to reduce the deterministic nature of note selection.

## Intervallic Distance and Late-Phrase Declination

The second stage outputs a score based upon the intervallic distance between the note directly previous and the candidate note. Small intervals are preferred over larger intervals. Therefore, the intervallic distance is assigned a score; higher scores for smaller intervals, lower scores for larger intervals. To recreate the pitch arch found in western melodic phrases, the melody as is split into two parts. Upward intervals are favoured in the first half, and downward intervals in the latter.

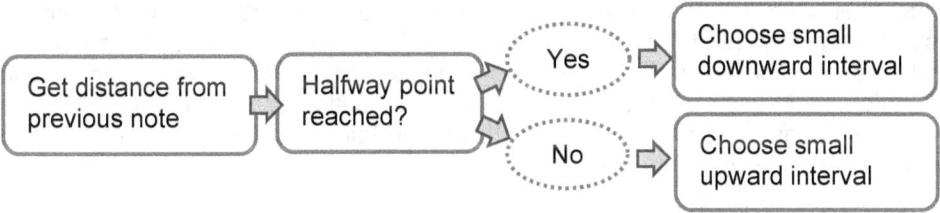

Figure 2. Intervallic Distance/Late Phrase Declination Algorithm

## Post-Skip Reversal

Listeners expect the direction of a melody to change after a large intervallic leap. If the system detects the interval between the previous two notes to be 7 semitones or greater, the algorithm weights in favour of a change in melodic direction.

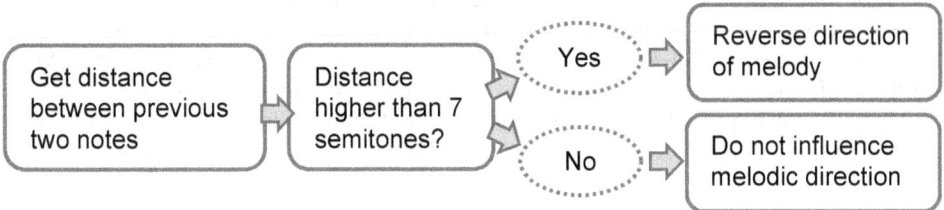

Figure 3. Post-Skip Reversal Algorithm

## Metric Salience

The system's choice of notes should vary in accordance with the metric position on which it occurs. Therefore, five weighting tables, which increase the weighting score for the most stable notes to the key [12] have been created. The weighting of notes with high tonal stability are increased for the stronger metric positions, with a gradual reduction in weighting through each salience rating.

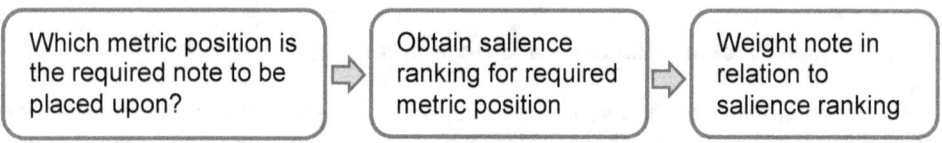

Figure 4. Metric Salience Algorithm

Once the required number of notes has been generated, the final melody is interlaced with the previously created rhythmic pattern and sent to the internal sequencer. As stated, the user input stage collects velocity, duration, and octave information is collected. Each sequencer step holds discrete octave, velocity and duration information. As the user plays, this information updates in real-time. This process intends to create a sense of rising and falling dynamics which follow the lead of the users' performance.

## 3.4 Learning Structure

The subsequent melodies generated by the rhythmic and melodic sections can be selected as chosen patterns by the user. These chosen patterns become the basis for future pattern generation. As the system generates each melodic passage, the note values are stored in a list. The user can identify 'favourite' sequences, which then form the training corpus for a Markov Model [28]. Markov Models work best with a large dataset, where smaller datasets provide predictable results with a high level of repetition. For this reason, the ability to activate the Markov structure is not available until a minimum of ten sequences have been entered as training data. After ten sequences have been sent to the Markov Model, the user can activate the output of the Markov Model, overriding any sequences generated in the compositional algorithm. The generation of rhythmic patterns remains the same. The number of notes required is collected at the output stage of the Euclidean rhythm generator. This value is sent to the Markov model, which outputs the required number of notes. This series of notes is stored within a list, and interlaced with the active step list, placing each note in the desired temporal position.

## 4. Objective Analysis

The algorithm was tested against each of the music cognition features implemented in the compositional algorithm.

### 4.1 Harmonic Compliance

A total of 3200 notes for each chord in the key of C major were generated; 100 groups of 32 notes (the maximum resolution of the step sequencer). All chords tested showed that the harmonic compliance algorithm was operating successfully, with the root $3^{rd}$ and $5^{th}$ of each chord featuring the most readily. Notes not present within the key were not selected.

### 4.2 Intervallic distance and Late Phrase Declination

The systems output was collected over 32, 16, 8 and 5 note phrases played over the chord of C major. A total of 100 phrases for each were collected. Each of the phrases showed a rise and fall in melodic contour. A notable arch shape can be seen in the longer phrases. As the length of the melody decreases, the arch shape is seen to dissipate.

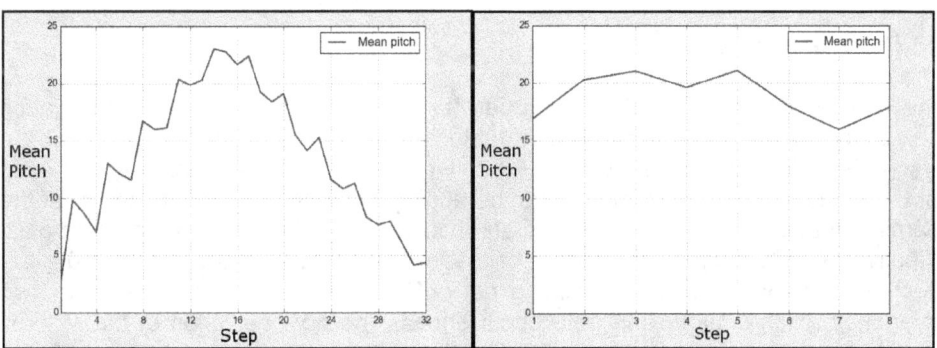

Figure 5 (left) and 6 (right). Pitch contour over 32 step and 8 step melodies.

### 4.3 Post-Skip Reversal

A series of two notes with an intervallic gap of one octave were input as the ultimate and penultimate notes. The resultant note was recorded and compared to its precursor for its registral direction. The algorithm operates with an extremely high success rate, with melodic direction changing after 96% of all large intervals input.

### 4.4 Metric Salience

The metric salience algorithm proved successful, with a high level of effectiveness found on lower salience levels (the strongest beats). This algorithm is of most significance on the strongest salience levels, aiming to provide a sense of structure and resolution to the melodic phrases generated. The algorithm successfully selects notes of higher tonal stability on the stronger metric positions.

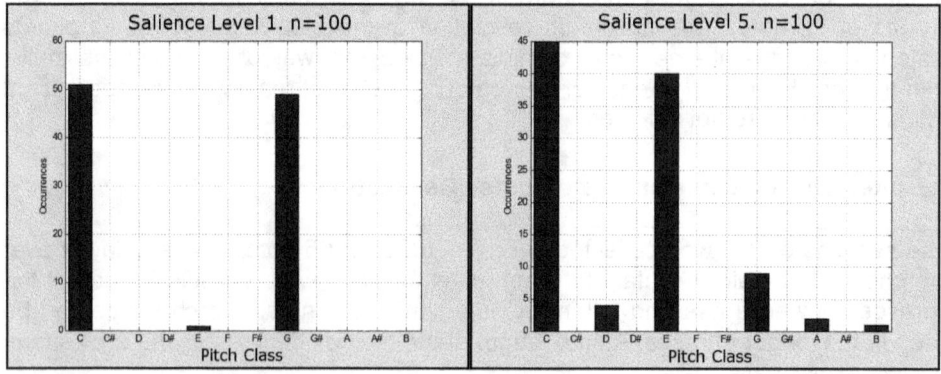

Figures 7 (left) and 8 (right). Note occurrences on salience levels 1 and 5.

### 4.5 Preference Learning Structure

The preference learning structure operates by building transitional information based upon a corpus of training data selected by the user. As the output of the system is entirely dependent upon the training data, the assessment methods used for the compositional algorithm cannot be applied. The objective assessment of the learning structure may be considered an observation, rather than assessment of its effectiveness. To monitor the output of the learning structure, a series of 100, 32-step melodies were input as training data. The output was monitored over two categories, pitch-contour and note occurrences. The note selection of the Markov model provided similar results to the harmonic compliance results of the compositional algorithm. However, the pitch contour (whilst displaying the preferred smaller intervals) does not display the notable pitch arch provided compositional algorithm.

## 5. Discussion

The objective analysis, supported by the results gathered in the subjective assessment, indicate the system performs with a reasonably high level of success. The implemented features (harmonic compliance, metric salience, post-skip reversal and intervallic distance incorporating late phrase declination) all function correctly, influencing note choice where appropriate. The created melodies have a sense of resolution, which change in relation to user input and correspond with the hierarchical structure of pitch music noted throughout the relevant literature [12] [13] [29]. The note choice of the system adapts to user input, selecting notes which are deemed most compliant to the chord. The output from the learning structure does not provide as pronounced a pitch arch as the compositional algorithm. This is due to the nature of implementing the Markov Model within Max. The model collects the data and processes a series of transitional steps. Once the data has been entered, the process is essentially 'fixed', not allowing for modification. In doing so, the benefits of the pitch arch algorithm is lost. However, the learning structure does produce similar melodies to those preferred by the user. The recurring patterns that are generated create a sense of a musical figure, which in turn give the impression of a musician experimenting with a theme.

The design and development of the system detailed in this paper raises some key issues. For a system to be 'generative', or create the illusion that it has the ability to create music of its own accord, it must be allowed to choose freely; a sense of spontaneity must be perceived by the listener. However, in order to meet the listeners' musical expectations, the system must adhere to the expectations of music naturally held by humans. In order to adhere to these musical properties, rules must be enforced to constrain the systems' freedom. Consequently, as each rule is added the system becomes less 'free', resulting in a more rigid, deterministic output. A successful system may be considered a balance between these two extremes.

## 6. Conclusions

Research in music cognition demonstrates that there are core aspects which underpin melodic construction. If these rules are used as a foundation for algorithmic composition, then 'realistic' performances which follow our understanding and expectations can be generated. The inclusion of user input creates an additional element which influences the melodic output. However, the preference learning structure may require further development to increase its connection to user input. Further investigation into stylistic traits found within specific genres may provide a means of creating a more refined system, tailored for specific musical accompaniment. The tonal relationship between successive notes may be considered a relevant feature to add for note selection, linking notes which have a strong musical relationship. Additionally, at present the system uses a maximum of two notes to generate the next. If a larger number of notes were considered, a greater sense of musical context may be achieved.

## 7. References

[1] Hiller, L., Isaacson, L.M. (1959). Experimental Music: Composition with an Electronic Computer. New York: McGraw-Hill Book Company.
[2] Roads, C. (1996). The Computer Music Tutorial. Massachusetts: MIT Press.
[3] Pachet, F. (2002). The Continuator: Musical Interaction with Style. Proceedings of the International Computer Music Conference, Gothenborg (Sweden).
[4] Thom, B. (2001). BoB: An Improvisational Music Companion. Available: http://reports-archive.adm.cs.cmu.edu/anon/2001/CMU-CS-01-138.pdf. [Accessed 24th Oct 2014]
[5] Fernandez, J.D. and Vico, F. (2013). AI Methods in Algorithmic Composition: A Comprehensive Survey. Journal of Artificial Intelligence Research. Volume 48, pp 513-582
[6] Rowe, R. (1993). Interactive Music Systems. Massachusetts: MIT Press.
[7] Winkler, T (2001). Composing Interactive Music. Massachusetts: MIT Press.
[8] Wigram, T. (2004). Improvisation: Methods and Techniques for Music Therapy Clinicians, Educators and Students. England: Jessica Kingsley Publishers.
[9] Johnson-Laid, P. (2002). How Jazz Musicians Improvise. Music Perception: An interdisciplinary Journal. Vol. 19, No.3, pp 415-442.
[10] Berenson, G. (2008). The joys of making music with others. American Music Teacher. pp 4-5
[11] Seddon, F. A. (2005) Modes of Communication During Jazz Improvisation. British Journal of Music Education. 22(1), pp 47-61.
[12] Krumhansl, C. L (1990): Cognitive Foundations of Musical Pitch. Oxford University Press.
[13] Huron, D. (2006): Sweet Anticipation: Music and the Psychology of Expectation. Massachusetts: MIT Press.
[14] Huron, D. (1996): The Melodic Arch in Western Folksongs. Computing in Musicology. Vol.10 pp3-23.
[15] Narmour, E. (1990). The Analysis and Cognition of Basic Melodic Structures: The Implication-Realization Model. Chicago: University of Chicago Press.
[16] Cuddy L & Lunney C. (1995). Expectancies Generated by Melodic Intervals: Perceptual Judgments of Melodic Continuity. Perception & Psychophysics. 57 (4), pp 451-462.
[17] Schellenberg, E.G. (1996). Expectancy In Melody: Tests of The Implication-Realisation Model. Cognition, 58 (1), pp 75–125
[18] Schellenberg, E.G (1997). Simplifying the Implication-Realization Model of Melodic Expectancy. Music Perception, Vol.14, No.3, pp. 295-318.
[19] Von Hippel, P. (2002). Melodic-expectation rules as learned heuristics. 7th International Conference on Music Perception and Cognition, Sydney, Australia.
[20] Elowsson, A. and Friberg, A. (2011): Algorithmic Composition of Popular Music. Proceedings of the 12th International Conference on Music Perception and Cognition. Thessaloniki, Greece.

[21] Parncutt, R. (1994a): A perceptual model of pulse salience and metrical accent in musical rhythms. Music Perception, Vol. 11, (04), pp 409-464
[22] Gabrielsson, A. (1993). The complexities of Rhythm. Psychology and Music: The understanding of melody and rhythm. Hillsdale, New Jersey: Lawrence Erlbaum Associates
[23] Ahlbäck, S. (2004): Melody Beyond Notes: A Study of Melody Cognition. Göteborgs Universitet: Humanistiska fakulteten
[24] Prince, J & Mark, S. (2012): The Tonal-Metric Hierarchy: A Corpus Analysis. Music Perception, Vol. 31. (3), pp254–270
[25] Elowsson, A. (2012): Statistical Analysis of Vocal Folk Music. Stockholm Royal Institute of Technology.
[26] Toussaint, G. (2005): The Euclidean algorithm generates traditional musical rhythms. Proceedings of BRIDGES: Mathematical Connections in Art, Music, and Science, Banff, Alberta, Canada, July 31 to August 3, pp. 47–56.
[27] Olsen. (2014). 11euclidean. Available: http://www.11olsen.de/code/max-objects/11euclidean. [Accessed 12th January 2015]
[28] Martin, A. (2014). VMM. Available: http://www.am-process.org/main/?portfolio=vmm. [Accessed 15th December 2014]
[29] Lerdahl, F., Jackendoff, R. (1983): A Generative Theory of Tonal Music. Massachusetts: MIT Press.

# Triple Helix Partnerships for the Music Sector: Music Industry, Academia and the Public

Carola Boehm

Department of Contemporary Arts, Manchester Metropolitan University, Crewe
Green Road, Crewe, UK
C.Boehm@mmu.ac.uk

## Abstract

*What kind of partnerships are best placed to drive innovations in the music sector? Considering the continual appetite for new products and services within our knowledge economy, how can we ensure that the most novel and significant research can be applied in and exploited for the market? How can we ensure that the whole music sector, including the not-for-profit sector, benefits and is engaged in new knowledge production?*

*This paper represents an exploration of a partnership model – the triple and quadruple helix – that is specifically designed to drive innovation. Applying this to the music sector, the presentation will provide case studies relevant for driving innovations in music technology, the creative sector and digital innovations. It will cover both the for-profit sector and social enterprise, and emphasize the importance of partnerships and community for maximizing sustainability when devising research and development projects using helix system models.*

## 1. Introduction and Background

All universities are involved in partnership work related to their research and enterprise interests. In the area of music technology this may include patenting music instruments, production of music scores, recordings and live performances and researching into new modes of composition and audio production. These activities are often contextualized academically as research and development (gadgets) or practice-as-research (engagement in creative processes). Within our own vision statement, we have a section that suggests we engage in 'transformational partnerships'. Like all other universities, we believe we make a real impact on the communities and commercial sectors with which we work.

This is specifically valid for the music sector, which interfaces heavily with external communities, related to cultural assets in forms of concert series, music in the community, music therapy or the music industry.

For academics and creative practitioners in the music technology sector, where subject matter straddles both science and art, technology and creative practice, often involving both commercial and social enterprise, there are questions about how to best to support partnership projects and how to improve the flow from a research stage to the application of these new insights into an external sector.

What makes the consideration of knowledge production in this area even more difficult is that within UK academia, there still seems to be an encultured difference between 'research' and 'enterprise', with the relatively new term on the block being 'knowledge transfer'. Universities may express their intention and policy of treating research and enterprise as a continuum, but just a brief look at career development opportunities within institutions, or research quality assurance frameworks, demonstrates a strong preference for basic research over enterprise. This represents a distinct disincentive for academia to engage more directly with industrial partners and/or communities representing end-users. This prioritization of basic research over applied research, or what has been termed as a prioritization of 'Mode 1' research over 'Mode 2 and 3' research, has the potential of slowing the knowledge exchange between academia and industry down, if not stopping it altogether.

Similarly, disincentive models exist in the area of social enterprise, often falling into the category of community engagement, widening participation and/or the 'civic duties' of a university. Many of these terms emphasize the perspective of the educating institution; they are university-centric and are conceptualized as activities that flow within and out of academia. It is this – an increasing number of academics and professionals would argue – which is problematic for forming partnerships that are impactful in allowing research and new knowledge to add significant value both to the sector and to society.

Specifically for music technology, the Higher Education sector divide between research and enterprise has meant that it is difficult for technological innovations coming out of universities to transfer quickly onto the market or external sectors. This difficulty in bringing an idea to the final market stage is perceived to be normal. The external sector thus often perceives universities as too slow to support innovation or to bring an application to market. The supporting structures and incentive models within academia often support the production of journal papers, but the journey from transferring this knowledge to developing a prototype, securing patents, developing market plans, designing for mass production and finally delivering a commercial product is so difficult that too many academically housed music technologists are opting for the traditional publish-a-paper route.

This situation does not need to be this way, and various voices from different sectors suggest that universities need to change the way in which they contextualize, value, incentivize and support research in order for the development of innovation and its application in society to happen much more instantaneously. Authors relevant for this debate are Etzkowitz [1], Carayannis and Campbell [2], Gibbons [3], Watson [4] and Boehm [5] among others, but there is also a wider relevant debate about the role of universities today, including contributors such as

Collini [6], Barnett [7, 8], Graham [9] and Williams [10]. The progressive terms relevant for the future are 'triple and quadruple helixes', 'Open Innovation 2.0' and 'Mode 3 research'.

To contextualize this in an example: if we look into the area of assistive music technologies, the market for technologies could be characterized as lacking competition and a consequently lacking diversity and choice. This is in an area where there is still a big end-user need. Supported by the research councils, the area of assistive music technology has always been one with a lively research and development community; many digital innovations are developed for specific special needs communities but they are far less often being turned into commercial products or refined towards mass production.

These challenges can be overcome more easily by having the right academia–business–government partnerships from the outset of a project, with a more collective and collaborative experience of both basic research and development, as well as application, commercialization and subsequent marketization. Additionally, with the new government-driven impact agendas for Higher Education, these issues are timely and relevant to a consideration of the role that universities play in society today. This paper thus focuses on communities, enterprise and the cultural sector involved in, or interacting with, music technological practices, making explicit the various interacting agendas with their respective stakeholders. It attempts to identify ways towards achieving a balance between inward- and outward-facing interests when considering collaborative projects that drive innovation.

The paper will use five main secondary sources: Etzkowitz [1], Watson [4], Carayannis and Campbell [2], Watson [11] and Gibbons [3]. These were written with a general academic perspective in mind, but I will apply the relevant themes in a specific music technology and arts context. The paper will apply these current concepts to innovation developments in music technology, covering both the for-profit and the not-for-profit sector. Providing example projects as case studies, I will suggest that triple and quadruple partnerships (e.g. helix models) between universities, industry, government and the civic sector (the not-for-profit and voluntary sectors) allow innovation to happen as a non-linear, collaborative process with overlapping processes of basic research, application and development. In this model, knowledge production (e.g. research) is not the sole concern of universities; and technology exploitation may not be the sole concern of industry; creating what has been called a 'socially distributed knowledge' [3] or a (Mode 3) 'Innovation Ecosystem' [2].

## 2. Research and Enterprise: A Personal Experience of Torn Identities

Universities are complex and diverse entities. Academics continually live in this 'super-complexity' [7]. They and their academic communities have shifting and changing agendas that – apart from education – allow individuals to engage in research, in enterprise and in community-facing activities. The increase in managerialism, professionalism and centralization has introduced larger amounts of accountability and measurement, and it has followed that activities in the area of enterprise and research are often treated separately, in order to be supported and measured in detail (see also [12]).

A current theme within our knowledge economy is that there are increasing demands on universities to have an impact on society, to interface with the business sector, to commercialize and to be enterprising, while still having supporting structures and incentive models that see civic engagement, enterprise, research and education as very different spheres, supported often by different sections and policies within the same university. Thus the government-driven impact agendas have, probably unexpectedly, resulted in highlighting that the neo-managerialistic cultures with their specific accountability measures are increasingly becoming the barrier to a more holistic consideration of impact – one that exploits the multidirectional benefits of engaging in research, enterprise and civic engagement all at the same time.

I started to consider questions of how best to support collaborative knowledge production and innovation projects a few years ago, when I had to justify yet again why I – an academic at a research-intensive university – was involved in projects that my university at the time classed as *not* research, but 'only' enterprise. I have been involved in MPEG7 developments for mp3 audio files, community engagement and patenting of instruments, but all of these were difficult to justify as falling under the category of Research with a capital 'R'.

I was confident to argue that all these activities produced new knowledge, and all resulted in peer-reviewed journal publications, the classic method for evaluating 'researchiness' in universities. However, there still seemed to be barriers within the university and the Higher Education quality frameworks to valuing something that does not show the classic linear progression from basic research, via dissemination through publications (co-authored in the sciences, single-authored in the arts and humanities), knowledge transfer and application, and external dissemination, to finally having some societal impact.

Similarly, until recently there were plenty of times when I had to argue that several of my projects which included communities and/or businesses were to be defined not only as exclusively 'community outreach' or 'enterprise', but actually as research in action. Even though there were publications as outputs, simply because the funding came from a heritage organization, or a business benefited from the knowledge produced, I seemed to be unable, or able only with difficulty, to collect those brownie points that would allow me to progress on my research-related ladder of academia. The incentives here were geared towards basic research, but not towards impactful community-facing or music-industry-facing product or service development.

This situation is changing fast, and I would suggest that now, after the first dust of the impact debate has settled, there is a real will to make university research (even) more impactful. One of the biggest shifts that allow universities to consider developing their research cultures into something different is the government's decision to make societal impact a substantial factor for evaluating the quality of research. This is important for universities because of the linked allocation of governmental research funding, now influenced not only by the peer-reviewed and perceived value of the piece of research as evidenced through academic publications, but also by the reach and significance that it has on the external sector, as evidenced through case studies.

Music technology academics have always found it hard to distinguish between technology and artistic practice, enterprise, community outreach and research. One simply has to consider the range of topics and diversity of speakers at the relevant international conferences in this area, such as the International Computer Music Conference, The Art of Record Production Conference or the new Conference for Innovation in Music. Many of the collaborative projects in the area of music technology simultaneously include partners from small and medium-sized businesses, cultural organizations and academia.

To make these developments even more impactful and effective, it is useful to consider partnership models in which knowledge production is not the sole concern of universities, just as technology exploitation may no longer need to be the sole concern of industry. Digital technology and the knowledge economy have allowed the spheres of academia and industry to be shifted, to be realigned. The question is, is this true of the research cultures within Higher Education? With knowledge traditions going back centuries, have they moved with the times, or are they possibly finding it too difficult to keep up with these societal developments?

The question emerged of what an ideal engaged *and* entrepreneurial university would look like, and this question involved dealing with understanding and resolving some of the tensions between outward- and inward-facing vested interests, research methodologies and how the quality of research and knowledge transfer is measured.

For each institution, there is the equilibrium of sustainability to be met in an ever-shifting climate of agendas – not a straightforward measurement, considering that the activities are often funded via a complex mixture of sources. This is where an explicit conceptualization of partnerships and vested interests helps.

## 2.1. Triple and Quadruple Helixes

The triple helix was first described by Etzkowitz in 2008 [1] and provided a conceptual framework for capturing, analysing, devising and making explicit various aspects of project partnerships, 'managing interactions among universities, business and government on common projects'.

The basic assumption of this conceptual model is that in our knowledge-based economy interaction between university, industry and government is key to innovation and growth. In a knowledge economy, universities carrying out research and development become a paramount asset in innovation-intensive production. This can be seen as a historical shift from industrial society, in which the primary institutions were industry and government, to the present knowledge-based society, where economies are much more tightly linked to sources of new knowledge and universities are becoming more important as structures with an everlasting flow of talent and ideas through their PhD and research programmes. Exemplars of this development can be seen in the emergence of university-owned and university-run science parks, incubators, cultural centres and enterprise hubs. Etzkowitz defines it as follows:

'The Triple Helix of university-industry-government relations is an internationally recognized model for understanding entrepreneurship, the changing dynamics of universities, innovation and socio-economic development.'[1]

Universities in this context of a knowledge economy have the big advantage that they have an inherent regular flow of human capital, such talent and ideas. This is a distinct difference from the research and development sections of large businesses and industry, where the employment structure creates much less dynamics or mobility within its own human capital.

However, in this new economy, the different spheres each also take the role of the other, and there is a much greater overlap of remits and roles than in prior centuries. In this model:
- Universities (traditional role: teaching and learning, human capital, basic research) take the role of industry when they stimulate the development of new businesses through science parks and incubation hubs.
- Businesses (traditional role: place of production, vocational training, venture capital, firm creation) develop training to ever higher levels, acting a little like educational establishments, even universities (e.g. higher apprenticeship schemes).
- Government (traditional role: regulatory activities, basic research and development funding, business support, business innovation) acts often as a public venture capitalist through research grants and studentships, including, for instance, knowledge transfer partnerships.

This overlapping of the formerly distinct roles of three different spheres (in the case of the triple helix) suggests that the traditional stages of knowledge transfer from
- Stage 1 government – university (example: research grant)
- Stage 2: university – business (example: incubator)

- Stage 2: government – business (example: business start-up grant)

overlap much more, and more often, than they have done traditionally.

Etzkowitz's model was expanded in 2012 by Carayannis and Campbell to include the third sector, and with it universities' own civic engagements. Watson [4, 11, 13] has foregrounded this latter role; his concept of the 'engaged university' proposes that social enterprise and the not-for-profit sector should be considered within the helix model. His international comparison of the way universities engage with their respective communities provides a strong articulation for academia to consider new knowledge production models that allow a greater interaction between universities on the one hand and both the public and industry on the other, for example for universities to become (even?) more engaged.

Various arts-related initiatives have attempted to use these models to initiate innovation [14, 15]. Similarly, because of their inherent use of inter-, multi- and trans-disciplinary knowledge production methods, the potential that helix partnerships provide for managing large-scale and multi-partner projects allow these concepts to come to the fore in considerations of the world's largest challenges. Addressing its impact potential on the socio-economic aspects, Watson suggested that in this new era universities have to become more 'engaged', and he specifically points his finger at universities in the northern hemisphere [4].

At the core of this debate stands the notion that our classic (northern hemisphere) research methodologies and their related cultures, frameworks and value systems are preventing us from increasing the impact on society. Universities that value socio-economic impact will thus always have an emphasis on partnerships between universities, industry, government and the civic sector (the not-for-profit and voluntary sectors).

Not only will these quadruple partnerships better support innovation, but they will allow innovation to happen in a non-linear, collaborative manner with overlapping processes of basic research, application and development. In this model research is not the sole concern of universities, and technology exploitation may be not the sole concern of industry, creating what has been called a 'socially distributed knowledge' [3] or a (Mode 3) 'Innovation Ecosystem' [2].

These debates feed into an ever-increasing discourse around the comparative appropriateness of various research methodologies for benefiting the real-life problems of society, from inter-disciplinary or trans-disciplinary methodological considerations to practice-as-research [16] and the creative practitioner; from the challenges of big, co-owned and open data or non-linear collaborative methods for producing knowledge.

What have given a renewed focus on how academia interfaces with communities outside of itself, allowing the Higher Education sector to produce knowledge that has real impact, are the last Research Excellence Framework (REF) in 2014 and the government-driven agendas concerning impact. The last REF could be seen as a collection of quality assessment methods that collectively have an inbuilt tension of, on the one hand, a more traditional, linear knowledge production culture (Gibbons's Mode 1 knowledge production model) and, on the other, an impact-driven, non-linear mode that values socially distributed knowledge more than discovery (Gibbons's Mode 2 knowledge production model) [5].

## 2.2. Gibbons, Carayannis and Campbell and their Knowledge Production Models

Mode 1 and Mode 2 were knowledge production models put forward by Gibbons back in 1994. Several authors of the past decade have picked up and further developed his concepts with relevance for the current impact agendas. The relevant works include Etzkowitz's 'The triple helix' [1], Watson's *The engaged university* [4], Carayannis and Campbell's *Mode 3 knowledge production* [2] and Watson's *The question of conscience* [11].

Gibbons conjectured that Mode 1 knowledge production was a more 'elderly linear concept of innovation', in which there is a focus on basic research 'discoveries' within a discipline, and where the main interest is derived from delivering comprehensive explanations of the world. There is a 'disciplinary logic', and these knowledge production models are usually not concerned with application or problem solving for society. Quality is primarily controlled through disciplinary peers or peer reviews; Carayannis and Campbell add that these act as strong gate keepers. Success in this model is defined as quality of research, or 'research excellence' and both Watson [4] and Carayannis and Campbell [2] suggest that our Western academic cultures still predominantly support the Mode 1 knowledge production model. The REF's focus on scholarly publication and its re-branding to include the term 'research excellence' may be considered as emerging from a culture surrounding the traditional Mode 1 knowledge production.

But Gibbons had already put forward a different way of producing knowledge, in which problem solving is organized around a particular application. He suggests that the characteristics of this mode are greater inter-, trans- and multi-disciplinarity, often demanding social accountability and reflexivity. The exploitation of knowledge in this model demands participation in the knowledge production process; and the different phases of research are non-linear, for example discovery, application and fabrication overlap. In this model, knowledge production becomes diffused throughout society for instance a 'socially distributed knowledge', and within this, tacit knowledge is as valid or relevant as codified knowledge [3]. Quality control is exercised by a community of practitioners 'that do not follow the structure of an institutional logic of academic disciplines' [3], and success is defined in terms of efficiency and usefulness in contributing to the overall solution of a problem [17]. Mode 2 is seen as a natural development within a knowledge economy, as it requires digital and IT awareness and a widely accessible Higher Education system. Research cultures using Mode 2 models often initiate a greater sensitivity of impact of knowledge on society and economy.

Obviously, the two modes currently exist simultaneously in various research communities, and have done so for a long time. Various terms emphasize the different nuances of the ongoing impact debate, from applied research, through knowledge exchange, to definitions of research impact. However, as Watson [4] contends, there is a distinct divide between the southern and northern hemispheres in how academia tends to see itself and its role in relation to society, and embedded in this is how research value is conceptualized.

In the northern hemisphere academia generally comes from a Mode 1 trajectory, that is, Mode 1 knowledge production is, more often than not, considered to be the highest form of research. This is reinforced by publicly funded research that creates a sense of entitlement [4], and generally there is more panic about the decline of interest in scientific and technological study, with many degrees being kept alive by students from overseas. For universities in the northern hemisphere, Watson's list of characteristics includes the following:

- They derive much of their moral power from simply 'being there'.
- They are aware of their influence as large players in civil society.
- They stress role in developing character and democratic instincts.
- They focus on contributions like service learning and volunteering.
- They see public support for the above as an entitlement.
- The main model of contribution is knowledge transfer.
- They have developed from a culture in which Mode 1 is valued as the highest form of research.

This cultural stance can also be detected in the role that universities play as cultural patrons. There is a sense that art is entitled to public funding, and there is a long history of publicly funded art – specifically in the UK.

For universities in the southern hemisphere, civic engagement is an imperative, not an optional extra. Watson writes that in his team's enquires, 'we were constantly struck in our Southern cases, by how much was being done by universities for the community with so little resources (and with relatively little complaint)' [4].

'Practical subjects' and 'applied' research take priority and with them comes a different value system for the role of research: the Mode 2 knowledge production model prevails [3, 4]. Thus Watson sees Mode 2 as a more progressive developmental stage of Higher Education in reference to societal impact and civic engagement. His list of characteristics includes:

- It simply is more dangerous – there is no comfort zone.

- There is an acceptance that religion and sciences should work in harmony.
- There is a general use of private bodies for public purposes.
- International partnerships are for assistance, not 'positioning'
- Challenging environments[1] where many attacks on universities seem to be connected to various governments' efforts to prevent opposition movements, restrict political debate or criticism of policies [18].
- There is frequently a central political drive for outcomes like 'transformation' (South Africa) or 'solidarity' (Latin America) (Leibowitz 2014:47).
- There is a privileging of 'development' (or social return) over 'character' (and individual return), of 'national cohesion' over 'personal enrichment'; and of 'employment' (human capital) over 'employability' (SETs (Science-Engineering-Technology) over arts).
- International partnerships are there for assistants, not 'positioning'.
- 'Above all "being there" doesn't cut much ice; there is a much greater sense of societal pull over institutional push' [4].

Thus, there is a predominant engagement with Mode 2 knowledge production.

In 2012 Carayannis and Campbell expanded the concept of Modes 1 and 2 to include a Mode 3 knowledge production model, defined as working simultaneously across Modes 1 and 2. Adaptable to current problem contexts, it allows the co-evolution of different knowledge and innovation modes. The authors called it a 'Mode 3 Innovation Ecosystem' which allows 'GloCal' multi-level knowledge and innovation systems with local meaning but global reach. This values individual scholarly contributions less, and rather puts an emphasis on clusters and networks, which often stand in 'co-opetition', defined as a balance of both cooperation and competition.

## 3. Case Studies

For the music sector, there are various opportunities that a more structured partnership approach can seize. Two of own research areas can act as examples of how Mode 3 thinking and a helix partnership approach benefit all the sectors involved – the music industry, the public, academia and government – with its societal and economic imperatives.

---

[1] For example, 2012 northern Nigeria, Federal Polytechnic in Mubi, 46 students killed, pretext student union election. 2013 Nigeria, gunmen killed at least 50 students. 2013 Syria, University of Aleppo, 82 students killed. 2014 Ethiopia, a bomb killed 1 and injured more than 70. 2015 Kenia, Nairobi, Somali militants burst into a university in eastern Kenya on Thursday and killed nearly 150 students. For a full report see Global Coalition to Protect Education from Attack, 'Education under Attack 2014', GCPEA, New York 2014. http://protectingeducation.org Last accessed 09/05/2015.

## 3.1. Case Study 1: Hard and Software Developments and Assistive Music Technologies

Music Technology is taught in the UK in various departments, according to UCAS by 103 providers to be exact, with more than 200 degrees situated somewhere within and between the disciplines of Computer Science, Electrical Engineering and the arts. Innovation happens in all of these, and specifically the more 'gadgety' type of innovation often needs industry-related experience and a knowledge of developing products from an idea to a mass-produced item for sale. Although in general Electrical Engineering and Computer Science departments have still more experience in these processes than arts and humanities departments, even here there are barriers that do not always allow good ideas to be developed into products. In view of the fact that our new knowledge economy needs *more* products, a more *diverse* range of products and *cheaper* products, the pathways from initial research to product really do need to be shortened. The industry sector is geared up for this, and modern innovations such as 3D printing and rapid prototyping have made the production of diversity in product development cheaper than it ever was before.

In fact, there have been plenty of individual instrument developments as part PhD studies and funded research projects; but of these, only the smallest number of ideas and prototypes have been developed towards industry exploitation. Plenty of examples exist where a prototype represents the final stage of the research project, and the lack of collaboration and/or incentives for individuals to develop it to marketization, as well as a real lack of incentive models within institutions, keep the knowledge just there with the individual. This individual often stays within academia, and is thus able to gain career advantages not by marketization, but by publication of the idea and concept. This may still be seen as a classic form of the ivory tower. Thus for the area of instruments or gadgets for special needs musicians, there is a distinct need to shorten the pathways from university research to market availability.

As one solution, we have been developing projects based on the quadruple helix model and a Mode 3 research methodology. In it we connect special needs communities with the micro and SME (Small and Medium Enterprise) market, supported by innovations derived from university research by PhD students and academics. The idea is for us academics to collaborate on developing a new series of digital innovations together with end-users and SME developers. Thus the knowledge will not be located only within the Higher Education institution, but will be shared among the partnership, and – importantly – between SME and Higher Education.

In Gibbons's terms, knowledge will thus be (more) socially distributed in this non-linear model, and discovery, application and fabrication will overlap. The control of quality will be exercised by the community of practitioners who (and I quote Gibbons again) 'do not follow the structure of an institutional logic of academic disciplines' [3]. These disciplines should not be relevant for evaluating the quality and success, as this is not defined by the Mode 1 model in terms of excellence (evaluated by peer review), but by Mode 3 models and in terms of efficiency, usefulness and contribution to an overall solution to a problem.

Obviously, university structures still tend to show some friction with these new conceptualizations of research and how to value it. But unless we want Europe to continue to fall behind in entrepreneurial and innovative activities, universities will need to find new ways in which to support and incentivize academics in a Mode 3 research model, in order to boost the economy of our knowledge society through real innovation based on knowledge production.

### 3.2. Case Study 2: Music- and Arts-Related Multi-Professional Work

Similarly, in another European project (see Figure 1) we are developing training packages for multi-professional or inter-agency community arts and community music workers. This project is simultaneously a community arts project in itself and a project to define and develop new multi-professional working skills and environments for professionals in art and social work.

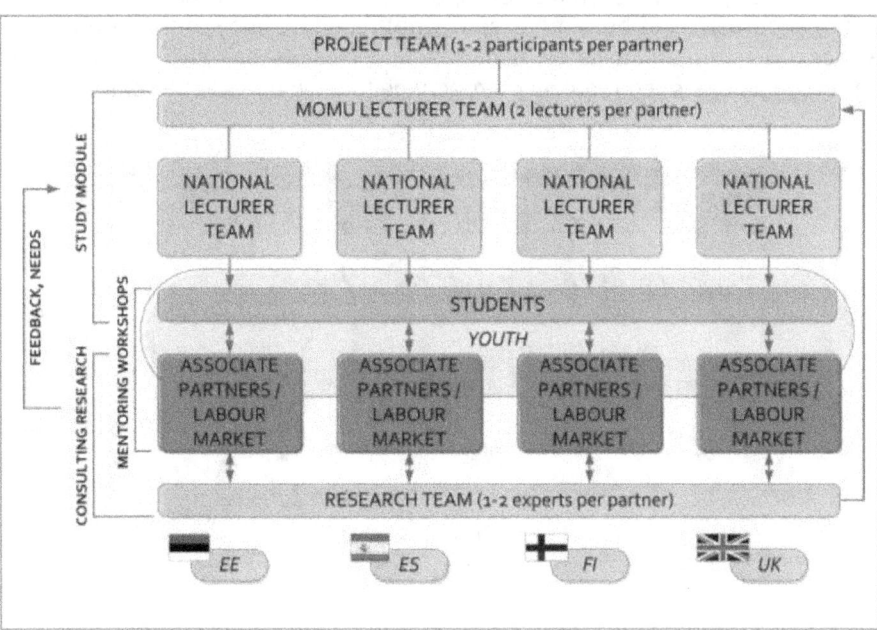

Figure 1. Structure of the MOMU project (multi-professional working skills for professionals in arts and social work)

Music of course has a big potential for engaging with external communities, whether it is in the context of being a cultural asset (concert series), a creative practice (music production, audio engineering, composition, performance), music therapy (assistive music technologies), music technology (plugins, apps), or simply being an anchor for economic regional growth and supporting new talent from all areas of the music industry and the creative sector.

In this project, however, the *new* knowledge (the definition and identification of skills and competencies in an inter-agency or multi-professional community arts setting) is gained within a partnership that includes:

- lecturers, representing academia;
- artists, representing the creative industry;
- end-users, community;
- and the European Commission, representing the governmental part of the helix.

It is no wonder that this is likely to be a Creative Europe-funded project, and not a Horizon 2020 project. Creative Europe, with its cultural and socio-economic mission, is perceived to be a more appropriate funding body to target projects that use Mode 3 research, as their activities and outputs are still considered more under the headings of community outreach, cultural work and enterprise.

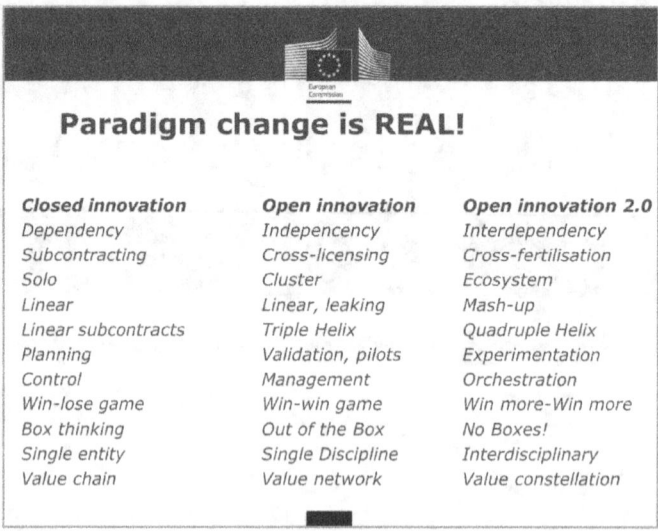

Figure 2. Bror Salmelin, director-general of the European Commission, discusses the differences between Closed and Open Innovation

However, even Bror Salmelin [19], a director-general of the European Commission, who presented at a European conference in Finland recently, emphasized the need for the European research community to embrace Open Innovation 2.0 models, including quadruple helix thinking (see Figure 2.)

## 4. Conclusion and Ways Forward

Bearing in mind Watson's suggestion that in the north we tend to engage predominantly in Mode 1 research (in contrast to the south's Mode 2), and thus are consequently somewhat less engaged in partnerships that could be considered triple, quadruple or even quintuple [2] helix models, it may be worthwhile to consider that even in the north, partnership work in publically funded research has been the norm. Thus, although they are not consciously implemented or explicitly formulated in policy, project parameters that conform to helix models can be identified extensively.

The concept itself, however, gives us various opportunities that have yet to be explored more widely, specifically in the music industry and cultural sector. The model has been evidenced to enhance innovation, and with the reduction of funding for the arts, universities – with their large sustainable amount of human capital – must increasingly become the place of viable patronage. Partnership models are thus increasingly important. The model also allows industry to have access to Higher Education research, without the more lengthy traditional routes of research – knowledge transfer – commercialization. In this model, the whole partnership will be (more or less) engaged in the research process, as well as in the commercialization. Where models have been adapted in other commercial sectors, the path to market has been shortened [14].

Project partnerships that have engaged in helix models report a better knowledge exchange and more effective partnership work for securing further funding to develop additional products. Helix partnerships help sustainable collaborations to emerge [14]. Finally, the powerful conceptual framework allows us to leverage stronger policy around research funding – allowing Mode 3 research partnerships to become more the norm and thus maximizing impact. Implicit examples for these can be seen in the EU's Creative Europe Programme.

The explicitness of the model allows the capture, analysis, reflection and explicit making of various aspects of project partnership work. With these in place, project interactions between universities, business, public and government can be managed in a rigorous framework of relationships.

With the realization that universities need to engage more, as evidenced by the current impact agendas within academia, and to maximize their impact of their own research, the debate on how to foster partnerships that more effectively turn new knowledge into benefits for industry and society has begun. Helix partnerships,

Mode 3 research models and Open Innovation 2.0 are the concepts that are currently considered to be a solution.

For the music industry, if the UK wants to exploit the talent and creativity it has within its midst, partnership work between SMEs, academia and the public is essential. Mode 3 research and triple and quadruple helix structures for partnerships are the best way forward.

## 5. References

[1] Etzkowitz, H. The triple helix: university-industry-government innovation in action. Routledge, New York (2008).
[2] Carayannis, E. G. and Campbell, D. F. J. Mode 3 knowledge production in quadruple helix innovation systems: 21st-century democracy, innovation, and entrepreneurship for development. Springer, New York and London (2012).
[3] Gibbons, M. The new production of knowledge: the dynamics of science and research in contemporary societies. SAGE Publications, London and Thousand Oaks, CA (1994).
[4] Watson, D. The engaged university: international perspectives on civic engagement. Routledge, New York (2011).
[5] Boehm, C. 'Engaged universities, Mode 3 knowledge production and the Impact Agendas of the REF' in Next steps for the Research Excellence Framework. Higher Education Forum. S. Radford, ed. Westminster Forum Projects, London (2015).
[6] Collini, S. What are universities for? Penguin, London and New York (2012).
[7] Barnett, R. Realizing the university in an age of supercomplexity. Buckingham. Society for Research into Higher Education and Open University Press, Philadelphia, PA (2000).
[8] Barnett, R. Reshaping the university: new relationships between research, scholarship and teaching. Society for Research into Higher Education and Open University Press, Maidenhead (2005).
[9] Graham, G. Universities: the recovery of an idea, 1st edition. Imprint Academic, Thorverton, England, and Charlottesville, VA (2002).
[10] Williams, G. L. The enterprising university: reform, excellence, and equity. Society for Research into Higher Education and Open University Press, Buckingham (2003).
[11] Watson, D. The question of conscience: higher education and personal responsibility. Institute of Education Press, London (2014).
[12] Deem, R., Hillyard, S. and Reed, M. I. Knowledge, higher education, and the new managerialism: the changing management of UK universities. Oxford University Press, Oxford and New York (2007).
[13] Watson, D. The question of morale: managing happiness and unhappiness in university life. McGraw-Hill, Maidenhead (2009).

[14] R. Clay, R., Latchem, J., Parry, R. and Ratnaraja, L. 'Report of CATH Collaborative Arts Triple Helix' (2015).
[15] Carayannis, E. G., and Campbell, D. F. J. 'Developed democracies versus emerging autocracies: arts, democracy, and innovation in quadruple helix innovation systems'. Journal of Innovation and Entrepreneurship, Vol. 3, p. 23 (2014).
[16] Linden, J. 'The monster in our midst: the materialisation of practice as research in the British Academy'. PhD thesis, Department of Contemporary Arts, Manchester Metropolitan University, Manchester (2012).
[17] Carayannis, E. G. Sustainable policy applications for social ecology and development. Information Science Reference, Hershey, PA (2012).
[18] G. C. t. P. E. f. Attack, "Education under Attack 2014," GCPEA, New York 2014.
[19] Curley, M. and B. Salmelin, B. "Open Innovation 2.0: a new paradigm'. 2015.

# Crowd-Sourced Learning of Music Production Practices Through Large-Scale Perceptual Evaluation of Mixes

Brecht De Man[1], Joshua Reiss[2]

Centre for Digital Music, School of Electronic Engineering and Computer Science,
Queen Mary University of London
[1]b.deman@qmul.ac.uk
[2]joshua.reiss@qmul.ac.uk

## Abstract

Mixing music is a highly complex and important part of the music production process, with a variety of creative and technical challenges, few of which have established solutions. Consequently, several approaches are viable for each given recording, and evaluation of differences in music production practices is therefore highly subjective. However, the study of perception of music production processes reveals that there is some degree of consensus on which mixes or specific parameter settings are preferred over others.

In this paper, we give an overview of prior work based on a dataset consisting of songs mixed by at least eight different mixing engineers, with extensive perceptual evaluation in the form of preference ratings and free-form comments. In contrast with most previous work in the area, we investigate realistic mixes as opposed to considering a specific process in isolation, which disregards the cross-adaptive nature of the mixing process. Furthermore, detailed perceptual evaluation of each mix allows to distinguish if the complete song or specific components thereof received a treatment that was perceived as positive or negative. Finally, having access to the original, raw audio as well as the exact parameter settings used on each processor, thorough analysis of the mix is possible.

## 1. Introduction

### 1.1. Innovation in Mixing Music

At the most basic level, the main tools at the disposal of the mix engineer are a multitrack recorder and medium, gain and level controls, pan pots, dynamic range compression, parametric equalisers [1], effect units such as reverberators, and automation of the parameters above. Most mix environments, be it a top tier or bedroom studio, are essentially an arrangement of these elements, each of which have been invented well before 1980 - and most of them much earlier. Aside from more recent developments such as the advent and widespread adoption of digital audio, the architecture of the recording studio and live sound rig have changed surprisingly little in the last three to four decades, while other parts of the music industry have seen major disruptions fuelled by new technologies.

At the same time, the music production process has been tremendously democratised to a point where the contemporary bedroom producer has access to a track count, audio quality and diversity of tools unparalleled by any recording studio in the eighties. Cheap or free digital audio workstation (DAW) software and inexpensive hardware have brought music production to the masses, but indeed the components of these studios are mostly identical in concept. Despite the immense analytical power of computers, few semantic technologies and intelligent tools have made it into the everyday arsenal of the sound engineer, meaning representation and manipulation of audio still happens at a very low level, through waveforms and filter gains. Recent years have seen a surge in research on automation of audio engineering tasks and even some commercial products with more high-level interface elements (such as a 'space', 'air' or even 'magic' control). However, for any of these technologies to be effective, both the meaning of such descriptors and the mix engineer process in general needs to be better understood.

## 1.2. Prior Work

Earlier work on mixing practices and the perception thereof has heavily contributed to the understanding of the many tasks that constitute mix engineering. Each of these deviate to some extent from what we intend to study, to make it possible to make claims about mixing practices and how they are perceived. For instance, much of these works focus on a single processor, often varying the parameters while keeping other aspects of the mix constant [2-5]. As a result, the potential interdependence of the many variables in a mix is ignored and statements about how parameters should be set are not necessarily valid when other parameters and features change. Similarly, testing a hypothesis on a (very) limited amount of musical content limits the transferability of findings to other situations [2, 6]. In general, acquiring data in a lab environment wherein the typical workflow of a mix engineer is not preserved, it is possible for the mix process to differ from a real-life, commercially relevant scenario. Finally, some algorithms, hypotheses or experimentally obtained values are not tested through subjective evaluation [7-10], meaning poor mixes or less than ideal parameter settings are potentially skewing the results.

## 1.3. This Work

Our goal is to understand mixing, to define descriptive terms frequently used to describe sound, and to help develop tools for the analysis and manipulation of sound at a higher, more abstract level than low-level features (e.g. level) and parameters (e.g. filter coefficients) allow us to do. In this work, we aim to provide an overview of our previous work in which collection and analysis of realistic mixes and evaluations thereof has allowed us to answer some of these questions, as well as to highlight some of the many questions that remain unanswered, and hypothesise how we may do so. By realistic mixes, we mean mixes that were produced using a commercially relevant set of tools, by someone who is used to using these, in a natural environment such as their home studio, a professional studio or institution's facilities.

We propose a methodology to derive the bounds of what are considered 'preferred' or 'acceptable' ranges of values of processing parameters and mix properties, from subjective evaluation of different mixes of identical and/or different songs. As such, we systematically learn from mixes of arbitrary quality to zone in on production practices that are perceived as good, obviating the need for exemplary productions to study the mixing process. On the contrary, a limited spread of parameter settings and mix features would impede a sufficiently accurate estimation of the lower and upper bounds of acceptable parameter ranges. As we learn how the bounds of these processing parameters or extracted audio features vary between different songs or genres, we identify zones wherein these values should lie in a majority of productions according to general perception.

In Section 2, we describe the process of collecting data for this research, from acquiring raw audio to be mixed, over producing mixes of this content, to the perceptual evaluation of said mixes. Analysis of this data is discussed in Section 3, where we explore the questions that the various types of data we collect can and - more importantly - cannot answer. Concluding remarks and a brief outline of future work are presented in Section 4. Finally, the reader is invited to use the resulting data for their own research, as well as to contribute to our dataset in Section 5.

## 2. Data Collection

### 2.1. Multitrack Audio Content

A first challenge we encountered when attempting to collect and analyse realistic mixes is the acute lack of available raw tracks, specifically those that have an open license that allows sharing the data for the purpose of sustainability and reproducibility. For this reason, we created the Open Multitrack Testbed[1] [11], a platform for hosting multitrack audio, including stems and mixes thereof. Rich metadata allows for searching and filtering of the content (e.g. 'multitrack containing bagpipes', 'track recorded with a Shure SM58 microphone', ...) that can be hosted locally or at the original website, depending on permissions. While

---

[1] multitrack.eecs.qmul.ac.uk

several projects have already made use of the data collected through and referenced from this platform, more contributions are still appreciated to ensure a large and diverse pool of multitrack audio.

## 2.2. Mixes

Having collected raw audio tracks of songs from a variety of genres and sources, we then had sound engineering students mix these in a specified digital audio workstation (DAW) using a restricted list of plugins. As such, we were able to analyse audio features and parameters from individual tracks and processors, allowing for extensive dissection of every mix.

Since then, engineers from sound engineering programs at schools in different countries have been added to the list, and we are still in the process of repeating these experiments with new songs, different engineers, and more subjects. As such, we are able to average out or indeed investigate the influence of location and background

## 2.3. Perceptual Evaluation

For reasons explained in Section 3, trained listeners provided ratings and comments of the different mixes per song that we collected.

We devised a listening test tool (MATLAB[2]- and browser-based[3] [12, 13]) for assessing these different mixes relative to each other, such that they are to be rated on a single axis, and with the possibility to write comments on each mix. The goal of providing text boxes for comments is

- to facilitate the tedious task of comparing as many as ten different mixes against each other by allowing the subject to take notes;
- to provide feedback for the respective mix engineers; and
- to give us more insight into the subjects' perception of the different mix decisions.

---

[2] https://code.soundsoftware.ac.uk/projects/ape
[3] https://code.soundsoftware.ac.uk/projects/webaudioevaluationtool

## 3. Analysis

In this section, we present an overview of prior and future work based on the data presented in Section 2. We show (or hypothesise) what we can learn from analysing the mix audio [14], subjective ratings [15], and ultimately comments [16], and how the combination of each of these provides more insight into the mix process than the individual elements.

### 3.1. Audio and Settings

Having access to not only the rendered mixes, but also the raw tracks and the DAW session files, it is possible to extract features from separate, processed tracks and look at the parameters of the different processors. As such, we are able to conduct a much deeper analysis of these mixes than what is possible with stereo audio files only [17]. In [14], we looked at a set of features extracted from lead vocal, bass, and various drum tracks (important tracks that were present in each of the considered songs) from mixes of eight different songs. For instance, Figure 1 shows the average loudness, relative to the total mix loudness, of the lead vocal, bass, kick drum, snare drum and rest of the drums. These results were since confirmed by [18] and correspond with [19].

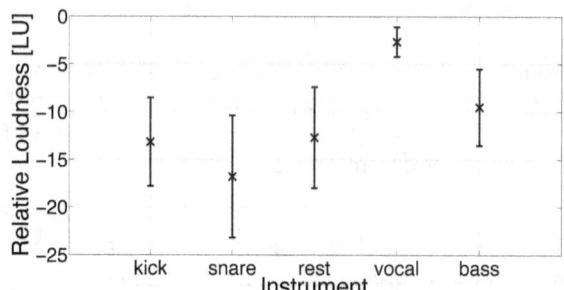

Figure 1: Average loudness of kick drum, snare drum, rest of drums, lead vocal and bass, relative to the total mix loudness (0 LU) - from [14].

However, analysing the audio or settings of the different collected mixes in isolation means that poor, unconventional or otherwise irrelevant mixes may add noise or skew our findings towards feature and parameter values that are less pleasing or typical of commercial mixes.

### 3.2. Ratings

Through perceptual evaluation in the form of ranking and/or rating of different mixes of the same song, it is possible to weed out poor mixes and investigate only mix settings and audio features of good ones, which are supposedly more similar to commercial mixes and more relevant to furthering our understanding of mix engineering. It even allows us to look at differences between highly and poorly rated mixes, and to some extent to answer the question of what makes a good mix.

Looking at ratings only, we have learned that mix engineers who also take part in the blind subjective evaluation of the different mixes tend to favour their own mix over others - see Figure 2 [15]. This suggests the mix engineer has a distinct preference for a certain mixing style, both when producing or assessing content, but it can also be influenced by the possible bias due to having mixed the song a couple of weeks earlier, or even downright recognising the mix as their own.

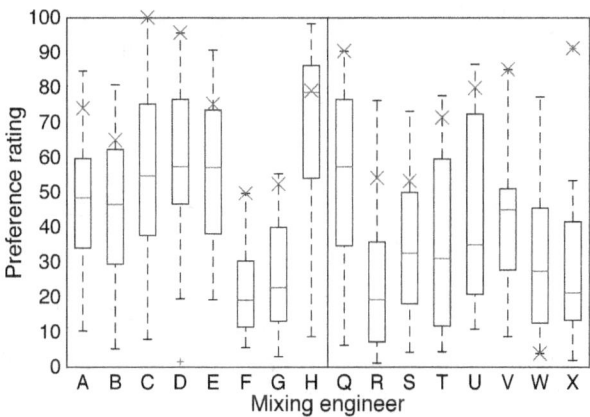

Figure 2: Ratings of own mix (red 'X') versus ratings by all participants of this mix (box plot) - from [15].

When combining the rating data with the extracted audio features [15] or workflow aspects [20], some correlations with preference ratings can be found that indicate a preference towards a higher dynamic range, a stronger central component, or a higher degree of grouping similar tracks together. However, to reliably infer which mix decisions are favoured over others, we would need to look at a very large and diverse set of evaluated mixes, and/or use specialised, complex, and perhaps perceptually motivated features. We do not know which specific features of which tracks to look at to understand which mixes or practices are perceived to be better, and the task of investigating the correlation of preference with every imaginable feature of every audio track is not only enormous, but comes with a near-certainty of overfitting the problem. After all, the chance of any of a million features (or a combination thereof) spuriously correlating highly with a limited number of preference scores is very high.

## 3.3. Comments

In [16], we investigated the comments assigned to the different mixes in the perceptual evaluation part of the experiment, and found the representation of different instruments and processors or features shown in Figure 3.

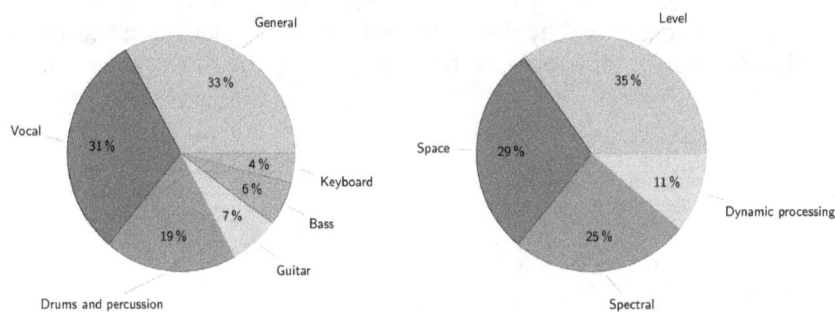

Figure 3: Representation of instruments and types of processing in statements about mixes - from [16].

At a lower level, we can look at which specific words occur most often, such as shown in Table 1. Looking exclusively at terms used to describe characteristics of sounds ('dry', 'bright', 'thin', ...), we learn how the processing on certain instruments in certain mixes is perceived - and, conversely, we may learn what these subjective words mean exactly by looking at the features of the sounds they were meant to describe - see Table 2.

| Term | # | % |
|---|---|---|
| vocal(s,ist)+vox+voc(s)+voice+singer | 1082 | 7.87% |
| rev(erb)(s,y)+reverber(ant,ated)+verb(y) | 412 | 3.00% |
| good | 350 | 2.54% |
| mix | 328 | 2.38% |
| balance+balanced+balances+balancing | 327 | 2.38% |
| drum(s) | 345 | 2.51% |
| loud | 264 | 1.92% |
| bass | 258 | 1.88% |
| nice | 246 | 1.79% |
| low | 171 | 1.24% |
| like(d) | 168 | 1.22% |
| snare | 164 | 1.19% |
| guitar | 160 | 1.16% |
| kick | 150 | 1.09% |
| compress(ed,ing,ion,or) | 141 | 1.03% |
| dry(ness) | 127 | 0.92% |
| lead | 116 | 0.84% |
| bright(er), brightness | 107 | 0.78% |
| thin(ner,ness) | 94 | 0.68% |
| weird(ly,ness,-sounding) | 87 | 0.63% |
| chorus(es) | 86 | 0.63% |
| instruments | 84 | 0.61% |
| dark | 79 | 0.57% |
| eq+eq'd+eq'ed+eqd+eqed+eqs | 79 | 0.57% |
| well | 78 | 0.57% |

Table 1: Top 25 most frequently occurring words over all mix comments.

| Term | # | % |
|---|---|---|
| dry(ness) | 127 | 0.9233% |
| bright(er), brightness | 107 | 0.7779% |
| thin(ner,ness) | 94 | 0.6834% |
| weird(ly,ness,-sounding) | 87 | 0.6325% |
| dark | 79 | 0.5743% |
| far | 52 | 0.3780% |
| soft | 52 | 0.3780% |
| muddy+mud+muddiness | 50 | 0.3635% |
| harsh(ness) | 47 | 0.3417% |
| room(-y,y) | 47 | 0.3417% |
| punch(y,ier,iness) | 46 | 0.3344% |
| quiet(er) | 43 | 0.3126% |
| wide | 41 | 0.2981% |
| big+bigger | 37 | 0.2690% |
| hot | 37 | 0.2690% |
| flat | 32 | 0.2326% |
| big | 31 | 0.2254% |
| mono(ish,-ish) | 30 | 0.2181% |
| definition+defined | 28 | 0.2036% |
| present | 28 | 0.2036% |
| presence | 26 | 0.1890% |
| narrow | 24 | 0.1745% |
| small | 23 | 0.1212% |
| weak | 23 | 0.1212% |
| forward | 21 | 0.1107% |

Table 2: Top 25 most frequently occurring descriptive terms over all mix comments.

For instance, 'bright' (and derivatives) and 'dark' occur 186 times combined over ca. 1400 mix 'reviews' - indicating these are popular terms to describe sound and in particular to note why a mix or the processing of a particular instrument is (dis)liked. Investigating what this term means may therefore be instrumental towards gaining understanding of sound, in particular in a music production context. Looking at the spectrum of the mix, or the instrument in relation to which it is used, we can then reveal e.g.

- what the average spectrum of a 'bright' and 'dark' sound looks like, as well as of sounds which elicit neither of these responses;
- if they are really used as each other's opposite (on average, or for the same person using the term);

- if they are indeed referring to the spectrum only, or if other features correlate with the description.

As an example, Figure 4 shows the objective features Brightness and Spectral Centroid of each of the mixes of ten different songs. Mixes which over 50% of the subjects found to be 'too bright', as understood from the comments, are above the upper dashed line, while mixes which they found 'too dark' are below the lower dashed line. This shows that with a large enough number of mixes and a large enough variance of the considered parameter or feature, it is possible to find the upper and lower bounds of its range of values deemed acceptable by the subjects - as long as there is enough consensus. As such, we can develop a 'mix space' of various parameters or features within which one can move while still maintaining a good sounding mix, and outside of which some mix decisions would be considered bold at best, and possibly poor. One of many challenges lies in taking the interdependence of some of these features into account.

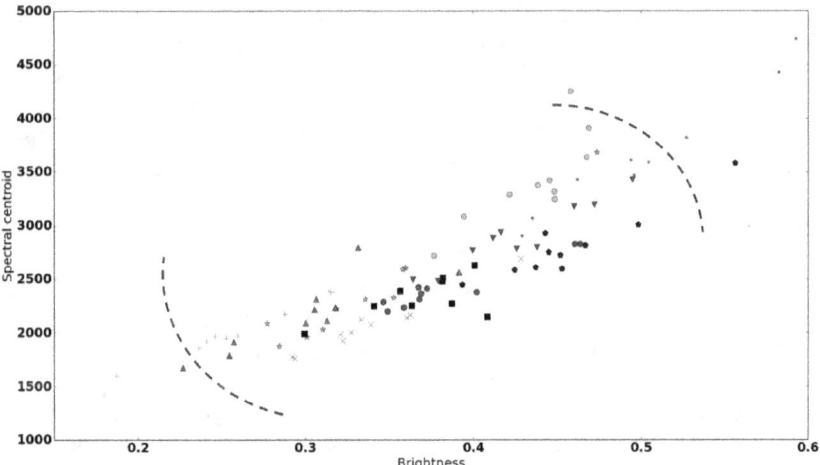

Figure 4: The evaluated mix fragments (each marker represents a different song) plotted as a function of the objective features Brightness (x-axis) and Spectral Centroid (y-axis). The dashed lines separate mixes which are labelled as too bright or too dark, respectively, by at least 50% of the subjects.

Looking at the comments that were written as part of this perceptual evaluation reveals which aspects of the mix prompted the subject to rate it highly or poorly, or in other words what problems and strengths the various mixes have. By combining assessments of different subjects, and preserving the salient comments, we can zone in on particular aspects of the mix that we assume to be true because of this consensus, and investigate them in isolation. This has the advantage that we don't need a mix to be 'good' in every way to learn what settings or features are perceived to be appropriate, but that we can learn even - or especially? - from poor mixes, where positive aspects ('punchy snare') denote appropriate settings but where negative features ('vocal too loud') can help find upper and lower bounds of the corresponding parameters. Taking preference ratings into account further helps understand which comments are likely positive or negative in nature, when it is not clear from the comment itself or its context.

Still, a thorough understanding of mix practices and their perception for arbitrary songs in different genres requires a very large dataset with a high number of highly diverse songs, mixed and evaluated by people from various backgrounds and locations.

## 4. Concluding Remarks

In this paper we have provided an overview of recent work on mix practices and the perception thereof, based on a dataset consisting of realistic mixes of high quality multitrack audio, and subjective evaluation of these mixes. We have shown that the combination of process parameters, audio features extracted from the mixes and individual processed tracks, subjective ratings, and/or comments on the mixes is more effective than each of those separately when deriving information from this data, and explored how it may be used for further research. This data is mostly available (insofar the license allows it) for other researchers to use. Furthermore, contributions to this data of any kind are also appreciated - see Section 5.

At this point, the number and diversity of songs, engineers and subjects limits the generality of findings inferred from this data. Therefore, we are in the process of repeating these experiments at various institutions, with new raw audio. This allows us to assess whether the discovered (and not yet discovered) trends in mix practices and perception of music production apply to engineers and listeners with different backgrounds and levels of experience, or, if not, what influence these factors have.

## 5. Call for Contributions

The Open Multitrack Testbed [11] welcomes any kind of multitrack audio, with or without mixes, which is already available for download on the internet or which has a license that allows for us to host it. As most licenses stipulate, content owners (as well as contributors) are acknowledged on the website[4].

---

[4] multitrack.eecs.qmul.ac.uk

Listening test tools developed for this type of research[5] [12, 13] are freely available including source code, and feedback as well as contributions are highly appreciated.

Furthermore, we are encouraging sound engineers and sound engineering students of various backgrounds, levels and locations to participate in further mix experiments and/or listening tests, to contribute (anonymously) to the aforementioned research as well as to be part of a unique critical listening exercise and to receive a wealth of feedback from a diverse and unbiased audience.

Further info and data is available at www.brechtdeman.com/research.html.

## 6. References

[1] G. Massenburg, "Parametric equalization," in 42nd Convention of the Audio Engineering Society, May 1972.

[2] S.-I. Mimilakis, K. Drossos, A. Floros, and D. Katerelos, "Automated tonal balance enhancement for audio mastering applications," in 134th Convention of the Audio Engineering Society, Audio Engineering Society, 2013.

[3] S. Hafezi and J. D. Reiss, "Autonomous multitrack equalisation based on masking reduction," to appear in Journal of the Audio Engineering Society, 2015.

[4] Z. Ma, B. De Man, P. D. Pestana, D. A. A. Black, and J. D. Reiss, "Intelligent multitrack dynamic range compression," Journal of the Audio Engineering Society, vol. 63, pp. 412–426, June 2015.

[5] E. Perez Gonzalez and J. D. Reiss, "A real-time semiautonomous audio panning system for music mixing," EURASIP Journal on Advances in Signal Processing, 2010.

[6] E. Perez-Gonzalez and J. D. Reiss, "Automatic gain and fader control for live mixing," IEEE Workshop on applications of signal processing to audio and acoustics, October 2009.

[7] J. Scott, M. Prockup, E. Schmidt, and Y. Kim, "Automatic multi-track mixing using linear dynamical systems," in Proceedings of the 8th Sound and Music Computing Conference, Padova, Italy, 2011.

[8] J. Scott and Y. E. Kim, "Analysis of acoustic features for automated multi-track mixing," in 12th International Society for Music Information Retrieval Conference (ISMIR 2011), October 2011.

---

[5] APE Audio Perceptual Evaluation toolbox (MATLAB): code.soundsoftware.ac.uk/projects/ape and Web Audio Evaluation Tool (browser-based): code.soundsoftware.ac.uk/projects/webaudioevaluationtool

[9] E. Perez-Gonzalez and J. D. Reiss, "Automatic mixing: Live downmixing stereo panner," in 10th International Conference on Digital Audio Effects (DAFx-10), 2007.

[10] E. Perez-Gonzalez and J. D. Reiss, "Automatic equalization of multi-channel audio using cross-adaptive methods," 127th Convention of the Audio Engineering Society, October 2009.

[11] B. De Man, M. Mora-Mcginity, G. Fazekas, and J. D. Reiss, "The Open Multitrack Testbed," in 137th Convention of the Audio Engineering Society, October 2014.

[12] B. De Man and J. D. Reiss, "APE: Audio Perceptual Evaluation toolbox for MATLAB," in 136th Convention of the Audio Engineering Society, April 2014.

[13] N. Jillings, D. Moffat, B. De Man, and J. D. Reiss, "Web Audio Evaluation Tool: A browser-based listening test environment," in 12th Sound and Music Computing Conference, July 2015.

[14] B. De Man, B. Leonard, R. King, and J. D. Reiss, "An analysis and evaluation of audio features for multitrack music mixtures," in 15th International Society for Music Information Retrieval Conference (ISMIR 2014), October 2014.

[15] B. De Man, M. Boerum, B. Leonard, G. Massenburg, R. King, and J. D. Reiss, "Perceptual evaluation of music mixing practices," in 138th Convention of the Audio Engineering Society, May 2015.

[16] B. De Man and J. D. Reiss, "Analysis of peer reviews in music production," Journal of the Art of Record Production, vol. 10, July 2015.

[17] P. D. Pestana, Z. Ma, J. D. Reiss, A. Barbosa, and D. A. A. Black, "Spectral characteristics of popular commercial recordings 1950-2010," in 135th Convention of the Audio Engineering Society, October 2013.

[18] A. Wilson and B. M. Fazenda, "Navigating the mix-space: Theoretical and practicallevel-balancing technique in multitrack music mixtures," in 12th Sound and Music Computing Conference, July 2015.

[19] P. Pestana and J. D. Reiss, "Intelligent audio production strategies informed by best practices," in 53rd Conference of the Audio Engineering Society, January 2014.

[20] D. M. Ronan, B. De Man, H. Gunes, and J. D. Reiss, "The impact of subgrouping practices on the perception of multitrack mixes," in 139th Convention of the Audio Engineering Society, October 2015.

# You Need Me Man, I Don't Need You: Exploring the Debates Surrounding the Economic Viability of On-Demand Music Streaming

Mathew Flynn[1]

[1] The Liverpool Institute for Performing Arts, Liverpool, UK
matflynn73@gmail.com

**Abstract**

*Streaming services have endured scrutiny and criticism from musicians and industry commentators as to the fairness, viability and sustainability of their economic and royalty distribution models. Streaming circumvents conventional unit capitalism, employing royalty distribution models that value each act or track by comparing their total plays against all the other acts or tracks on the platform. Whilst affording record companies an unprecedented opportunity to perpetually monetise their entire catalogues, at the same time, music streaming services offer acts far less in immediate royalty returns than the unit model. As streaming services continue to struggle to post profits, it is difficult to ascertain if the innovation of streaming's royalty distribution models are productive ones. Despite the very public concerns of acts and their labels, music users are increasingly adopting streaming as a way of listening to music. This paper considers the choice music users face between freemium and premium subscription models and provides an overview of the implications of those choices for record labels, acts, advertisers and the streaming platforms.*

## 1. Introduction

With the launch of Apple Music into a maturing music streaming market, 2015 sees music streaming emerging as a mainstream option for listening to music. In the UK, across the main platforms Apple, Tidal, Deezer, GooglePlay and Spotify, average total weekly streams have reached five hundred million [1]. Music streaming is shifting recorded music consumption from the need for music users to acquire and store recordings, to one where they just access them on demand.

Mulligan [2] asserts that, 'Streaming is not a product nor is it a business model. Instead it is simply a technological means of getting music onto people's digital devices. In fact consumers should not even have to understand the difference between a download and a stream.' Whilst streaming is not a business model, the hundred year old record industry business model of selling units does not readily transfer to servicing streams. Whereas it may not be important for music users to understand the impact of how they choose to listen to music, their choices have ramifications for the record industry's entire value chain.

As Nowak [3] observes, 'Research on music consumption must take into consideration the materiality of the technologies... in order to grasp upon how it participates in the emotional responses to music.' Streaming music, particularly on smartphones, has affected a fundamental shift in the demand for music. The emotional and technical distinction between acquiring a unit and accessing a stream, and the relative economic value of the two processes, means the future of the recorded music economy demands innovation in its business models to match those in the technology. Despite removing the costly functions of packaging and replication and sales and distribution [13] from the record industry value chain, the uncertainty as to whether or not a sustainable streaming economy can be fashioned is a crucial area of contention and debate across the music industry and amongst scholars. By analysing commentary and data from industry organisations and practitioners and situating those debates within business and industry theory, this paper offers an initial overview of the contradictions and conflicts between record labels, acts, streaming services, advertisers and consumers, as the record industry transitions from selling units to selling use.

The first section evaluates industry reaction, commentary and analysis on current market leader Spotify's 'freemium' business model, where music is given away for free to a large group of users to sell a premium service to a smaller fraction of the user base [65]. The purpose of the section is to outline how Spotify blends Longtail [4] and Blockbuster [5] business strategies to drive subscriber uptake, whilst also critiquing its royalty distribution model. The second section considers Apple Music's premium only streaming offer. This section outlines the differences and distinctions in the choice music users face between freemium and premium subscription, and the implications of that choice for the business models of content creators and owners. The conclusion argues that in pursuing a business strategy that insists consumers pay a monthly subscription for music on-demand, the major record labels risk alienating consumers and conceding market power to the streaming platforms.

## 2. Spotify Shifts the Format to the Platform

According to Venture Consulting [62], despite growing rapidly to a $1.5 billion market by 2012, sustainable profitability in music streaming remains elusive. There are two key debates surrounding streaming's economic viability. The first of these is; are enough consumers willing to pay for a monthly subscription [60]? The second debate considers steaming's viability within the wider concerns of the record industry. Can streaming generate sufficient revenue to initially offset and then recover the decline in annual record sales revenues [63]? Early analysis by Hardy [7] was pessimistic, 'Whatever increased revenues Spotify might represent, it was never going to be enough.' (p.286) The 'enough' Hardy refers to is the difference between total unit sales prior to the emergence of streaming, and the continued decline of unit sales that streaming revenue has failed to offset. However, since 2013 examples from a range of European markets including Sweden [8] and Spain [9] indicate lost unit sales are recoverable. As the current dominant market player, to date, Spotify has been the focal point of the streaming revenue debate. This first section will analyse Spotify's significance in innovating a viable, but as yet unprofitable [64], streaming business model.

Radiohead frontman Tom Yorke infamously expressed early concerns, 'I feel like as musicians we need to fight the Spotify thing [10].' Like Yorke, many artists view Spotify's freemium tier as displacing precious unit sales and research by Aguiar and Waldfogel [63] supports this perspective. Acts such as Coldplay and Adele have engaged in the practice of windowing, where the record release is held back from being available on Spotify for a few weeks or months until substantial unit sales have abated. Some acts, such as the Black Keys, The Beatles and until recently AC/DC have gone even further by refusing to license their catalogue to Spotify at all.

The debate around the viability of streaming exploded in 2015, when Taylor Swift caused a media sensation by removing her entire five album catalogue from Spotify. In explaining her reasoning Swift [11] stated, 'I'm not willing to contribute my life's work to an experiment that I don't feel fairly compensates the writers, producers, artists and creators of this music.' In further justifying the decision, Scott Borchetta [12], owner of Swift's record label Big Machine, stated, 'If this fan went and purchased the record, CD, iTunes, whatever, and then their friends go, 'Why did you pay for it? It's free on Spotify, we're being completely disrespectful to that superfan who wants to invest.' For the acts and industry executives caught between the unit and use models, outselling the competition still defines success. Elberse [5] describes this Blockbuster business model as, 'Winner Takes All.' For Swift [11], becoming a historic winner, as the first act to achieve three first week million selling albums in the USA, evidently framed her decision to remove freemium access to fifth album 1989 via Spotify. Swift couldn't risk cannibalising first week unit sales. Swift's decision typifies the dilemma all acts and their label investors face in 2015. How to reach as many fans as possible, as they migrate to streaming platforms, whilst maintaining the level of sales revenue from unit sales. In achieving the million first week sales, Swift reinforced the pervasiveness of the record industries continued unit based approach to defining commercial and cultural success. The uncertainty as to the level, type and value of demand for streaming has, to date, prompted the majority of the record industry to quantify the music use model through the mechanised accountability of the unit economy. One obvious example is the sales chart, where streams are calculated by equating a specific number of plays to one unit sale.

Likewise, for music users, legally acquiring units is a relatively straightforward process. Dubber [14] summarised the process of buying units of music as, 'Hear - Like - Buy.' However, as Tschmuck observed of physical format buying, 'Consumer sovereignty [was] limited to the ability to choose from a pre-selected pool of products, which in turn encourages conservative buying habits [15] (p.242).' In complete contrast to units, Spotify both aspires to afford access to the entire pool of commercially available products and encourages liberal consumer sovereignty, as there is no economic cost to a risky or poor choice. Streaming services operate on what Anderson [4] has defined as the Longtail business model. The theory advocates it is as profitable to sell one of a million things, as it is a million of one thing. Spotify has in excess of thirty million tracks available to satisfy the listening demands of all its users.

Anderson, Dubber & James [16] state, 'Streaming is analogous to listening to music on the radio, though a consumer can choose his or her own playlists of music.' (p.96) However, unlike radio, with streaming there is no need for the consumer to purchase the track to be able to access it on-demand. At the premium tier, streaming completely reverses Dubber's 'hear - like - buy' unit maxim to 'buy - hear - like'. The streaming provider is subscribed to in advance and the user then selects and listens via radio settings, playlists, by track, artist, genre, context or activity. As expected, differing demographics of user display hugely varied tastes in the music they play. However, superstar acts such as Taylor Swift, Beyoncé, Bruno Mars and Daft Punk have a place on the average playlists of all demographics of user [17]. As Elberse [5] asserts, 'Assortments may become more and more expansive, but the importance of the few titles at the very top keeps growing.' Just like the unit model, becoming a heavy rotation act is fundamental to streaming success. As Negus [50] observed when discussing the industrial logics of record companies during their CD era heyday, 'Stars require substantial investment but their profile and market dominance enables the production of profits to finance further acquisitions and expansions.' (p.48) And despite the shift from format to platform, the major record companies continued control of the core function of A&R in the value chain [15 & 46], means they remain uniquely placed to discover, develop and deliver stars in the streaming era. However, as Wade Morris and Powers [54] observe, 'The line between Spotify as a distribution outlet and Spotify as a promotional intermediary,' (p.8) is blurring. Spotify is continually enhancing its capability to exert influence over the star making process.

Ed Sheeran is a prime example of a cross demographic heavy rotation act that, in contrast to Swift, has embraced streaming to bolster his burgeoning international career. [18] Music Business Worldwide calculates Sheeran's 2 billion stream count, when multiplied by Spotify's purported headline 0.007 per stream royalty, has earned Sheeran £9 million since his debut album appeared on the platform in 2011. [19] Whilst alluding to the financial viability of billions of streams for a superstar artist, by their own admission MBW's figures are a crude estimation of Sheeran's royalty income, not least because Spotify doesn't actually calculate or pay royalties on a per stream basis. As Spotify state on their website for artists, 'we personally view "per stream" metrics as a highly flawed indication of our value to artists'. [20] Spotify's subscription business model pays 70% of the platforms total monthly subscription revenue from users and advertisers to rights holders, by calculating an artist's "market share" of the total revenue by dividing an artist's streams by the total streams on Spotify.

In critiquing the fairness of the market-share approach to independent acts, musician and industry blogger Sharky Laguna [21] argues, 'That royalties should be paid based on subscriber-share, not overall play share.' He contends subscriber-share is a fairer system as it distributes the royalties from the subscription fee of each user to the acts that user has actually played. Under the market-share system, the majority of the subscription fee goes to the most popular acts. Conversely, for the most popular acts, in addition to the risk of displacing unit sales, the royalty value of their popularity is not defined by their number of streams, but is proportional to the popularity of other acts on the platform. The market-share system appears to disadvantage acts at both ends of the spectrum of success.

Maasø [51] and Rex Pedersen [52] compared the market and subscriber-share models by applying both calculations to the same set of streaming data. They concluded whilst subscriber-share slightly advantaged the top acts and was effectively neutral in terms of revenues to the major labels, it would be an advantage to indie and lesser known emerging acts. An obvious contention here is that Spotify could pay by subscriber-share, as they certainly have the information to be able to account at a subscriber use level. Recent calculations on website Rockonomics [22] concluded that overall the distinctions between the two royalty distribution models is economically neutral, but Maasø and Pedersen's analysis seemingly justifies the concerns of smaller acts over the equity of the market-share model to them. It also begs the question, if Spotify's approach squeezes the value delivered to the platform's primary content creators at both ends of its Longtail, why does it operate a market-share model?

Spotify employs market-share remuneration because it disproportionately favours the most the popular artists by valuing their subscription driving power. Continually increasingly its subscriber base is crucial for Spotify. Not just for its own growth purposes, but to fulfil the contractual obligation it has to the major record labels. The leaked Sony Music / Spotify 2011 [23] content license agreement clearly outlined the contractual obligations of Spotify to achieve monthly subscriber and conversion goals. Spotify was tasked with adding one million new subscribers in the USA each month, in addition to, converting at least 10% of its ad-funded freemium users into paying, premium, subscribers. Spotify's self-published subscriber data shows as of November 2015 it had 75 million active global subscribers of which 20 million were paying users. [20] As Peter Drucker [24] observed, primarily business exists to create a customer (p.35), from this perspective it would appear Spotify is succeeding. However, for the major record companies who license the majority of the popular content to streaming services, the volume of conversions from freemium to premium is far from satisfactory.

The fact that almost 80% of Spotify's users continue to subscribe for free, is increasingly viewed as a problem by the major record companies. Lucian Grainge,

CEO of Universal Music, stated, 'The ad-funded part of the music ecosystem – that's on-demand, ad-funded – as I've said before, is not something that is particularly sustainable in the long-term [25].' However, Spotify's insistence on not only retaining their freemium tier, but also guaranteeing that all content on the platform is available on it, if only in a limited capacity, suggests Spotify is acting in accordance with McLuhan's [26] assertion that, 'The owners of media always endeavour to give the public what it wants because they sense that their power is in the medium, not in the message or the programme.' (p.235) Spotify risks the periodic criticism from acts and record labels, because controlling a medium that delivers a network of 75 million potential fans means only the very few superstars, like Taylor Swift, can culturally and economically afford to circumvent their platform.

For the record companies, whose business is fundamentally in exploiting the use of its catalogue, arguably streaming is the ultimate business model. Through recommendation algorithms, contextual based playlists [27] and curated content, record companies have the opportunity to effortlessly monetise previously economically dead recordings without any additional marketing or promotional spend. The availability of a Longtail of catalogue creates a potential Longtail of listening. Under streaming, unlike with units, records and acts don't fail to sell. And the more subscribers actively using the platform, the more likely the depth and breadth of a record company's catalogue can generate reciprocal revenue. Furthermore, it is not just the number of customers Spotify is creating, but the type of customer.

Much of the tension between the content providers and streaming platforms is how the distinct constituencies value the consumer. Whereas, 'The music business never cared what consumers thought, it cared instead what retailers and radio thought.' (Faxon cited [2]) Streaming platforms place as much value upon how their subscribers pay attention as they do to how much they pay. As Tim Anderson [53] has observed, the streaming platforms capture every moment of their subscribers listening to build user taste profiles and continually generate new relationships between the data and the user (p.24). Whereas listening on a format was a personal and completely private experience, platform listening automatically captures and curates user listening to continually enhance the user-experience. Data capture and manipulation is one of the key points of distinction between recorded music's unit model and use model. As Fornaciari observes, 'Framing individuals as consumers, possibly, contributed to focusing one's attention on practices of e-commerce. Labelling them as users, instead, shifted the focus from the economic value of purchasing to the economic value of disclosing [28].' Streaming services understand the value of disclosure, not only in keeping users connected to their platform, but also being able to package user data so that it appeals to the targeted reach of advertisers. Despite the recent launch of YouTube's own premium subscription service 'Red', advertising remains YouTube's primary revenue stream. Robert Kyncl Chief Business Officer at YouTube, currently the worlds most used platform for streaming music, maintains,

'Our free ad-supported business is growing incredibly fast. We'll always have that: that's our core, and we'll never stop focusing on it [36].'

Streaming platforms deliver programmatic advertising which, 'Allows brands to use audience insights and technology to tailor messages to the right person, at the right moment, in the right context [32].' Global advertising revenue has risen from $481 billion in 2011 to $574 billion in 2015 and is expected to rise to $667 billion by 2018 [29]. In 2015 in the UK 50% of advertising spending was attributed to online mediums. Whilst the UK is way ahead of the global figure of 30% [30], the trend for advertising spending to migrate to mobile devices is compelling, especially as advertising within apps isn't as susceptible to the use of Adblocker software [31]. Currently only 10% of Spotify's total annual revenue is derived from advertising spend, but that did increase 53% in quarter one of 2015 [33]. Spotify isn't just creating customers that use music, it is creating a customers that appeal to advertisers. As Christensen asserts when highlighting barriers to innovation, 'Parallel value networks, each built around a different definition of what makes a product valuable, may exist within the same broadly defined industry [6].' Spotify is creating parallel value networks around the user. Their business model is to manage the attention of each user and move that data to make free access pay and paid access profitable. Hence a recent addition to their strategy is Spotify for brands. In light of streaming's emergence Taplin, somewhat pessimistically, observes, 'We made a decision societally to do a wholesale reallocation of revenue from people who made content and owned content to people who owned platforms [37].' If, as Taplin suggests, consumers are unwittingly conceding power to the platforms, where does this leave music companies and acts as the record industry transitions from format to platform.

## 3. The Power Accord

In his 2009 book Communication Power, Manuel Castells [38] argues that political influence is afforded to those constituencies that control the means and modes of communication. It enables the holders of communication power to decide what is valuable. Viewed from Castells' perspective, the programmers of streaming services influence the networks of communication between content creators, content owners music users and advertisers. This affords the platforms significant influence in deciding what is valuable in the streaming era. Either in attention or money, subscribers are primarily paying to use the platform not the music. Therefore, the fundamental choice for the 21st century music user is to which platform to subscribe.

Most audio streaming platforms offer a similar service and almost identical catalogue at the same headline price of £10 per month. Therefore, they predominantly compete for market dominance across territories through differentiating the user experience of the platforms interface, quality, taste and control [54]. Deezer and the majority of other platforms pursue a similar model to

Spotify. They cater to the demands of the majority of consumers by offering a freemium tier as an essential part of the service and argue freemium is the best conduit to converting free users into premium subscribers. Like YouTube, this group of platforms predict a viable ad-funded model can be built. In contrast to Spotify, Apple Music launched without an on-demand ad-funded tier. Apple and Tidal's [39] business philosophy aligns more closely with the record industry's contention that on-demand music should be paid for and therefore, after a free trial period, both platforms only offer a paid for subscription option. The fundamental difference between the platforms is whether they offer a freemium tier of access. This is significant for creators and owners of recordings, because a freemium philosophy defines the platforms business model.

Despite devising a business model that ensures on-demand streaming is paid for, like Spotify, Apple has elected to employ a pro-rata market-share approach [41]. However, Apple caused great controversy by initially intending not to pay independent labels or acts for the right to license their music during the platform's free trial launch. Once again Taylor Swift intervened to persuade the technology giant to change tact and promise to pay royalties [40]. Swift's Spotify and Apple protests demonstrate the influence superstar acts can wield in the development of the streaming market. In both instances, Swift's underlying message was music needs to be paid for and musicians need to be paid. Given that both platforms operate a similar market-share royalty model, Swift's decision to make her catalogue available on Apple Music implies the only experimental element of streaming she doesn't feel fairly compensates creators is Spotify's freemium offer. Despite its nobility, the contradiction in Swift's stance is that it appears to serve the agenda of the major record companies far more than it does acts or small catalogue owners.

Lohan Presencer, CEO of Ministry of Sound, the UK's biggest independent record label, suggests it is the three major record companies Universal, Sony and Warner who dictate the streaming platforms system of subscription and royalty distribution [42]. As the three majors are the rights holders of almost 80% of the annual commercially viable recorded music catalogue, to have any success a streaming service must be able to license the majority of the majors' catalogue. Presencer observed, 'It's split up at $10 a month because that favours the three biggest players in the game [42].' Catalogue control ensures the major labels receive a guaranteed fee from each streaming service, irrelevant of the streaming platforms market success. As Marshal observes when commenting on the major labels equity share in Spotify, 'The recorded music landscape in the streaming era is beginning to bear many similarities to that of the CD era: financial success depends upon scale and catalogue, the major labels have a stake in distribution networks, and the vast majority of artists don't make any money [61].' (p.15)

Despite the similarities, the streaming era economy functions differently. Whereas with the unit model profits were, and still are, generated by continually investing in individual stars, with streaming combined back catalogue play becomes as valuable as any one off hit record or act. As every play increases the major labels market-share of a contractually bound increasing pot of monthly subscriptions, arguably, investing in generating subscribers, as much as stars, seems the smarter and safer strategy toward increasing profits. The contradiction is that in transitioning unit consumers into paying subscribers, the record companies risk too quickly displacing current physical and digital file unit sales that still constitute almost 70% of the global market [55]. The major labels are caught in what Christensen defines as the innovators dilemma. This is where, 'Successful companies populated by good managers have a genuinely hard time doing what does not fit their model for how to make money [6].' This strategic conundrum is compounded by the fact that most streaming subscribers will try freemium before graduating to premium tiers, and with only a current 20% conversion rate on Spotify, the risk for the record labels is that unit buyers just become free subscribers. From this perspective, Grainge's [25] anti-freemium stance is self-evident but still inherently problematic. Firstly, because without a freemium option consumers simply won't sample music streaming platforms, especially as YouTube already offers easy access to most music for free without subscription. Moreover, the £10 per month subscription fee demanded by the major record labels is just below the £14 UK consumers spend on average on music annually [56]. This pricing gap [57] means that heavy unit consumers can spend significantly less annually, but for the occasional unit buying majority, paying a month what they usually pay in a year, means freemium is the obvious default option.

Although the primary unit to use dilemma is making subscription and subscribers pay, that is not to say that superstar acts aren't important to record labels under the use model. Whilst Ed Sheeran's two billion plays is valuable to him, it is also very significant for Warner, his parent label. Not just in the revenue each play of Sheeran's recordings generates but in the fact that if music users are listening to Ed Sheeran, it means they cannot pay attention to an artist on Universal or Sony. Whilst a depth of catalogue increases the chances of play and a breadth appeals to the widest possible range of tastes, the most valuable catalogue is defined not by the number of recordings, but by the number of listens. Owning the rights to the records that are listened to most, at the expense of everything else, is where the secondary value is for the majors. The competition for market share of catalogue use between the majors is a zero sum game, where the value of superstar acts, 'is to stand out from the competition – to win the battle for attention [5].' Likewise, for the stars, the record companies investment and marketing expertise remains crucial.

However, unlike under the unit model, which split the percentage of sales success between act and label, under the use model, the label and the act are potentially operating at cross purposes. Whereas the label generates an aggregate sum for the monthly use of the entire catalogue, the greater the number of acts played in a market-share calculation, the less each act in the catalogue receives for their share of the royalty revenue. The conflict for the major labels, particularly with superstar acts, is that even as winners, each act risks taking less and less. The caveat to this conundrum is that research by Salganik, Dodds and Watts [43] [44] recognises popularity drives popularity. So it is feasible that superstar acts command an ever greater share of an increasingly expanding pot of subscription royalties. Even if this isn't quite winner takes all, it is certainly winner takes more. Yet, the lack of clarity in the new royalty relationships devised around streaming could certainly lead established superstar acts to question the value of their contractual relationships with record companies. Jay Z's re-branding of streaming service Tidal attempted to capitalise on the influence of exclusive star power with a launch event [58] that had a clear artist owned agenda. With the likes of Madonna, Chris Martin, Jack White and Alicia Keys, amongst others, appearing to take control of their own streaming destiny by all signing up as equity share owners in the platform.

Irrelevant of how successful an individual act is, ultimately acts cannot compete with catalogue. The major record companies currently control the majority of catalogue on the streaming networks and influence the negotiations over subsriber value. As Apple's initial free trial stance exemplified, the problem for small or individual catalogue owners is the absence of demand means streaming services do not consider their catalogues sufficiently valuable in their own right. It was only Swift's public protest that triggered a u-turn by Apple. Yet her claim, 'These are the echoed sentiments of every artist, writer and producer in my social circles who are afraid to speak up,' [40], was indicative of the uniqueness of her situation. Swift could only negotiate terms with Apple and remove her music from Spotify, because as a reported equity owner of her record label Big Machine, Swift controls her own catalogue. The majority of her superstar contemporaries do not, and most likely never will. Even if they did, most couldn't afford the risk of not being available on Apple Music or Spotify. In the future, many more artists may seek to retain or regain ownership and control of their recordings and remove, as Prince did recently [45], or renegotiate the licence to use their catalogues on platforms. But until then, even superstar artists, unless they own the platform like Jay Z does with Tidal, will, in Castellion terms, only ever exert influence over the network, not control.

Whilst artists lack control of the network, like the major record labels, streaming platforms need superstar acts to drive and maintain the attention of users. A Jones [46] asserts, being current is currency in an attention economy. Whereas Laguna argues it is unfair the most popular acts receive a disproportionate share of royalties, it is the popular catalogue that maintains the platforms value. Under the subscriber-share model, each user is a distinct and dislocated node on the network. However, a market-share distribution of monies connects all the nodes in the system to give the platform its popularity promoting power. Whereas subscriber-share would more equitably remunerate emerging acts and re-establish the direct economic relationship between fan and act [51], to the platforms, their only value is that they deepen and broaden the available catalogue. Most importantly, platforms don't distribute royalties to acts but to rights holders. A subscriber-share model would risk the major record labels allocating revenue away from themselves and their superstar acts to smaller rights holders and acts, thus conceding network power and influence in the process. For these reasons it is unlikely major labels will advocate for a subscriber-share model or that the platforms would countenance it.

What is clear is Apple's premium only model aligns far more comprehensively with the streaming agenda of the record industry than Spotify's freemium model. The emergence of Apple as the primary competitor to Spotify has seen the major labels attempt to assert their network power. Universal Music's advocacy of Apples approach has led to accusations of anti-competitive collusion in the USA courts. [47] Yet, despite their public protestations that on-demand music must be paid for, only 59% (6.5 million subscribers) of Apple Music's initial eleven million free trialists opted to retain their £10 per month subscription [59]. Although considerably better than Spotify's conversion rate, the majority of early adopters will have been from Apple's existing database of 800 million account holders. This suggests, that priced at ten times the average annual UK consumer spend, premium fees are either too high for many consumers or non-subscribers elected to maintain their existing subscription with a competitor platform. Therefore, at the time of writing, Spotify is the on-demand streaming platform that makes the most money for the record industry. With 20% of premium subscribers generating over 80% of Spotify revenues, there is validity to the argument that it would be in Spotify's own financial interest to abandon their freemium tier [48]. However, as Spotify's revenue and reach data is broadly consistent with the 80/20 Pareto Principle [49], if it remains so, there is validity in Spotify's assertion that freemium drives premium uptake. Moreover, with increasing freemium subscribers come higher advertising revenues. The IFPI [55] estimates $227 million in advertising spend was lost to illegal file sharing sites in 2014. Most importantly, without Apple's market advantage of a hardware business that could afford to treat Apple Music as a content loss leader to drive device sales, for Spotify, freemium is the only model that can create customers and grow their business. For all the stand alone music platforms, like Spotify, conversion is the key to success and so streaming's viability and sustainability depends on its freemium offer. Consumers must first be convinced of the value of paying attention before they can be convinced to pay.

In the context of a unit based business model, freemium streaming is evidently unsustainable because it is like equating the revenue from commercial radio to that of unit era record sales. This analogy emphasises the fundamental problem of measuring and discussing the value of music use, predominantly, in terms of unit sales. The very premise of debates that equate selling recorded music products to delivering recorded music services are fundamentally flawed. However, because there should be no difference to the consumer between the experiences of downloading to that of streaming, comparisons are continually made. As long as the displacement of the unit remains the prism through which the economics of streaming are viewed, it matters little whether consumer choice is freemium or premium subscription, or royalties are distributed on market or subscriber-share, none of these use models will satisfactorily fit into the pervading unit model thinking of how to make money.

As a business model based upon use, the economic viability of streaming rests on two key metrics, the numbers of users and the value of their use. The streaming platforms understand the parallel values of their network. The economic value of disclosing in a freemium model, that in turn funnels users toward the economic value of purchasing a premium subscription. Established as a legal alternative to online piracy, the platforms communication power is in the fundamental message that they connect the user with the music they love for free. Conversely, in withholding or windowing their catalogues of superstar acts from streaming platforms, the message the major record labels and their acts are sending the consumer is you have to pay to listen, on our terms. Given the enhanced sovereignty of the consumer in the digital era, the attempt to dictate the terms of how and what users stream, in the same way the record industry dictated the products and price in the CD era, is arguably counterproductive to promoting streaming and growing a subscriber base that will ensure steaming is viable and sustainable.

By continuing to act in their short term interests designed to squeeze the remaining value out of the unit model, the major labels are curtailing streaming growth. In the acts they invest in and promote the labels have the most direct and compelling conduit to the influence the behaviour of consumers. Unfortunately, at present, the narrative as to the virtues of freemium streaming are dominated by the attitudes exemplified by Taylor Swift more than Ed Sheeran, and even Sheeran's advocacy doesn't extend to outright support [66]. Yet nearly twenty years of digitisation and on-line piracy means rights holders and creators can no longer demand or even expect consumers to pay for a listening experience. Instead, record labels need to adapt to meet the evolving demands and derive value from how consumers want to experience listening. Freemium streaming is the new entry point to the record industry's value chain and, despite their ongoing attempts, acts and record companies lack the communication power to convince consumers otherwise. Only in fully embracing the use model as distinct from the unit, and building business models out from that premise, can rights holders and creators begin to solve their innovator's dilemma.

## 4. Conclusion

The shift from format to platform is not just a fundamental change in the structure of the record industry's value chain, it is a complete reordering of its economic structure. Streaming requires Longtails of both catalogue and user-attention to function, but ultimately depends on Blockbuster acts and tracks to keep platforms current and viable. In negotiating licenses, major labels can exert a degree of control over the viability of streaming services. Likewise, occasionally superstar acts can influence the actions of both the platforms and consumers. However, the change from unit to use ultimately affords the consumer greater sovereignty to decide music's value. In freemium and premium streaming, consumers have a choice between two distinct but interrelated business models that represent differing values from each other and the purchase of a unit. It is the users relationship to music, not the music itself, that has value in the streaming era. Whereas in the unit era, record companies could afford not to care what consumers thought, as long as they bought, in the streaming era, insisting users pay for an experience, as if it is a unit, is arguably what is most disrespectful to the fan who wants to invest. Unless the record companies can shift their unit mindset and start investing in subscribers as much as they do stars, it will be the streaming platforms, who use data to give the customer what they want, who will eventually emerge as the winners who take all.

## 5. References

[1] Pakinkis, T. 500m weekly streams landmark breached in UK for first time. Accessed 2015 from http://www.musicweek.com/news/read/500m-weekly-streams-landmark-breached-in-uk-for-first-time/062381
[2] Mulligan, M. Awakening: The Music Industry in the Digital Age, CreateSpace Independent Publishing Platform (2015), loc 512 & 3630.
[3] Nowak, R. Investigating the interactions between individuals and music technologies within contemporary modes of music consumption. Accessed 2015 from http://firstmonday.org/ojs/index.php/fm/article/view/5550
[4] Anderson, C. The Longtail: Why the Future of Business is Selling Less or More, Random House Business, London (2008).
[5] Elberse, A. Blockbusters: Why Big Hits? and Big Risks? Are the Future of the Entertainment Business, Faber & Faber Non Fiction, London (2013), loc 2575.
[6] Christensen, C. Innovator's Dilemma: When New Technologies Cause Great Firms to Fail (Management of Innovation and Change), Harvard Business Review Press (2013), loc 950 & 4317.
[7] Hardy, P. Download!: How the Internet Transformed the Record Business, Omnibus Press, London (2012), p286.
[8] Ingham, T. Sweden is Back on Track: Music Market up 4.2% in First Half of 2015. Accessed 2015 from http://www.musicbusinessworldwide.com/sweden-is-back-on-track-music-market-up-4-in-first-half-of-2015/
[9] Pakinkis, T. Spanish Music Market up 10.9% Thanks to Streaming. Accessed 2015 from http://www.musicweek.com/news/read/spanish-music-market-up-10-9-thanks-to-streaming/062404
[10] Yorke, T. Thom Yorke calls Spotify The Last Desperate Fart of a Dying Corpse. Accessed 2015 from http://www.theguardian.com/technology/2013/oct/07/spotify-thom-yorke-dying-corpse
[11] Willman, C. Taylor Swift on Being Pop's Instantly Platinum Wonder... And Why She's Paddling Against the Streams. Accessed 2015 from https://www.yahoo.com/music/bp/exclusive--taylor-swift-on-being-pop-s-instantly-platinum-wonder----and-why-she-s-paddling-against-the-streams-085041907.html

[12] Sisario, B. Chief Defends Spotify After Snub by Taylor Swift. Accessed 2015 from http://www.nytimes.com/2014/11/12/business/media/taylor-swifts-stand-on-royalties-draws-a-rebuttal-from-spotify.html?_r=1
[13] Wheeldon, J. Patrons, Curators, Inventors and Thieves: The Storytelling Contest of the Cultural Industries in the Digital Age, Palgrave and Macmillian, Hampshire (2014), p63-90
[14] Dubber, A. 20 Things You Must Know About Music Online (2007). Accessed July 18, 2014, from New Music Strategies: http://newmusicstrategies.com/wp-content/uploads/2008/06/nms.pdf
[15] Tschmuck, P. Creativity and Innovation in the Music Industry. Heidelberg: Springer, 2nd ed (2012), p242.
[16] Anderton, C., Dubber, A., & James, M. Understanding the Music Industries, Sage, London (2013), p96.
[17] Lamere, P. Exploring age-specific preferences in listening. Accessed 2015 from http://musicmachinery.com/2014/02/13/age-specific-listening/
[18] Press Association. Sheeran defends Spotify payments. Accessed 2015 from http://www.dailymail.co.uk/wires/pa/article-2871548/Sheeran-defends-Spotify-payments.html
[19] Ingham, T. Ed Sheeran Tracks have made $14m on Spotify. Accessed 2015 from http://www.musicbusinessworldwide.com/ed-sheeran-tracks-have-made-14m-on-spotify/
[20] Spotify. How to Spotify Contributing to the Music Business. Accessed 2015 from http://www.spotifyartists.com/spotify-explained/
[21] Laguna, S. How To Make Streaming Royalties Fair(er). Accessed 2015 from https://medium.com/cuepoint/how-to-make-streaming-royalties-fair-er-8b38cd862f66
[22] Rockonomics. Popularity versus Demand: Looking further into the fair distribution of streaming wealth Accessed 2015 from http://rockonomic.com/
[23] Singleton, M. This was Sony Music's contract with Spotify: The details the major labels don't want you to see. Accessed 2015 from http://www.theverge.com/2015/5/19/8621581/sony-music-spotify-contract
[24] Drucker, P. The Practice of Management, Routledge (2007), p35.
[25] Ingham, T. 7 Times Lucian Grange Bashed Freemium at Code/Media. Accessed 2015 from http://www.musicbusinessworldwide.com/7-times-lucian-grainge-bashed-freemium-at-codemedia/
[26] McLuhan, M. Understanding Media: The Extensions of Man, McGraw-Hill, Canada (1964), p235.
[27] Wikstrom, P. A Typology of Music Distribution Models, International Journal of Music Business Research, vol. 1 no. 1, (2012) Accessed 2015 from https://musicbusinessresearch.files.wordpress.com/2012/04/ijmbr_april_2012_patrik_wikstrom1.pdf
[28] Fornaciari, F. Pricey Privacy: Framing the Economy of Information in the Digital Age. Accessed 2015 from http://firstmonday.org/ojs/index.php/fm/article/view/5008/4184
[29] The Statistics Portal. Global advertising revenue from 2007 to 2016 (in billion U.S. dollars). Accessed 2015 from

http://www.statista.com/statistics/237797/total-global-advertising-revenue/

[30] Strategy Analytics. Digital to Account for 50% of UK Ad spend in 2015. Accessed 2015 from https://www.strategyanalytics.com/strategy-analytics/news/strategy-analytics-press-releases/strategy-analytics-press-release/2015/03/02/digital-to-account-for-50-of-uk-adspend-in-2015#.VbzeofQ7uWJ

[31] Baker, D. Why Ad blockers should Scare the Shit Out of the Media World. Accessed 2015 from http://contently.com/strategist/2015/07/10/why-adblockers-should-scare-the-shit-out-of-the-media-world/

[32] Google. A Brand Marketer's Guide. Accessed 2015 from https://www.thinkwithgoogle.com/programmatic-guide/

[33] Hanley, J. Spotify ad revenue grows 53% in Q1 2015. Accessed 2015 from http://www.musicweek.com/news/read/spotify-ad-revenue-grows-53-in-q1-2015-compared-with-same-period-last-year-2/061525

[34] Franck, G. Modern Science: A Case of Collective Intelligence? On the Roleof Thought Economy and Gratifying Attention in Knowledge Production. Accessed 2015 from http://www.researchgate.net/publication/227177403_Modern_Science_A_Case_of_Collective_Intelligence_On_the_Role_of_Thought_Economy_and_Gratifying_Attention_in_Knowledge_Production

[35] IFPI. Global Music Sales. Accessed 2015 from http://www.ifpi.org/global-statistics.php

[36] Dredge, S. YouTube trains its sights on traditional TV: 'It's a no-growth business'. Accessed 2015 from http://www.theguardian.com/technology/2015/jun/02/youtube-future-small-screens-mobile-robert-kyncl

[37] Taplin, S. Sleeping through a Revolution. Accessed 2015 from https://vimeo.com/122361826

[38] Castells, M. Communication Power, Oxford University Press, Oxford (2009), p46.

[39] Mag, F. Jay Z Interview with Fader Mag. Accessed 2015 from http://www.neogaf.com/forum/showthread.php?t=1022008

[40] Helman, P. Taylor Swift's Open Letter to Apple Music. Accessed 2015 from http://www.stereogum.com/1810310/read-taylor-swifts-open-letter-to-apple-music/news/

[41] Resnikoff, P. F*&k It: Here's the Entire Apple Music Contract for Indies... (2015) Accessed 2015 from http://www.digitalmusicnews.com/2015/06/17/fk-it-heres-the-entire-apple-music-contract-for-indies/

[42] Stassen, M. Lohan Presencer: Subscription Model Only Favours 'the three biggest players in the game'. Accessed 2015 from http://www.musicweek.com/news/read/lohan-presencer-subscription-model-only-favours-the-three-biggest-players-in-the-game/061788

[43] Salganik, M., Dodds, P., & Watts, D. Experimental Study of Inequality and Un predictability in an Artificial Cultural Market. Science, 311, 854-856. (2006) Accessed 2015 from http://www.princeton.edu/~mjs3/salganik_dodds_watts06_full.pdf

[44] Salganik, M. J., & Watts, D. J. Leading the Herd Astray: An Experimental Study of Self Fulfilling Prophecies in an Artificial Cultural Market, Social Psychology Quarterly, 71(4), 338-355. (2008) Accessed July 18, 2014, from http://www.princeton.edu/~mjs3/salganik_watts08.pdf

[45] Pakinkis, T. Prince releases new track on Spotify only weeks after pulling catalogue from streaming. Accessed 2015 from http://www.musicweek.com/news/read/prince-releases-new-track-on-spotify-only-weeks-after-pulling-catalogue-from-streaming-2/062454

[46] Jones, M. The Music Industries: From Conception to Consumption, Palgrave Macmillan, Hampshire (2012), p94.

[47] Ingham, T. Google Loves Spotify, Which is Hurting Apple, Which is in a War for Global Domination Against...Google. And People Say Music's Lost its Value. Accessed 2015 from http://www.musicbusinessworldwide.com/google-loves-spotify/

[48] Hirschhorn, J. Less Money, More Music and Lots of Problems: A Look at the Muisc Biz. Accessed July 2015 from https://www.linkedin.com/pulse/less-money-mo-music-lots-problems-look-biz-jason-hirschhorn

[49] The Pareto Principle. Accessed July 2015 from https://en.m.wikipedia.org/wiki/Pareto_principle

[50] Negus, K. Music Genres and Corporate Cultures, Routledge, London (1999), p.48.

[51] Maasø, A. User-Centric Settlement for Music Streaming: A report on the distribution of income from music streaming in Norway, based on streaming data from WIMP, Clouds and Concerts, Oslo (2014) Accessed 2015 from www.hf.uio.no/imv/forskning/prosjekter/skyogscene/publikasjoner/usercentric-cloudsandconcerts-report.pdf

[52] Rex Pedersen, R. Music Streaming in Denmark: An Analysis of listening patterns and the consequences of a 'per user' settlement model based on streaming data from WIMP, Roskilde University, Roskilde (2014) Accessed 2015 from rucforsk.ruc.dk/site/en/publications/music-streaming-in-denmark(d553b4dc-4e68-4809-a4ba-67da99a2122a).html

[53] Anderson, T.J. Popular Music in a Digital Music Economy: Problems and Practices for an Emerging Service Industry, Routledge, London (2014)

[54] Wade Morris, J. & Powers, D. Control, curation and musical experience in streaming music services, Creative Industries Journal, 10 (2015)

[55] IFPI. Digital Music Report 2015: Charting the path to sustainable growth, London (2015) p.6&7. Accessed 2015 from http://www.ifpi.org/downloads/Digital-Music-Report-2015.pdf

[56] Ingham, T. Why Norway and the UK produce the world's most valuable music fans. Accessed 2015 from http://www.musicbusinessworldwide.com/norway-uk-produce-worlds-valuable-music-fans/

[57] Mulligan, M. Rdio Goes After the Sqeezed Middle Accessed 2015 from https://musicindustryblog.wordpress.com/2015/05/14/rdio-goes-after-the-squeezed-middle/

[58] Ingham, T. Tidal: 16 superstars grab equity in Jay Z's 'United Artists of music' Accessed 2015 from http://www.musicbusinessworldwide.com/tidal-16-superstars-grab-equity-in-jay-zs-united-artists-of-music/

[59] Mulligan, M. Apple Music By The Numbers Accessed 2015 from https://musicindustryblog.wordpress.com/2015/10/20/apple-music-by-the-numbers/

[60] Giletti, T. Why Pay if it's Free? Streaming, downloading, and digital music consumption in the "iTunes era", Media@LSE, London (2012) p.30. Accessed 2015 from www.lse.ac.uk/media@lse/research/mediaworkingpapers/mscdissertationseries/2011/71.pdf

[61] Marshall, L. 'Let's keep music special. F--- Spotify'. On-demand streaming and the controversy over artist royalties, Creative Industries Journal 8:2 p1.13 (2015) p.15.

[62] Venture Consulting. Will Music Streaming Ever be Profitable? (2013) Accessed 2015 from www.ventureconsulting.com/assets/Streaming-Article-vfinal2.pdf

[63] Aguiar, L. & Waldfogel, J. Streaming Reaches Flood Stage: Does Spotify Stimulate or Depress Music Sales? European Commission, Spain (2015) Accessed 2015 from https://ec.europa.eu/jrc/sites/default/files/JRC96951.pdf

[64] Ingham, T. Spotify Revenues Topped €1bn in FY2014 – but losses grew 77% to €165m Accessed 2015 from
http://www.musicbusinessworldwide.com/spotify-revenues-top-e1bn-fy2014-losses-grow/

[65] What Is Freemium. Accessed 2015 from http://www.freemium.org/what-is-freemium-2/

[66] Palermino, C.L. Spotify Superstar Sheeran Claims he doesn't Stream Anything Ever. Accessed 2015 from www.digitaltrends.com/music/spotify-superstar-ed-sheeran-doesnt-use-streaming-services/

# Real-time long-distance music collaboration using the Internet

Paul Ferguson[1]

[1]Edinburgh Napier University, Edinburgh, UK
p.ferguson@napier.ac.uk

## Abstract

The recent but rapid adoption of networked audio systems such as RedNet within the commercial and education domains is, as yet, limited to Local Area Networks (LANs) or Campus Area Networks (CANs). However, the increased connection bandwidth offered to individuals and studios by Internet Service Providers is opening up the potential for audio and video-based remote collaboration in the arts. The commercial opportunity this bandwidth and performance improvement presents can be evidenced by collaboration-focused tools such as Source-Connect and by the new cloud-based workflows in Pro-Tools 12. Neither of these are real-time however, and incur latency times measured in seconds rather than the tens of milliseconds we require when musicians actually play together.

To see where we might end up given sufficient network performance we need only to look at research using the high-speed National Research and Education Networks (NRENs) found in many countries. These networks offer speed and jitter performance far in excess of their commonly available commercial counterparts and they allow us to do research and to develop collaborative practices that will ultimately be available to us all once the commercial networks achieve similar levels of performance.

## 1. Introduction

Five years of research with the LoLa (Low Latency) system [1] over NRENs in Europe and America shows us that real-time performance across Europe (and further) is unquestionably possible. The question that then arises is "how do we ensure that the collaboration result is worthwhile?" For example, how do factors such as audio latency and the visual representation of the remote artist affect the performers and therefore the quality of their musical performance?

## 2. Background

The LOLA low-latency audio/video streaming system is the product of a research partnership between Conservatorio Tartini and network engineers at GARR, the

*Copyright © 2015 Future Technology Press and the authors*

Italian NREN. In September 2012 the first UK test of LOLA took place between Edinburgh Napier University and The Janet Arts and humanities streaming workshop hosted in the Royal College of Music, London [5]. This and subsequent demonstrations together with those of early adopters of LOLA in other countries show that real-time performance and rehearsal between musicians is unquestionably possible over distance up to 3000 kilometers. The experiment described in section 4.3 shows that even greater distances may be feasible.

## 3. Considerations

### 3.1. Latency

Prior to LOLA, low-latency audio-only long-distance networked audio was possible using JackTrip [1] but systems incorporating video typically introduced 200ms to 500ms delay. To reduce the effect of these delays videoconferencing systems usually incorporated echo-cancelling techniques that worked well with speech but not music. The aim of the Tartini/GARR partnership was to reduce this delay to the point that remote musicians could successfully play together. Chew et al [4] suggest that 50ms is the maximum acceptable figure although research by Chafe and Gurevich [3] determines 11.5ms as the optimal one-way latency. To put this into context, the latter figure is equivalent to acoustic musicians playing 12 feet apart. Or, for anyone using computer-based audio, it is equivalent to the latency added by a 512 sample audio buffer running at 44100 sample rate.

### 3.2. The importance of video

Edinburgh Napier University's early LOLA experiments used standard-definition (VGA) cameras running at 60fps and used 24" CRT-based monitors to reduce latency. Most of the interviewed musicians found the picture to only be essential when the music required non-verbal cues between musicians. Some considered it to be of little importance the remainder of the time. The introduction of high-definition (HD) 720p video to LOLA in 2014 allowed picture quality to be changed during experiments. Early results show that HD picture coupled with careful camera placement and lighting allows the remote musician to be portrayed with increased realism. This appears to considerably increase the musicians' sense of engagement with one another.

### 3.3. Audio and video synchronisation

LOLA can process audio using a 32 sample buffer which results in an audio latency of 0.7ms plus the operating system overhead. Video acquisition is not as fast however: Video frame grabbers and fast USB3 cameras allow a best-case video latency of nearer 5ms. This audio/video synchronization difference is compounded on output where the TV or projector can add an additional frame of processing latency which equates to 20ms at 50fps. This offset between audio and video was detected by the professional ensemble in experiment 4.2 below.

## 4. Experiments

Three of the Edinburgh Napier University LOLA experiments conducted between 2012 and 2015 have been chosen for discussion:

### 4.1. Real-time remote recording and mixing between Edinburgh and Prague

This experiment took place in December 2014 and differs from the more usual remote 'musicians playing together' performance, rehearsal or masterclass. Instead, this experiment mimics a radio broadcast with an outside broadcast truck mixing multiple microphones on stage. The difference being that the performance was in Edinburgh and the virtual 'truck' was a recording studio in the Academy of Performing Arts in Prague. The connection was via the JANET, GEANT and CEZNET NRENS which gave an each-way network latency of 16ms. It should be noted that LOLA requires symmetrical outbound and inbound network routes as well as equal upload and download bandwidths.

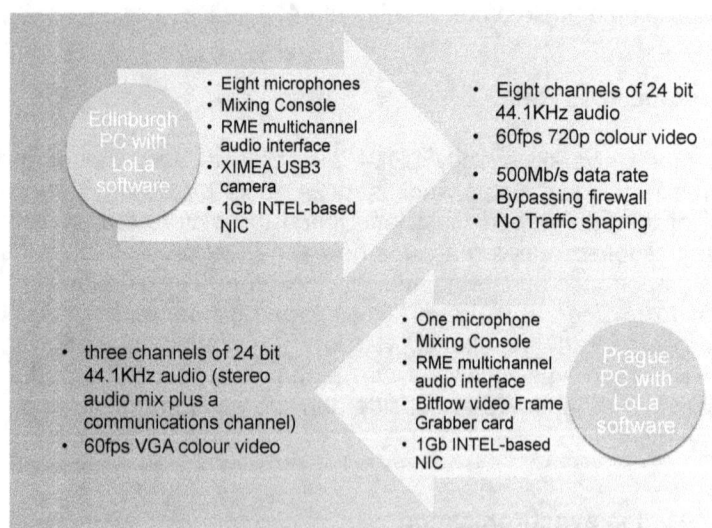

Figure 1. Edinburgh to Prague real-time recording experiment

Students and lecturing staff judged the experiment to be successful from both a technical and a teaching standpoint. In order to achieve the lowest possible latency performance LOLA has no error-recovery protocols in the event of lost or delayed data packets. This can result in audible glitches and this affected the mixed audio returned to Edinburgh towards the end of this experiment. Because audio was recorded locally in Edinburgh and Prague the final result was unaffected. A follow-on experiment will use LOLA as a real-time link between two remote AVID Pro Tools systems running a cloud-hosted session.

### 4.2. Near real-time pipes and drums performance: Edinburgh and Chicago

This experiment used LOLA to transmit a drum core in 5.1 surround sound. More significantly, it shows that distances greater that 3000km (corresponding to latencies exceeding the commonly agreed 30-50ms maximum) may be possible. For this test an Edinburgh drum core led by former British Army Senior Drum Major Brian Alexander played with a Chicago piper (thanks to LOLA support by Dan Nichols from NIU). Despite the round-trip latency time of 140ms, Alexander found it useful to hear the delayed piper even the delay time bore no obvious relationship to song tempo. The student members of the drum core found it almost impossible to play whilst hearing the piper and resorted to watching and following their drum major. On interview Alexander stated that the scenario was not unlike a live performance at the Edinburgh Tattoo where the echo times are constantly varying as the band marches between buildings. In Brian's words: "you just learn to get on with it".

### 4.3. Professional Ensemble masterclass between Edinburgh, Trieste (Italy) and London.

This May 2015 experiment was the first UK test of LOLA by a professional ensemble and composer James Macmillan CBE. Emphasis was put on creating a more immersive audio and video representation of the remote horn players in Trieste and London. Loudspeakers faced forwards and backwards to mimic the horn and the player was represented life-size on a portrait-oriented TV monitor. Early in the experiment the ensemble noticed the offset between audio and video discussed in section 3.3 and this caused them to become more reliant on listening. However most of the ensemble were aware of a realistic connection to the remote player.

### 5. Conclusions

These recent experiments show that there is potential for incorporating LOLA as a real-time link in professional workflows providing that backup audio recording is taking place locally. There is potential for research to see to what degree musicians can adapt to latency but most significant is the work to be done in terms of the User Experience (UX) by giving an artist a more immersive (and synchronized) sense of the remote musician or musicians.

## 6. References

[1] Caceres, J., Chafe, C. Jacktrip: Under the hood of an engine for network audio. In Proceedings of the International Computer Music Conference 2009, Montreal, Canada. (2009)
[2] Carôt, A., Reizner, J. A Telematic Approach for Mass Music Ensembles. Re-New Conference and Digital Arts Festival, Copenhagen, Denmark. (2013)
[3] Chafe, C., Gurevich, M. Network Time Delay and Ensemble Accuracy: Effects of Latency, Asymmetry. Proceedings of the AES 117th Convention, San Francisco. (2004)
[4] Chew, E., Kyriakakis, C., Papadopoulos,C., Sawchuk, A., Zimmermann, R. Distributed Immersive Performance: Enabling Technologies for and Analyses of Remote Performance and Collaboration. Distributed Immersive Performance (D.I.P.) California, USA. (2004
[5] Ferguson, P. Using low-latency net-based solutions to extend the audio and video capabilities of a studio complex. Proceedings of the AES 134th Convention, Rome, Italy (2013)

# Integrating the Spatiality of Live Performers within the Imaginary Spatial Image of a Pre-Recorded Electroacoustic Part as a Compositional Premise

Timothy Cooper

The Royal Conservatoire of Scotland, Glasgow, UK
t.cooper@rcs.ac.uk

## Abstract

*Composing mixed-media music (involving live instrumentalists and electroacoustic sounds projected by loudspeakers) presents unique issues for the composer. How can these two parts relate spatially in order to coherently present sounds produced live on stage and illusory sounds projected by loudspeakers? What kinds of relationships can succeed and how are they managed compositionally and in performance?*

*This paper will explore my approach to space within my 2012 composition, Fata Morgana, for four clarinets and pre-recorded electroacoustic music. The spatial perspectives are intrinsically linked to the musical materials in the piece, particularly the perspectives created by combining the real and illusory sounds.*

*The live presentation of mixed-media music is a delicate and important aspect in successfully realising a work. This should directly relate to the spatial and musical aspects of the composition and I will discuss how this is managed in the live performance of Fata Morgana.*

## 1. Introduction

This paper is concerned with the spatial aspects of my 2012 composition *Fata Morgana* for four clarinets and electroacoustic music. Through the paper I will describe the spatial aspects at play and how I approach space as a compositional parameter. I will conclude with an outline of how I approach the live performance of the electroacoustic materials. The musical ideas are given shape by theories posited by Denis Smalley, Frank Ekeberg Henriksen and Simon Emmerson [1] [2] [3] [4] [5].

## 2. Mixed-Media Space

As Henriksen points out '"space" is a very complex term in the context of electroacoustic music, where it refers to many different things that for the most part can be discussed as if they were separate entities, but which in reality are intertwined and cannot be experienced in isolation.' His framework for analysing sound spatially provides strong definitions for contextualising space in my own work.

Within electroacoustic music, space is a tangible and controllable parameter for musical expression. Beyond the aesthetic interest it carries it plays an essential role in coherently combining instrumental and electroacoustic resources in mixed-media music. Spatial relationships need to be established in order for the other, more traditional relationships (pitch, time, timbre etc), to be understood. It is crucial to carefully realise these relationships when presenting the music to an audience in a larger public space (what we will later go on to discuss as *perceived space*). [1] [4]

Mixed-media music poses some very specific problems for the composer and the audience surrounding how we process the two different sound-worlds as related. There is a tension between live and illusory sounds that is both a problem and a creative opportunity for the composer. With the compositional materials at hand it is important to be careful about how suitable they are for combining.

This applies as much to spatial relationships as it does to the more traditional relationships. In fact, one must be even more careful to coherently use space as a parameter. Being able to discreetly compose with space is not an add-on to be carelessly played with, but an intrinsic and important part of the composition that must relate to the materials and contribute to structuring the work. Just because a composer can produce a certain spatial effect does not mean that it is an appropriate spatial effect for the materials in question, especially in relation to any on stage instrumentalists.

In my compositional process I view this is as extremely important. The spaces I create are not super-imposed upon the sounds. They are drawn from the materials themselves. Spaces and motions are suggested or implied by the sounds and I view it as my role to support and enhance these, rather than superimposing new spatialisations upon the sounds. This approach separates space (how we experience sound) and spatialisation (how that experience is mediated). Space is the area of artistic interest and spatialisation tools allow me to create and support these spaces.

In order to coherently create an overall sound-world between the instrumental and electroacoustic materials it is worth acknowledging the separate spaces at play in a mixed-media work:

1. The spaces apparent in the electroacoustic materials.
2. The spaces apparent in the instrumental materials.
3. The spaces made by combining the instrumental and electroacoustic materials.

4. The spatial characteristics of the larger public performance space (what Henriksen calls the *listening space*) and how they interact with the *composed spaces*. This combination Henriksen terms *perceived space*. [4]

Having introduced some wider views on the role of space in mixed-media music I will now explore the aesthetic and compositional aspects of *Fata Morgana* before discussing the technological solutions and how I approach the public performance of this work.

## 3. Perspective in Fata Morgana

Denis Smalley describes perspectival space as:

'...the relations of position, movement and scale among spectromorphologies, viewed from the listener's vantage point. I say 'viewed' because although the acousmatic image may be invisible, one can also, depending on the nature of the spectromorphologies and their contextual relations, locate and track their positions in a quasi-visual manner.' [5].

Perspective is particularly important in mixed-media music – and in *Fata Morgana* – because of the privileged role the instrumentalists take in relation to the electroacoustic part. The audience's attention is drawn to the ensemble, visible on stage. As Emmerson says 'in live works the instrument is the anchor and we can never for long leave the realm of its influence...' [1]. In *Fata Morgana* I rely on this. The audience observes the ensemble from their vantage point. The fixity of the ensemble's positioning means that the electroacoustic materials are positioned, relative to the ensemble. This perspective means that the audience's vantage point is fixed. This helps in the translation from the studio to a larger public space. Spaces in the electroacoustic material occur relative to the ensemble. They are relatively more distant, present, wide or narrow than the ensemble visible on stage.

Perspectives in *Fata Morgana* result from layering various instrumental materials and electroacoustic materials. The layers and perspectives are conceived in stereo and explore depth and width, rather than surrounded-ness. I approach mixed-media space in this way because of the role of the ensemble drawing the listener's attention forwards and because of my interest in sound as landscape. I think of the stage as a frame for the musical action to occur within, extending the sphere of the instrumentalists and focusing the action on them, rather than drawing the audience's attention away from the ensemble.

There are a number of reasons I have tended to approach space, in a mixed-media context, in this way:

1. The visual role the ensemble plays on stage firmly centers the audience's attention forwards. Sounds that are dislocated from the ensemble spatially

raise questions that I was not seeking to address in this work. Importantly, the materials I made did not imply surround-sound spaces. [1]

2. My own personal interest is in sounds that change depth in the stereo image from distant to proximate or proximate to distant. I am less interested in lateral positioning. Left-Right or Right-Left motion is a tool, whereas, my experience of sounds approaching or receding is that they create more of an emotional or physiological response than sounds that move across the sound stage.

The British sculptor Richard Long also influences my approach. First noted for his 1967 work *A Line Made by Walking* [6], Long's landscape work is characterised by his interactions with places and spaces. In his outdoors sculptures he has two primary modes of working. In the first (as in *A Line Made by Walking*) he imprints marks upon the ground by repeatedly walking over the same area. In the second Long moves and arranges objects within the place or space, usually large stones or boulders as in his 1974 work, *Stones in Iceland* [7]. The environment he finds himself in determines the scale of a work, ranging from relatively intimate to vast. In Long's work there seems to be a similar play with reality as in my spatial approach. The unique character of every stone that, whilst similar to its neighbours, is still unique, finds its equivalent in the sounds that create a sense of space in *Fata Morgana*. The sounds are similar enough to maintain a consistent sense of environment, but different enough to be perceived as evolving, natural and not synthesised.

What draws me to these works is a sense that the sculptures are not out of place. A number of them even appear totally natural and not composed. They are seamlessly integrated into the environment, as though they existed without human interference. They are a part of the wider landscape and seem, to me, to be integrated within it. The notion of acting upon a landscape greatly appeals to me as a composer. My preference has always been for spaces within sound that are conceivably real or surreal, rather than contrived or synthesised spaces. In all of my electroacoustic music there are believable spaces that seem to have clear boundaries. This places the listener either within, or in a position of observing, the composed space(s).

The image created in *Fata Morgana* is one of an evolving landscape. If this was a visual artwork its equivalent would perhaps be something like a time-lapse video where the framing remains the same but the activity and change within that frame is detailed and dynamic. The textures and gestures evolve, sometimes slowly and sometimes quickly. However, the frame created by the stage and the anchoring role of the quartet maintains the sense that the space created is of one shifting landscape rather than many different landscapes occurring one after another. This relates back to the fixed vantage point of the audience and the fixity of the ensemble. If the vantage point and overall framing does not shift then the spatial structuring relies on the action within the frame articulating the space.

In *Fata Morgana* this spatial structure supports the relatively organic overall structure. In this case it is not useful to describe this structure blow by blow. However, the way the layers interact determines how the spatial structure evolves and I will introduce the different kinds of materials and some of the more significant ways that they are combined [5].

## 3.2 Electroacoustic Materials

There are a number of materials that make up this overall sonic landscape. The layers of electroacoustic materials have separate spatial characteristics. I will use Henriksen's terminology here to frame the spatial characteristics:

- *Non-directional* sounds that fill the stereo image. These sounds tend to inhabit *intrinsic orientations* that are described as 'based on the perception of internal spatial components'. Or *spectral orientations* that are described as 'a vertical space in which sounds are localised on the basis of spectral emphasis, such as pitch or nodal spectrum') *orientations*. The *intrinsic* and *spectral* characteristics in *Fata Morgana* tend to be related. Because the source materials for the electroacoustic materials are mostly pitch based, their *intrinsic* qualities are, by their nature *spectral* and *harmonic*. The sounds do not exhibit the same kind of spatial activity other *intrinsically oriented* sounds might afford [4].
- *Directional-sounds* that frame the image. These are very granular sounds that inhabit *extrinsic space*. These sounds tend to hold a very intimate, close proximity and are spatialised to mark the edge of the stereo image laterally or to circle the space, marking the periphery of the width and depth of the *composed space*. (sound example 2) (ibid.)
- *Directional-sounds* that are more gestural in character. These sounds move across and through the image and also inhabit *extrinsic space*. They are more soloistic and are directly relatable to the live clarinet sounds. (sound example 3). (ibid.)

## 3.3 Instrumental Materials

Defining spatial characteristics for live instrumentalists is a more complex issue. Their presence and activity allows us to see where the sound was made and we attach those sounds to the players. However, changes in timbral characteristics framed by the electroacoustic sounds can be suggestive of different spatial characteristics.

### *Intrinsically Oriented* Instrumental Materials

In these materials the clarinets tend to be used homophonically. The way the parts are shaped dynamically is suggestive of the *non-directional* electroacoustic sounds. When framed by those electroacoustic materials there is a sense that they extend or reveal the interior of the harmonic instrumental passages.

Spatially these materials can appear more or less present. The clarinetists either play with an open or closed timbre. The closed sound is less bright and can disappear or recede behind the electroacoustic materials, particularly when the electroacoustic materials have brighter spectral content. When played with a more open sound the materials sound stronger and occupy space more confidently. This occupation of the foreground, and the use of less spectrally bright electroacoustic sounds, causes the listener to perceive the electroacoustic materials as occupying the background of the sound stage.

These materials do become more linear, but the motion does not contribute to the materials becoming *extrinsically oriented*. Because the spatial framework has been established these more linear parts are perceived as being developed from the static harmonic passage. The motions within the clarinet parts are perceived more like spectral fluctuations within the established *intrinsic space* rather than the instrumental lines becoming overly *directional* and *extrinsic*.

In sound example 4 you can hear a transition from held to linear. Initially the performers act together but gradually, initiated by the bass clarinet, they become more independent of one another.

### *Extrinsically Oriented* Instrumental Materials

In these clarinet materials collective gestures are made up of very short, spectrally dense clarinet notes. The short notes take the form of agglomerations, described by Smalley as sound 'accumulating into a mass'. The gestures play on the directional nature of these clarinet sounds. Each sound is *directional* and there is a sense of gestural and spatial interactivity within the ensemble [8].

In sound example 5 you can hear three agglomerations that lose intensity through the passage.

### 3.3  Combining Instrumental and Electroacoustic Materials

Having identified the different spaces inherent in the instrumental and electroacoustic materials and their characteristics I will now explore the ways these are combined.

(It should be noted that within generally *intrinsic* or generally *extrinsic* sections there are of course elements of spatial layering that include *extrinsic space* within generally *intrinsic* sections and vice-versa.)

## Both Parts Sharing the Same Spatial Characteristics

There are sections where the two parts act together relatively equally, playing material that behaves similarly as well as following relatively the same phrasing. In order to support the traditional musical development they also share the same spatial characteristics.

In sound example 6 they both play continuous but dynamic material. Accents in the music tend to come together in this section between the two parts. However, the quartet bounce accents off one another to create longer, more dynamic gestures in the instrumental part.

Spatially the two parts are more *intrinsic* in orientation. The electroacoustic materials develop relatively organically (although the phrases are punctuated by more *extrinsic* gestural material and the clarinet accents). The continuity of the instrumental material when framed by the electroacoustic material allows the listener to perceive the instrumental group as an individual sound source, rather than as four individual clarinetists. A solo line of this material would tend to move towards the foreground because of the perspectival expectations set up by including a soloist. With just one clarinet the part would become spatially foregrounded rather than the integrated result using a quartet affords.

Importantly, within this shared *intrinsic space* the two parts can support one another. The clarinet materials can come into the foreground because of how they occupy *spectral space* and vice-versa.

## *Spectral Space* and Perspective in *Intrinsically Oriented* Sections

The difference between combinations of materials, particularly the more sustained clarinet and electroacoustic materials, tends to be subtle. The differences are usually in the behaviour of the materials, the spectral occupancy of the electroacoustic materials and the timbre of the clarinet materials.

Sound example 7 is from the opening section transitioning into the second part. Here the clarinet and electroacoustic materials are *intrinsically oriented*. It begins with the clarinets alone before the electroacoustic part enters to support the clarinet materials. It may seem similar to the sustained material in sound example 8, however there are a number of key differences:

1. There is no proximate material in this example in the fixed part. This is partly to do with an absence of sounds occupying a more intimate perspective. The electroacoustic materials here spectrally lack detailed high frequency content, which provides proximity cues for the listener [5].
2. The shape of the clarinet parts defines the structure of this passage; the way their lines unfold is supported, not directed by the electroacoustic part.

3. In the previous example the clarinets short gestures helped frame the phrasing in the electroacoustic material rather than lead the phrasing.
4. The clarinets initiate the first significant change that occurs around two minutes into the example. When the fixed part becomes more active just after the first big gesture it is the first time the fixed part has behaved in this way rather than simply providing an evolving space for the clarinets to inhabit.

## *Intrinsic* Electroacoustic Materials, *Extrinsic* Clarinet Materials

In these passages the electroacoustic phrases are punctuated by the clarinet gestures.

In sound example 8 the clarinets move from marking the space between electroacoustic gestures through short agglomerations before they recede behind the fixed part and gently highlight the more interesting fixed material. This is an example of the clarinet materials transitioning from *extrinsic* to *intrinsic orientation*. In the second part of this passage the clarinets play with a closed sound that allows the brighter electroacoustic materials to hold the foreground.

## *Ensemble Space*

The spatial combinations I have described exist within *ensemble space* that Smalley describes as:

'*Ensemble space*, within which individual gestural spaces are nested, is the personal and social space among performers: a group of performers produces a collective performed space. This is revealed both visually (seeing proprioception at work, and knowing how it works) and in the music (hearing proprioception at work). In duos or small ensembles the space is more personal...' [5].

This is the principal "space" that the clarinet materials occupy in *Fata Morgana*. Generally they work as a unit in order to create fully formed textures of their own in order to interact with the fixed part on an equal basis.

*Ensemble space* is also the principle space that the instrumental and electroacoustic materials interact within. The two parts can work together, support one another or act upon one another within *ensemble space*. This also supports the important notion of landscape within the work. The detail is within the landscape rather than being positioned in the foreground. Within this zone roles are exchanged and perspectives defined by the proximity of the electroacoustic materials in relation to the physical presence of the ensemble and in relation to the spatial behaviours of the materials.

In *Fata Morgana*, there are passages where the source of the sound is less identifiable. These passages suggested the title *Fata Morgana*, and the development of further spatial illusions. At the point where the sound is neither identifiably played by the instrumentalists or projected by loudspeakers subtle changes in performance, spectral shaping or energy allow the perspectives to momentarily shift, before blurring again. This perspective allows for the materials to become re-defined and their role and importance re-contextualised. It is in these passages that different materials are usually resolved and concluded or gain a new role. *Ensemble space* contributes to the illusion. As Smalley says, 'Sound can bind spatial zones when like behaviour creates a sonic contiguity where we cannot separately identify individuals...' [5].

These combined spaces only exist through performance. Each element requires the presence of the other for the full context to be understood by the audience. Having identified the spatial relationships in the work it is crucial to carefully consider how these are realised in performance, in a larger public space.

## 4. Mixed-Media Presentation

Presenting mixed-media music in a live context is a delicate task. In the composition of *Fata Morgana* I made a number of conscious decisions in order to facilitate the presentation of the composition. The goal was to reproduce the spatial perspectives composed in the studio and to blend the two parts so they share a coherent sound world.

It is important to unpack what this sound world involves, especially in light of the sounds produced by the live performers. In terms of acousmatic music Henriksen describes the combination of *composition space* – the space/spaces inherent in the electroacoustic materials – and *listening space* – the space that the sounds are presented in – as *perceived space*. This is the complex result of how the acoustic sound of the performance venue and the sounds projected by the loudspeakers interact in order to realise, or articulate, through diffusion the spatial characteristics of any given work.

Henriksen's descriptions – which were made in response to acousmatic music – elegantly summarise the relationship between acousmatic sounds and performance venue. However, this does not fully address the issue facing mixed-media music. Into this equation we must enter the sounds produced by the live performers. The live sounds are part of the overall composed space of the work. But because of the visual presence of the performers on stage complicate the overall performance of the work and how this can be realised in a public venue.

To address this issue in *Fata Morgana* I have taken a number of steps in order to ensure that the materials remain musically distinct (where appropriate) yet can be blended within the same apparent space. These are amplification, multi-channel realisation of the electroacoustic materials and diffusion.

## 4.1 Amplification

Amplification is often an important tool in mixed-media performance. In *Fata Morgana* the clarinets are amplified through loudspeakers adjacent to the ensemble. The role of the amplification is not to make the instrumentalists louder but to add clarity and bring their sounds' into the domain of the electroacoustic materials. The amplification aids in blending the two sound worlds together and allowing the detail present in the performers sounds to match the detail of the electroacoustic materials.

How loud to amplify the performers is a venue specific issue. However, because of the importance of space and how the electroacoustic spaces relate to the on-stage performers I would usually not amplify the performers to the point where the sound is identifiably projected by the loudspeakers. Amplifying below this level allows the sound of the clarinetists to still appear to emanate from their playing positions, maintaining their spatial positioning and the integrity of the spatial relationships.

## 4.2 Multi-Channel Electroacoustic Materials

In *Fata Morgana* I distribute the different electroacoustic materials using four-channels. Rather than the more traditional four-channel positioning of left, right, left surround and right surround I use a pair that are positioned close to the ensemble (these loudspeakers also receive the amplified clarinet signals) and a wider pair of loudspeakers (Figure 1).

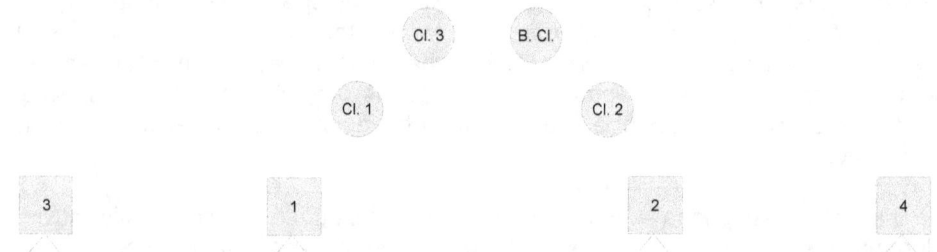

Figure 1. Rehearsal Layout

Channels one and two carry the electroacoustic sounds that are clearly relatable to the sounds of the instruments. Channels three and four carry the electroacoustic sounds that are more abstracted from the sound of the clarinets themselves.

The pairs of channels have distinct roles and carry contrasting materials. The pair positioned adjacent to the ensemble frames and extends it. The sounds are relatable to the live clarinet materials. These materials tend to exhibit the more extrinsic spatial characteristics and act as a bridge between the instrumental and electroacoustic materials. The relatively tight positioning of the main pair adjacent to the clarinets means that the stereo image maintains its coherency, partly due to the visual presence of the clarinets.

Sounds that are not directly relatable to the clarinet sounds are sent to loudspeakers three and four. These sounds usually exhibit the more intrinsic, harmonic and environmental spatial characteristics described earlier.

## Diffusion

Diffusion is the live presentation of electroacoustic music using a loudspeaker system in a public venue. The aesthetics of acousmatic diffusion are well documented (by for example Smalley and Harrison) [8] [9] and the act of diffusion has been described by Smalley as '...the most crucial of all' [8]. The importance ascribed to diffusion is not overstated. A poor diffusion can completely destroy the spatial characteristics of a composition and it is extremely important that the diffuser is sensitive to the work at hand. I will outline my aesthetic approach to mixed-media diffusion, which differs subtly from acousmatic diffusion, and then outline a potential performance solution for *Fata Morgana*.

## Diffusion in a Mixed-Media Context

Where mixed-media diffusion differs from acousmatic diffusion is clearly in the presence of the live performers. The diffusion must take into account the musical and spatial relationships between the instrumental and electroacoustic materials. My approach in my compositions so far, and in performing the work of others, is summed up by my strategies when performing *Fata Morgana* and I will describe this strategy whilst referring to some further ideas Henriksen has outlined.

Henriksen describes diffusion as 'a musical performance in which the combination of composed space and listening space is such that the integrity and meaning of the work are retained and coherently communicated in the specific listening space.' This implies that in acousmatic music the composed space carries the spatial information necessary for the diffuser to analyse and, sensitively, reproduce the work in a live performance.

'Knowing and understanding the musical content of the work is therefore a key issue. A successful performance requires that the sound diffusionist is intimately familiar with the work in question, and has analysed it in terms of its structurally significant spatial components' [4].

Much of this applies to mixed-media diffusion. The recorded spaces are still apparent and a diffuser can create a convincing performance of the electroacoustic materials simply from familiarising themselves with the fixed-media part. Where the diffusion of mixed-media music becomes more complex is in ensuring that the performance of the electroacoustic materials makes musical sense in the context of the live performers on stage. In the score for *Fata Morgana* I do not notate the diffused performance. In mixed-media performance the analysis of the work must take into account the materials played by the live performers as well as the spatial characteristics of the electroacoustic materials.

Related to these ideas is the notion of portability or the potential for my work to be heard in different venues with different performers. It is my view that my compositions should be portable. I do not want my work to be limited to a certain venue or ensemble because I believe that different performers, spaces and contexts bring new and different aspects to my work. In a practical sense, this means that I do not expect to always diffuse my own work.

The score for *Fata Morgana* provides written guides for the diffuser and suggests potential speaker placements and tactics for the diffusion. However, the relative balances for the instrumental and electroacoustic materials are not made explicit from moment to moment and this could be an area where my performance materials could be developed. It would be impossible, and probably not particularly useful for the diffuser, to notate dynamic contours for every sound in the dense textural parts. Nor is a specific diffusion notated, in part because a diffused performance will be necessarily different from one venue to another. However a notion of the overall balance may aid another diffuser in performing the work.

## A Potential Speaker System for *Fata Morgana*

In a studio setting sensitive amplification and careful balancing of the four-channel part over four loudspeakers should result in a musically coherent performance. In a concert situation in a larger, public space a more radical approach is necessary. Adding additional loudspeaker pairs in strategic positions allows the more abstracted sounds to be 'moved' in relation to the ensemble. It is these sounds that contextualise the clarinet materials and the electroacoustic materials that are directly related to the clarinet sounds, creating the spatial perspectives. Adding additional loudspeakers (Figure 2) allows the sound diffuser to realise these perspectives that are so important to the music meaning in the composition. The loudspeaker pairs should be carefully positioned, more distant pairs (loudspeakers five and six) might be angled dramatically off-axis or directed away from the audience to attenuate the higher frequencies that provide proximity cues for the listener making them sound more believably distant. Loudspeakers might be added to "flood" the sound stage (loudspeaker seven and eight). Directing these loudspeakers at the sidewalls may create a stereo image where the sounds are less discreetly locatable. This image would be useful in passages containing sustained, harmonic spectra that fill the stereo sound stage.

Integrating the Spatiality of Live Performers within the Imaginary Spatial Image of a Pre-Recorded Electroacoustic Part as a Compositional Premise
*Timothy Cooper*

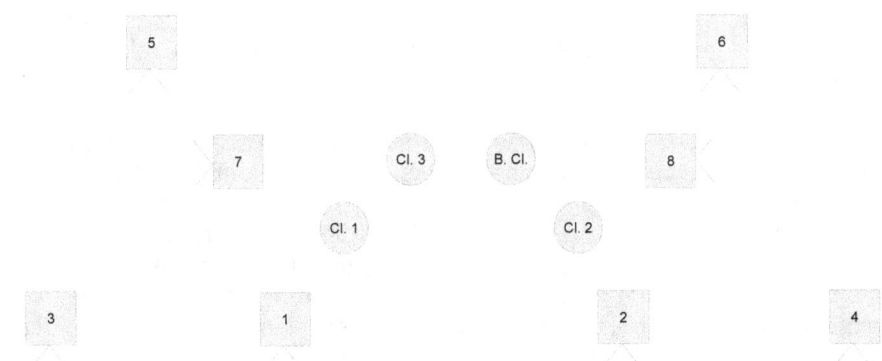

Figure 2: Potential Performance Setup

In diffusion height can be an interesting perspective to add. However, in the diffusion of mixed-media music it is important to take care when adding high loudspeakers. Different venues will afford different solutions for different music. In *Fata Morgana* it is important not to dislocate the sound of the electroacoustic part from the sphere of the clarinet ensemble. The diffusion should support the structure of the work and adding height, whilst attractive, should be done thoughtfully, with regard for the spatial characteristics of the work.

It is important to note that the success, or not, of the diffused performance is in how it is perceived. The theoretical thinking that shapes the strategy must be applied carefully and tested through detailed listening to the final result.

## 5. Summary

Using a stereo sound stage afforded the composition of a work that explores notions of landscape and illusion. Spatialising the electroacoustic materials over four channels and diffusing this aided the clarity of the reproduction and facilitated interesting spatial relationships.

Presenting *Fata Morgana* with speakers surrounding the audience would distort the composed spaces and sever the spatial relationships between the instrumental and electroacoustic materials. It is important to remember both in the composition and performance of a work that space is not an arbitrary parameter, but is intrinsic to how we perceive and relate to a composition.

Moving forwards I am interested in how some of these ideas could be applied or re-imagined in surround sound mixed-media works. I am interested in the kinds of spatial relationships that can coherently bind the dislocated sounds back to the performer(s) on stage. I can imagine spaces or motions related to human experience such as throwing, stretching or scattering that could be successful.

These spatial behaviours would require materials that suggest these motions in order to be coherent. These behaviours will also need to be relatable to the performer(s), who ordinarily play from a fixed position.

My approach to sound diffusion has been successful in the case of my mixed-media works and a number of other works I have performed. The process of ensuring that the sounds remain connected to the live performer(s) applies to surround sound works. However, the role of the diffuser is further complicated by the use of surround techniques. Balancing the technological and musical requirements will require careful planning and rehearsal and the use of performance spaces that are flexible enough to install larger loudspeaker systems and are acoustically appropriate.

## 6. References

[1] Emmerson, S. Acoustic/Electroacosutic: The Relationship With Instruments, Journal of New Music Research, 27:1-2, 146-164, DOI: 10.1080/09298219808570742, (1997)

[2] Emmerson, S. 'Live' Versus 'Real-Time', Contemporary Music Review, 10:2, 95-101, DOI: 10.1080/07494469400640331, (1994)

[3] Emmerson, S. Living Electronic Music, Ashgate Publishing Limited, Aldgate, (2007)

[4] Henriksen, Frank Ekeberg. Space in Electroacoustic Music: Composition, Performance and Perception of Musical Space. PhD Thesis, City University, London, (2002)

[5] Smalley, D. Space-Form and the acousmatic image, Organised Sound, Volume 12, pp 35-38, DOI 10.1017/S1355771807001665, (2007)

[6] Long, R. A Line Made By Walking, Accessed November 2015 from http://www.richardlong.org/Sculptures/2011sculptures/linewalking.html, 1967

[7] Long, R. Stones in Iceland, Accessed November 2015 from http://www.richardlong.org/Sculptures/2011sculpupgrades/iceland.html, 1974

[8] Smalley, D. Spectromorphology: explaining sound-shapes, Organised Sound, Volume 2, pp 107-126, DOI 10.1017/S1355771897009059, (1997)

[9] Harrison, D, J, T. Sound, space, sculpture: some thoughts on the 'what', 'how' and 'why' of sound diffusion. Organised Sound, 3, pp 117-127, (1998)

# Interactive Digital Music: Enhancing Listener Engagement with Commercial Music

Justin Paterson[1], Rob Toulson[2], Sebastian Lexer[1], Tim Webster[2], Steve Massey[1], Jonas Ritter[1]

[1] London College of Music, University of West London, UK.
justin.paterson@uwl.ac.uk

[2] CoDE Research Institute, Anglia Ruskin University, Cambridge, UK.
rob.toulson@anglia.ac.uk

## Abstract

*Listeners have long been inspired to interact with music and create new representations of popular releases. Vinyl offered many opportunities to reappropriate chart music, from scratching and tempo manipulation to mixing multiple songs together. More recently, artists could engage their audience to interact with their music by offering mix-stems online for experimentation and sharing. With the extended processing power of mobile devices, the opportunities for interactive music are dramatically increasing.*

*This paper presents research that demonstrates a novel approach to interactive digital music. The research looks at the emergent format of the album app and extends existing paradigms of interactive music playback. The novel album app designed in this research presents a new opportunity for listeners to engage with recorded content by allowing them to explore alternative takes, renditions of a given song in multiple genres, and by allowing direct interaction with embedded mix-stems. The resultant audio remains true to the artist and producer's studio vision; it is user-influenced, but machine-controlled. The research is conducted in collaboration with artist Daisy and The Dark and was funded by the UK Arts and Humanities Research Council.*

## 1. Introduction

This paper presents the work in progress of a research project that was designed to develop a unique interactive music album format that represents a new paradigm in the way we listen to and engage with digital music. The research focuses on identifying and evaluating new modes of engagement between popular artists and audiences, whilst simultaneously identifying a bold new business model for the music industry. In general, digital platforms have been designed in an attempt to replicate and replace the linear analogue music formats; however, modern digital playback systems from mobile devices to networked hi-fi systems are extremely over-engineered for simply 'playing' music and audio. Such devices offer far more creative processing capabilities and are, as yet, underexploited commercially.

A principal objective was to investigate the opportunities for popular music playback to be interactive and malleable, whilst retaining and extrapolating the artistic vision of the musicians and producer. The greater investigation was centred in two specific areas – what are the capabilities of available technologies and the subsequent opportunities for artists, and what is the audience and consumer response to these novel creative approaches? This paper is centred upon the former.

### 1.1. Modes of Variable Playback

*Interactive music* can be defined as music in which it is the user's intention to change the nature of the audio, whereas variation in *dynamic music* is primarily a function of some other variable or state [1], for instance user-engagement with a video game. Interactive music can be considered from two different viewpoints. An example of *produced interactivity* enables a listener to manipulate the musical elements of a song in a number of different ways. The song might be an upbeat rock track including drums, electric guitars, vocals and a string section. Consider however, that at any point whilst listening, the listener might prefer to hear the song in a more relaxed manner without disrupting the flow of the music. They may prefer to listen to a stripped down version, perhaps with the electric guitars being replaced by acoustic versions, the drums becoming hand percussion and the strings taking a more prominent role in the mix. Similarly, the listener might select an electronic version of the song, which introduces programmed drumbeats and synthesized sounds. The musical content might have changed, but it is still the same song, and by employing combinations of bespoke alternative audio content created in the studio, the musician's artistic vision is maintained.

There are further opportunities to interact with the music within either a specific and fixed genre, e.g. there could be multiple vocal takes which the listener can choose from, or different guitar or drum parts that represent the song either subtly or dramatically differently. The term produced interactivity is used because the artist still has control of the boundaries for playback, deciding what genres and instrumentation they create as a palette, and they will also define the default playback setting – the version released for conventional sale and distribution.

Algorithmic music is well established and in this, an algorithm maintains full control over what variation of the audio content is being played back; this might include motifs, timbres, rhythms and other musical content. *Algorithmic interactivity* can represent a form of interactive music in that it is processed predominantly with input from mathematical and statistical algorithms, but with user-influence on the result. The listener might select genres and playback styles as with the produced method, however this system responds subtly differently. For example, a number of gestures that a user might make could be automated into a unique sequence, or algorithmic components might include preset modes of real-time processing, enabling the listener to trigger the application of these at will.

## 1.2. Further Aspects of the Project

It is also necessary to consider the tools required for musicians, music producers and importantly, record labels to develop their own interactive music. This requires a content management system (CMS) that allows consistently repeatable population of the format – an operational paradigm with a simple user interface design that facilitates building of bespoke interactive music releases. Standard industry procedure involves matching the relative loudness of tunes in an album at the final mastering stage. A large number of different combinations of audio files in combinations that might change dynamically are a heterodox to this. Additionally, in bringing interactive music systems to a diverse audience with different preferences and behavior patterns, it is useful to be able to gather data on the nature of the user response to this new medium. The last two areas are beyond the scope of this paper.

## 2. Background and Related Work

### 2.1. Game Audio

Computer games have featured dynamic (often referred to as *adaptive*) music since the 1980s. LucasArts used their iMuse engine [2] in many of their games. This system chose from multiple MIDI sequences that were triggered on demand by a number of pre-programmed decision points that could steer the compositional direction through a 'tree' of sequences. This developed into horizontal re-sequencing systems that re-ordered pre-composed blocks of music in response to the user's gaming decisions and situation [3]. Vertical re-orchestration utilized a number of concurrent layers of music which could be added to or taken away, again in response to gaming activity [3].

Albeit in the context of games, in 2012 Berndt et al. highlighted the negatives of static and repetitive music, and produced a survey of approaches to remedy this with dynamic technologies, pointing out that "neither fully static compositions nor completely unrelated (random) music do an expedient job" [4, p. 62]. This paper implies the readiness of the modern consumer for greater variation in the listening experience and further, looked forward towards the development of more sophisticated audio engines that might deliver this. In 2014, Gasselseder [5] produced a scientific study which confirmed that game players experienced a greater degree of immersion when experiencing dynamic music.

## 2.2. The Album App Format

One emerging format of music delivery is the mobile application (often referred to simply as an *app*). The *album app* format is valuable since it allows unique artistic and interactive content to be distributed alongside a collation of audio, supporting the notion that an album is more than just a collection of songs, but potentially a representation of artistic vision which may include artwork, photography, lyrics, video, animation, gaming, social networking and crucially – interaction. The album app is also an incredibly attractive method for music delivery because it is secure, i.e. once the app is created it generally cannot be tampered with, ensuring both digital integrity (as opposed to MP3s) and added piracy resilience, since apps are much harder to duplicate and distribute than simple audio files. Ultimately, the concept of the format could extend into adoption by smart TVs and games consoles. Streaming music services are nowadays also adding additional media content to albums, such as song lyrics and extended artwork. It is therefore possible that album apps and audio streaming applications could become merged in future innovations.

## 2.3. Previous Interactive and Album App Releases

Bands such as Rush have previously offered combined (static) music and media apps as far back as 2010, and in 2014 Paul McCartney re-released five of his solo albums as album apps; however, few interactive music applications have been released in recent years. Bjork's 2011 *Biophilia* album is perhaps the most recognized to be released to date. Alongside music, artwork, credits and animations, the app also introduces interactive elements for each song, allowing the user to engage with different aspects of sound and visualization with respect to the album content. Similarly Peter Gabriel's *Music Tiles* app, although not an album itself, allows the user to interact with the music and produce unique (albeit basic) mixes of the tracks, and is designed to be more of a game than a playback medium. Jorge Drexler's *n* app also features songs written specifically for interactive playback, attempting to utilize the full processing capabilities of digital mobile devices. Gwilym Gold's *Tender Metal* used an algorithmic system to play back synthesized backing differently every time, although without user control. The Jammit series [12] of teaching tools that started in 2012 allowed muting and volume control of the individual stems, slowing down of the music, notated transcriptions and recording of the user playing along. Pitbull's *Planet Pit* offers many interactive multimedia features, but ultimately is a promotional tool since it only features excerpts of the actual music. 2013 saw the release of DJ Vadim's *Don't Be Scared* and *This DJ* via the Immersive Album LTD system. These are apps that play back video and allow users to engage with features on the screen and change elements of the music and video simultaneously, effectively substituting audio stems to change vocalist or drumbeat. The company Reactify [16] have a number of apps including *VW & Underworld: Play The Road*, in which the interaction comes not from the human, but from whatever is being done with the car to control a live remix of the band Underworld.

Many new developments happened in 2014. Reactify also released the remixing app *CTRL*, which allowed a number of time-synchronized DJ effects to be applied to the tracks of a number of popular artists. Shakhovskoy and Toulson [17] defined a potential album-app model with artist Francois and the Atlas Mountains for their album *Piano Ombre,* developed by Script. It was regarded as the world's first chart-eligible app and is recognized as the foundation software platform for which the interactive app described in this paper is built upon. Bernhoft Islander released his self-titled album as an app, including interactive features that allow the listener to manipulate the balance and panning of instrument stems and to experiment with looping motifs and phrases from his songs [18].

### 2.4. Multi-Track Music Formats

A number of multi-track audio formats have been created, and have been documented by Redhead [19] and Taglialatela [20] amongst others. iKlax [21] is a file format that allows the clustering of up to 10 audio tracks (in a mobile app – more on a desktop machine) and offers the developer the chance to mute, solo and adjust the volume of the individual tracks. iKlax has been implemented in apps such as *Perform A Track*, which is targeted at those wishing to play along in a *music minus one* [22] fashion. The Audizen company developed a similarly specified system to iKlax called *Music 2.0,* and in 2010, the best features from each were adopted into the MPEG-A Interactive Music Application Format (IM AF). This was specified [23] to offer: multiple audio tracks and a definition of their hierarchical structure, data that pre-defined mixing information and rules that introduce user-interaction data, along with timed text, images and metadata. Any interactive music player that supported this format would be able to offer both preset 'producer' versions of songs, and also allow users to create their own unique mixes.

Various other formats have also been created. MXP4 was released in 2009, and this offered video streams and consumer-focused metadata such as artist biographies. Another multi-track format is the open-source MOGG [24], which supports multiple Ogg Vorbis files, although it was not widely adopted. Song Galaxy also produced a multi-track format called MTF (Multi Track File) [25] targeted at the karaoke market, but also allowing certain remix-type actions, including transposition. Yet another format is iXMF, which is a wrapper for both audio and MIDI files, and contains cue sheets that allow specific events to be triggered at a particular point in time. The MIDI/audio engine that powers *Tender Metal* [26] is the BRONZE Format [27], developed at Goldsmiths University in 2012. In 2015, Native Instruments released *Stems*, a DJ tool that offers manipulation of four separate tracks, packaged in a MPEG-4 Container [28]. This system works with their Traktor Software, and also comes with a CMS that allows musicians to create and package their own material for subsequent manipulation.

## 3. Research Methodology and Application Design

### 3.1. Research Objectives

The key project objectives and research questions were defined by the overriding aim to investigate new ways that contemporary music-playback platforms can potentially:

1. Support novel playback paradigms that can engage listeners and hence generate new revenue streams for the commercial music industry

2. Create a more intimate and creative connection between the artist and their fan base

In order to evaluate these research objectives, a methodology to design, build, test and evaluate a new interactive digital music platform was identified, as shown in Figure 1.

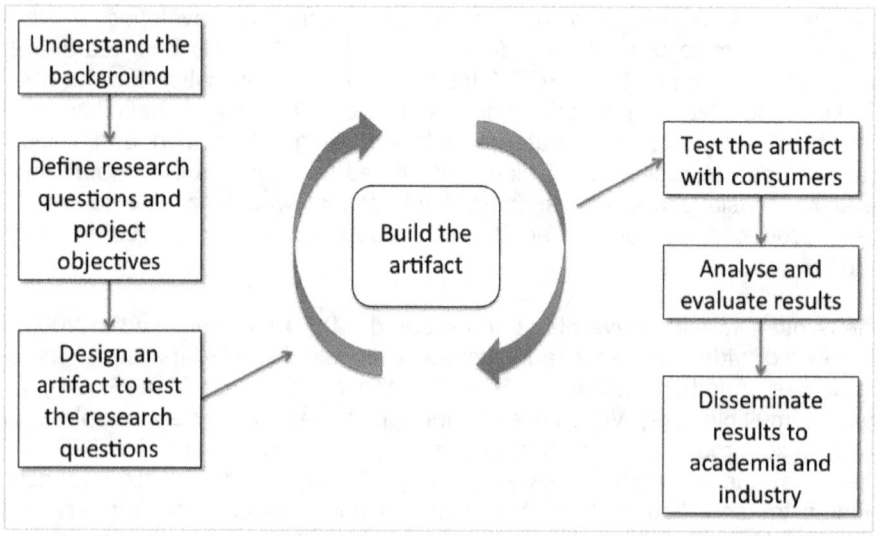

Figure 1. Research methodology for the album app design project

## 3.2. Application Design and Implementation

The development team agreed functional design specifications during an early brainstorming stage of the project, and these were then implemented in the agile and iterative development build-cycle shown in the centre of Figure 1. The iterative development process is shown in more detail in Figure 2, which also represents the seven-month app-development cycle. The initial brainstorming and prototyping phase was intended to evaluate a number of interactive playback paradigms that could potentially be used in a mobile music application. The prototyping stage was conducted in a number of high-level audio manipulation packages including Max/MSP, Pure Data, Logic and Abelton Live, as well as engineering packages including Matlab and Xcode. On development of the high-level prototypes, a review process, including feedback from the collaborating artist Daisy and The Dark, was required to decide which specific prototypes would be taken forward to the final application design and developed in the Objective-C language (in Xcode) for implementation on Apple iOS devices, specifically the iPhone and iPad.

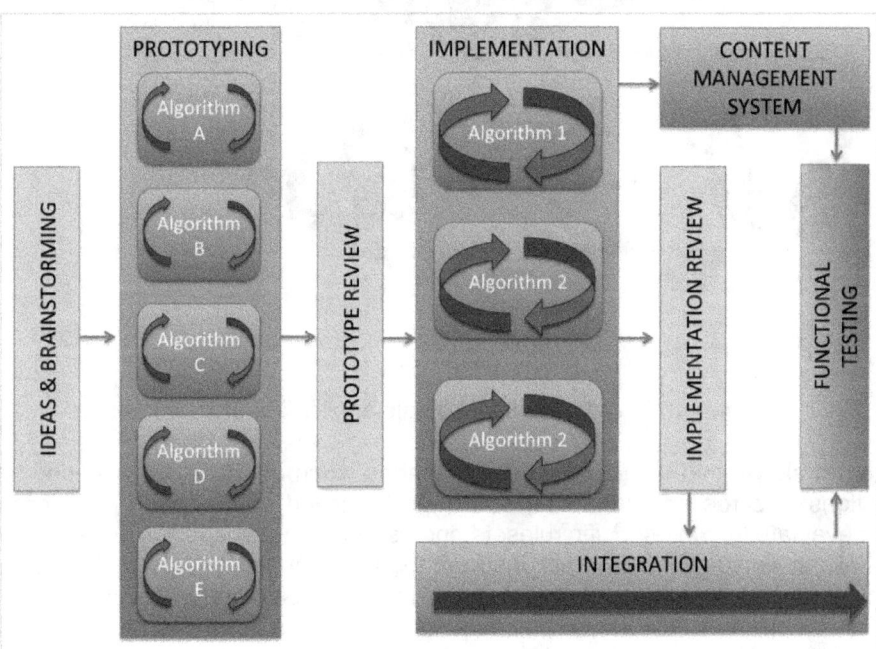

Figure 2. Iterative application development process

The integration phase of the project involved the repurposing of the album app platform originally developed by project collaborator Script [17]. This was to implement the new interactive music features and to populate the platform with the audio and visual assets of Daisy and The Dark. Alongside the integration phase runs a prototype CMS development process, which is intended to define and test the features that are required in order to develop a platform that any music artist or record label might populate with their own audio and visual media.

The functional design for the interactive album app's music playback features is built upon a three-layer architecture. The architecture defines the linking of *graphical user interfaces* (GUIs) with an advanced *audio playback engine*, via a *rulesets* layer that defines the specific interaction operations and the user controlled features, as shown in Figure 3.

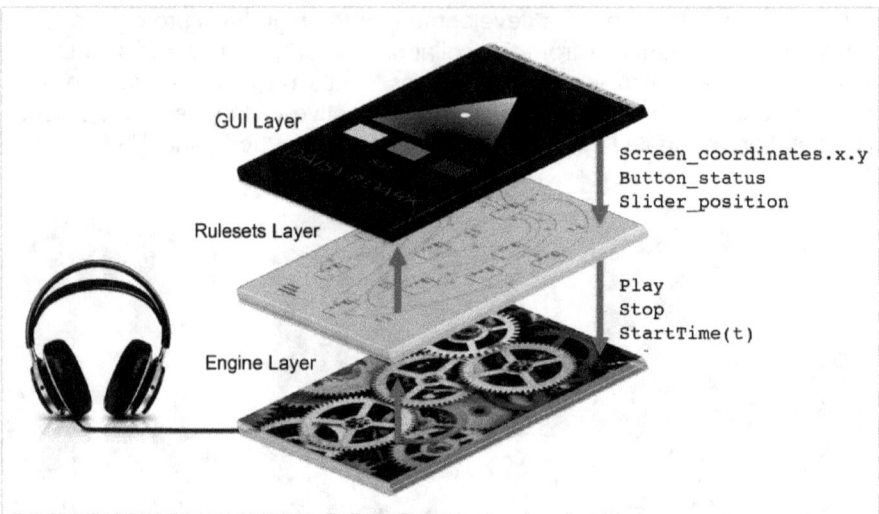

Figure 3. Interactive digital music application architecture

Figure 3 shows that user-interaction messages, such as those representing touch locations of screen co-ordinates, button presses and control slider positions are then evaluated by the specific rulesets and used to request specific audio playback and digital signal processing actions from the audio engine. Additionally, the audio engine reports its status to the rulesets layer, which informs the GUI layer to update whenever audio playback is modified, such as a new track starting or when an algorithmic interaction is implemented.

## 4. Functionality and Operation

### 4.1. Audio Playback Engine

The design concept of the audio engine is to allow simultaneous playback of 36 audio files, which is the maximum number imposed by the CPU capability of the iPhone 5, the earliest device for which compatibility was sought. A given song uses six stem families, for instance: vocals, guitar, bass, drums, strings and keys, although the actual instrumentation is different for each song and song version. This allows 36 combinations of the six stems to be available to the user in real time, although only six could be heard at any one point. This was achieved by the implementation of a 36-track audio player, designed using the Audio Unit *AUFilePlayer* library – part of Aple's iOS.

Developed in the Objective-C programming language in the Apple Xcode programming environment, the audio engine consists of two major bespoke components (classes): the *SLAudioEngine* object and the *SLtimer*. The SLAudioEngine implements 36 AUFilePlayers, taking their source audio as specified by a file URL supplied in the *songName.plist*. These players connect to a 36-input *AUMixer* object, which facilitates control over audio playback. The SLtimer controls synchronization and scheduling.

Within in the SLAudioEngine are fade engines that allow the design of *transitions*, i.e. the timed fade to a defined volume level, with one for each stem. Transition profiles (are stored in the songName.plist preset file and are created by using the custom-built CMS system – the user selects suitable profiles from a pre-defined palette. Each transition is defined by a mix level in dB, and the signal is assumed to be silent if it is at a level below –99 dBFS and is flagged accordingly. Each transition allows either a linear or equal-power fade curve, and steps through 100 increments within a definable time. Fades can start on any of these steps, as well as stop at any step greater than the start.

The current implementation of the algorithm allows CMS-user-definition of 36 transitions. Upon triggering by the end-user's gesture, each fade engine evaluates whether the current volume of the corresponding mixer input needs to be adjusted to reflect the volume level defined in the specified transition. If the defined volume level is greater than the current volume level, an increase will occur over the range between the defined start and end steps. Conversely, if the desired volume value is lower, a fade out will occur between the defined steps.

As the transition time is variable, the app GUI may supply and influence the transition time. The CMS also allows quantization or limiting of the moment of triggering within a calibrated range of settings, to force transitions to occur in time with the tempo of the song and in a musically appropriate fashion. Transitions can also be triggered by intelligent computer control, either randomly or in response to some other algorithmic event.

## 4.2. Interactive User Interfaces

A number of interactive GUIs were prototyped and four were chosen to be included in the final application. These were those referred to as *stem faders, stem switches, manual mix crossfades* and *intelligent mix crossfades*.

The most simple user interfaces were those that allowed fading and on/off switching of audio stems. Figure 4a and Figure 4b show the *stem faders GUI* for a single song (in this case the song *Red Planet*). Each vertical slider allows manipulation of the playback volume of a particular audio stem. For example, *Red Planet* is made up of audio stems representing drums, bass, synthesizers, cellos, strings, and vocals.

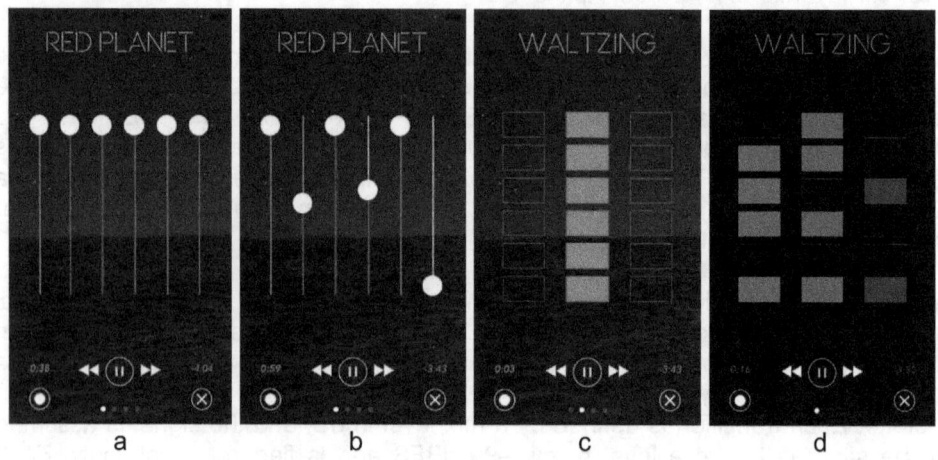

Figure 4. Stem faders and stem switches GUIs

It is apparent that the user could create a unique mix of the stems to their own preference, but it is also possible for a single instrument stem to be muted, in order for the listener to sing/play along. It is also possible to mute multiple stems and leave a single stem active in solo, e.g. the listener might wish to solo the bass guitar in order to learn how to first mimic, then ultimately play along with the full track, replacing the original part.

The *stem switches* implemented on the GUI for the song *Waltzing* allows the user to manipulate three different versions of the same song. When the six central stem buttons are active (as in Figure 4c), the main radio mix of *Waltzing* is heard (stems representing two piano lines, cello, synthesizer, electric guitar and vocals). An electronic remix is controlled by the left column buttons (drums, bass, piano, synthesizer, electric guitar and vocals) and the right columns activate an orchestral version (made up of different cello, violin and vocal lines). The user can chose to play back one of the three produced versions of the song, or they can manipulate their own mix made up of a combination of the stems across all three song versions (as shown in Figure 4c and Figure 4d). The stem fader positions also influence all different combinations of the stem switches.

The *manual mix crossfades GUI* design is implemented for both the *Ghost* and *Red Planet* songs, though in different geometries, as shown in Figure 5a and Figure 5b. *Ghost* uses a triangular cross fade mixer which incorporates three versions of the song. When the small white cursor (the *mix control*) is at the top point of the triangle, the main radio mix of the song is played back, whereas the bottom corners engage acoustic and electronic versions of the song. The listener can choose to move the mix control towards any corner to a position that blends between two or all three versions. Tapping the mix control toggles the vocals on and off, effectively allowing an instrumental version of the song to be played, although again the stem faders can also influence operation.

The *Red Planet* GUI (Figure 5b) works similarly, though with a circular design. The main radio mix of *Red Planet* is heard when the mix control is positioned in the center of the circular interface. Acoustic, electronic, dub and choral interpretations are positioned at 0, 90, 180 ad 270 degree positions on the circle perimeter.

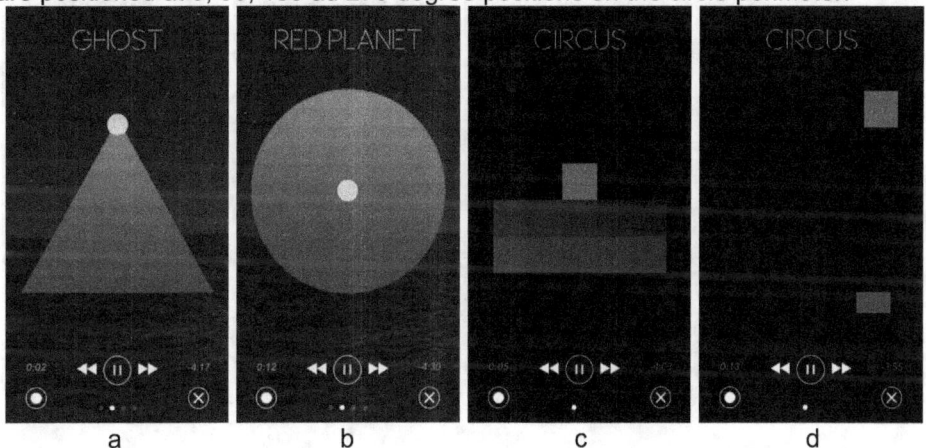

Figure 5. Manual and intelligent crossfade GUIs

The Circus user interface is an *intelligent mix crossfade GUI*, implemented as a matrix of 25 different cells, each representing a different mix (as shown in Figure 5c). Different mixes can be engaged by tapping or dragging around the matrix interface. Initially the mix control is positioned in the center, which is the position for the main radio mix of the track. Each corner of the matrix represents an alternative mix of Circus, including acoustic, and electronic remixes; towards the corners, each matrix cell plays a subtly different mix. When a new mix is selected, a unique cross-fade algorithm smoothly transitions the music from one mix to another. The Circus interface also has a unique *variPlay* feature, which is activated by any of the four buttons beneath the main matrix (as highlighted by Figure 5d). When variPlay is active, a quadrant of the matrix is highlighted, and from it, an intelligent algorithm automatically selects new mixes at various points in the song, ensuring that a unique experience is heard on each listen. There are four variPlay modes, each presenting a different quadrant of the matrix.

### 4.3. Additional Album App Features

The app has a number of additional rich media features that are intended to enhance the listener's overall user-experience. The main home screen (Figure 6a) and home menu allows the user to select different features of the app by dragging menu items to the center of the screen. This launches a short animation and opens the selected app page. The music album page (Figure 6b) gives access to the four tracks of the EP. Any song can be selected, which automatically launches the associated song-player user-interface.

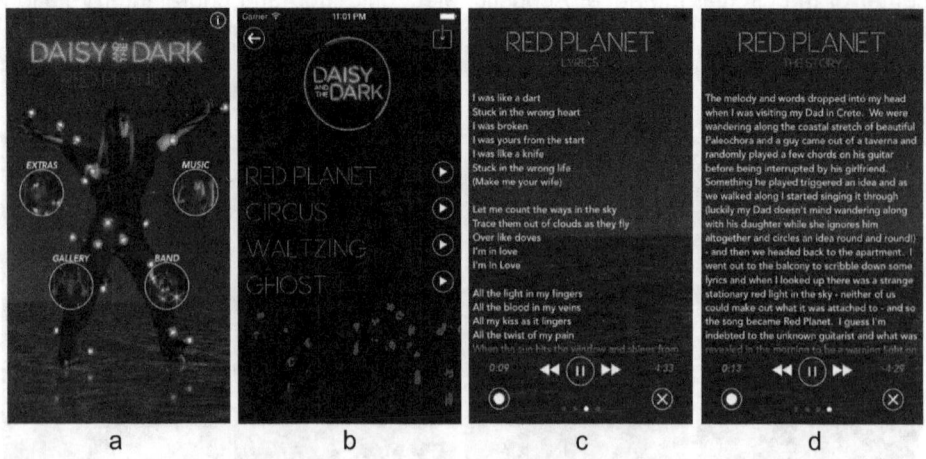

Figure 6. App home screen, music album, song lyrics and song description

While in the song-player interface, the user can also swipe left and right to access additional features including the song lyrics (Figure 6c) and a detailed narrative on the song and its origin (Figure 6d).

The band section of the app (accessed from the main home screen) allows the user to read the full artist biography of Daisy and The Dark, as well as scroll through a number of artist images. Additionally the user can access performer and production credits for the EP. A gallery section contains a number of images from the album artwork, and live performances by the artist. A extras section also links to a number of and social network related features.

## 4.4. Data Collection

Data analytics are built into the app using the propriety Flurry protocols [20]. The data analytics allows collection of user interactivity for a number of aspects of app engagement, menu selections and song interaction. It is therefore possible, with enough app users, to gather meaningful quantitative data on the sections, which receive the most user engagement and the duration spent by the user on each app feature. Additionally it is possible to gather and analyze data of which songs were played the most and the frequency of interaction with individual GUIs and playback features.

The app also includes a built-in research questionnaire which assesses the listener's user-experience in both a qualitative and quantitative manner. Questions include asking users to rate the interactive album app features, to comment on their overall impression of the app, and whether they would be willing to purchase commercial music in this format in the future.

## 4.5. Content Management System

A CMS is required to enable content providers such as music producers or record labels to integrate their audio into a final compiled app. The CMS allows its user to: specify combinations of stems to be played, trim volumes, set parameters for the fade times between audio stems and to define how the app reacts when different buttons are pressed. The transitions between different song sections could also be auditioned, and variPlay structured. When doing all this, it is essential that the user is able to get instant results that emulate the behaviour of the final app, both to provide feedback to fine-tune the mix and enable experimentation.

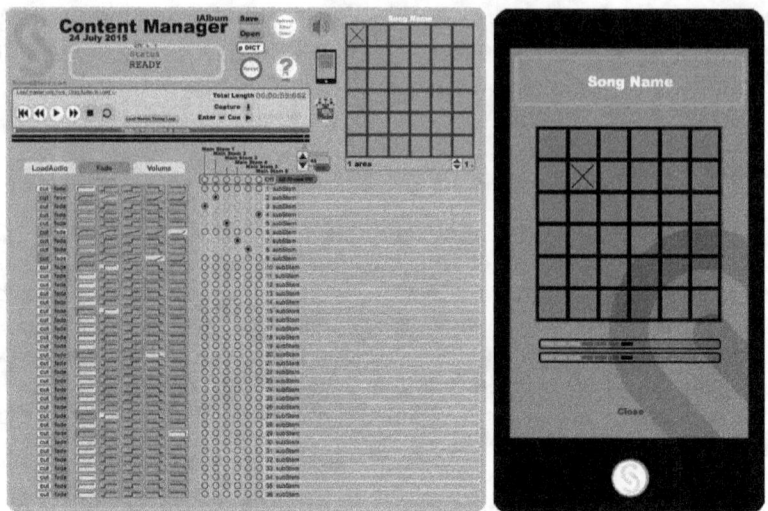

Figure 7. The CMS GUI and iPhone simulator window

The *Content Manager* was created in Max/MSP because this rapid-prototyping program is versatile enough to control audio, capture multi-touch data and format it into a JSON file that could be read by the app. The GUI can be seen in Figure Figure 7 (left), and one of a number of pop-up sub-windows that represents an iPhone user's view (right).

## 5. Discussion and Conclusions

The app holds data for a total of 96 audio stems and it was chosen that 256 kbps MP3 data compressed files - as opposed to lossless pulse-code-modulation (PCM) - data, would be used to keep the total size of the app to a minimum. The total app size when downloaded from the iPhone app store is 790 Mb, which is slightly smaller than Bjork's *Biophillia* app that has a data size of 849 Mb.

Most commercial iOS apps play back audio using AVPlayers from the AVFoundation library. The AVPlayers only offer non-synchronous playback, and so were not suitable for the 36-track parallel architecture required here. It was for this reason that a low-level (Audio Unit) audio engine had to be designed with bespoke players. The SLAudioEngine also proved much more CPU efficient. The multi-track audio formats discussed in Section 2.4 where evaluated and deemed unsuitable for a context such as this due to lack of controllability in the highly parallel architecture.

There is an opportunity to perform future listening tests to quantitatively evaluate the sound quality loss of using data compressed audio files in this application.

However, audio testing by the development team revealed that the overall quality of mixing stem files in MP3 format to a stereo monitoring stream proved noticeably superior to mixing down the equivalent PCM audio stems and converting the result to MP3. This result is unsurprising given the nature of data reduction in the MP3 codec, which appears to work much more transparently on (unmixed) instrument files. Similarly, the loudness levels of all audio files in the app have been carefully controlled in order to give a smooth sonic experience for the user. There are a number of interesting observations from a loudness analysis perspective, which will therefore be quantitatively evaluated and disseminated in future research publications by the investigating team.

A number of different interactive music GUIs have been developed for the app. The Stem Fader mode of operation is in line with that of some of the apps referred to in Section 2.3, yet maintains relevance here as part of a varied suite. The GUIs all behave rather differently, and are likely to appeal to different people, and again, this aspect will be evaluated in future research tasks. In particular, a full and thorough analysis of the Flurry-gathered user data will be conducted in order to reveal which GUIs have been engaged with the most. This exercise will be supported by the running of focus-group workshops which will allow users to both feed back directly and by completing the built-in app questionnaire. The full evaluation of the user-experience will therefore be disseminated in future publications by the investigating team.

As demonstrated in Section 2.3, to date there are few album app releases and defining a unifying format for the future could hold potential benefit before too many variants emerge. Of course, interactive music is in its naissance and its evolution is likely to involve in a number of different paradigms of varying success, however, this research does offer a functional model that could be developed to evolve further. Commercial exploitation of any such single format would also increase profit margin as releases proliferate, since development costs will have already been covered. Further, lead times to release will be dramatically reduced.

In particular, there is an opportunity to develop more advanced graphic designs that animate alongside the sonic experience, utilizing visual programming techniques that have been developed within the mobile games industry. Interestingly, the games development community has experienced difficulties currently associated with cross-fading between disparate pieces of music, as Gungormusler notes: "one major drawback of the approach is the lack of smooth transitions between the different selections of musical pieces, which is said to be left as future work." [21, p. 3] It is therefore conceivable that the audio mixing architecture and associated algorithms developed in this research might also serve valuable purpose in future games audio systems.

## 6. References

[1] K. Collins, Game Sound: An Introduction to the History, Theory, and Practice of Video Game Music and Sound Design. MIT Press, 2008.
[2] M. Z. Land and P. N. Mcconnell, "Method and apparatus for dynamically composing music and sound effects using a computer entertainment system," US5315057 (A), 24-May-1994.
[3] K. B. McAlpine, M. Bett, and J. Scanlan, "Approaches to Creating Real-Time Adaptive Music in Interactive Entertainment: A Musical Perspective," presented at the Audio Engineering Society Conference: 35th International Conference: Audio for Games, 2009.
[4] A. Berndt, R. Dachselt, and R. Groh, "A Survey of Variation Techniques for Repetitive Games Music," in Proceedings of the 7th Audio Mostly Conference: A Conference on Interaction with Sound, New York, NY, USA, 2012, pp. 61–67.
[5] H.-P. Gasselseder, "Dynamic Music and Immersion in the Action-adventure an Empirical Investigation," in Proceedings of the 9th Audio Mostly: A Conference on Interaction With Sound, New York, NY, USA, 2014, pp. 28:1–28:8.
[6] Jammit, "Jammit | Jam with your Favorite Band." [Online]. Available: http://www.jammit.com/. [Accessed: 06-Aug-2015].
[7] "Reactify," Reactify. [Online]. Available: http://reactifymusic.com/portfolio/. [Accessed: 05-Aug-2015].
[8] J. Shakhovskoy and R. Toulson, "Future Music Formats: evaluating the 'album app,'" Journal on the Art of Record Production, no. 10, Jul. 2015.
[9] D. Greeves, "Can The App Save The Album?," Sound On Sound, Oct-2014. [Online]. Available: http://www.soundonsound.com/sos/oct14/articles/apps.htm. [Accessed: 06-Aug-2015].
[10] T. Redhead, "Composing and Recording for Fluid Digital Music Forms," JARP, no. 10.
[11] C. Taglialatela, "MPEG-A Interactive Music Application Format (IM AF) Encoder," Seconda Universita' Degli Studi di Napoli, Naples, Italy, 2012.
[12] "iKlax multitrack music file format - Get the SDK for encoding and decoding." [Online]. Available: http://www.iklax.com/. [Accessed: 05-Aug-2015].
[13] Music Minus One, "Music Minus One - musicminusone.com." [Online]. Available: https://www.musicminusone.com/. [Accessed: 06-Aug-2015].
[14] MPEG, "Interactive Music Application Format." [Online]. Available: http://mpeg.chiariglione.org/standards/mpeg-a/interactive-music-application-format. [Accessed: 05-Aug-2015].
[15] "MOGG Files - Multitrack Digital Audio Format," MOGG Files - Multitrack Digital Audio Format. [Online]. Available: https://moggfiles.wordpress.com/. [Accessed: 05-Aug-2015].
[16] "Music Software Song Galaxy Online Shop," Song Galaxy. [Online]. Available: http://songgalaxy.com//software.php. [Accessed: 05-Aug-2015].
[17] "Gwilym Gold." [Online]. Available: http://gwilymgold.com/. [Accessed: 12-Feb-2014].

[18] M. Grierson, "BronzeFormat," 2012. [Online]. Available: http://bronzeformat.com/. [Accessed: 12-Feb-2014].
[19] Stems-Music, "Stems is for DJs," Stems, 2015. [Online]. Available: http://www.stems-music.com/stems-is-for-djs/. [Accessed: 05-Aug-2015].
[20] magicspark, "Flurry Analytics," Flurry, 28-Mar-2014. [Online]. Available: http://www.flurry.com/solutions/analytics. [Accessed: 10-Aug-2015].
[21] A. Gungormusler, N. Paterson-Paulberg, and M. Haahr, "barelyMusician: An Adaptive Music Engine for Video Games," presented at the Audio Engineering Society Conference: 56th International Conference: Audio for Games, 2015.

# Author Index

Adelman-Larsen, Niels   103
Averell, Edward   116

Boehm, Carola   128

Canfer, Tim   26
Choi, Chang Seok   88
Colin, McRae   64
Cooper, Timothy   179

De Man, Brecht   144
Don, Knox   116

Ferguson, Paul   174
Flynn, Mathew   157

Jonas, Ritter   193
Joshua, Reiss   144

Leml, Esthir   64

Marrington, Mark   52
Martin, Bryan   14

Nicholas, Ward   36

Paterson, Justin   193

Reed, Esslinger   64
Richard, King   14
Rob, Toulson   193
Robert, Sazdov   36
Ronan, Malachy   36

Sebastian, Lexer   193
Shelvock, Matthew   75
Steve, Massey   193

Tim, Webster   193

Toulson, Rob   1